FATAL DREAMS

FATAL DREAMS

Joanne Bario

THE DIAL PRESS
Doubleday & Company, Inc.
GARDEN CITY, NEW YORK
1985

The names of some characters and locations have been changed—
though not those of the principals.

Library of Congress Cataloging in Publication Data
Bario, Joanne.
    Fatal dreams.
    1. Bonnano, Salvatore. 2. Narcotic enforcement
agents—United States—Biography. 3. Bribery—Texas—
Case studies. 4. Prison homicide—Texas—Case studies.
5. Bario, Joanne. 6. Narcotic enforcement agents'
wives—United States—Biography. I. Title.
HV8079.N3B663   1985   363.2'092'4 [B]   84-12071
ISBN 0-385-27938-8

An excerpt from *Present Past, Past Present* by Eugene Ionesco is reprinted with permission from Grove Press, Inc.

Published by The Dial Press

Copyright © 1985 by Joanne Bario

PRINTED IN THE UNITED STATES OF AMERICA
ALL RIGHTS RESERVED
FIRST EDITION

For David
and my parents

Acknowledgments

I would like to thank the following people for their belief in me and in this book:

As always, Nancy and Jerry Tumolo gave me their time, energy, and love.

Richard Ben-Veniste offered friendship and his very considerable legal skills, for which I could never repay him.

Clyde Taylor, my agent, stuck by this book for what felt like forever. The staff of Bread Loaf Writers' Conference honored it when it didn't have a publisher. Joyce Johnson, my editor, heard what I meant to say and coaxed form and clarity from me.

Many friends provided encouragement and good advice, especially Linda Fite, Alan and Marilyn Levitt, Lizzie Mansfield, and Mark Jonathan Harris.

I owe a special debt to the members of Sante Bario's family, who have accepted me as one of their own.

We are like Cinderella, who lived her life expecting a transfiguration of the world, who lived her life expecting a few hours of glorious, sumptuous festivities; the rest of the time we are there in rags, in the dirty shanties of reality.
—Eugene Ionesco,
Present Past, Past Present

I

It was July 1964, and Sante Bario was relieved to be out of the heat of Washington, D.C. He adjusted the air vent above his seat and sat back for the short flight to Boston. He was out. He couldn't believe it. He had told the manager of the Sheraton Hotel to shove his night auditor's job. He had told his wife that he would call when he could but that it might not be often. He had gotten himself a job with the Treasury Department as a special undercover agent in Boston's Little Italy, where it helped to be Italian. Until he checked into his temporary room in the North End, he was between lives and finally free enough to look at where he'd been and where he was so dramatically going.

At twenty-eight he was impatient for success. He had lost three years since moving to the States. For two years in Detroit he had been no better than a common immigrant, long on talent and short on English. He had waited tables, sold Fuller brushes, and taught Italian at Berlitz before moving to Washington with his wife and small son, so she could take a political writer's job on the Hill while he kept books part-time for the Sheraton Hotel. They had been demeaning years, and he still felt the sting of them. No matter how hard he tried, he couldn't seem to sell himself for what he knew he was. Until the interview at IRS Intelligence he hadn't been able to translate his skills into the kind of job he deserved and wanted.

He could admit now that he had counted too heavily on easy past successes as his father's most charmed and charming son, winning his way into the Carabinieri Academy in Rome and taking all the prizes. It might not have been exactly what he wanted, but he had enjoyed a certain status in the Carabinieri. A graduate with his standing was recognized as somebody in Italy, where the best young officers became political attachés in foreign embassies. He thought he had earned the right credentials. At twenty-two he made the front page of all the Roman dailies by saving the lives of several tourists in a hotel fire. Off-duty theatrics, his friends had teased. He had played short but heady undercover roles at work and anticipated a diplomat's career in Paris. The academy's stiffest courses had been a piece of cake for him. He was fluent in French, passable in Spanish, and good with people. Even his father, the stern, implacable police chief of Vieste, their small town on the Adriatic, had set his sights high for "Santino." His father and his fiancée's father openly competed setting goals to fix his life. Lela's father held up the family's flourishing vineyard in the south like a carrot on a stick to hook him. In 1960 his choices had been laid out like complicated courses on a banquet table. He could stay in the diplomatic service as his father wished, playing out his time in Rome and eventually working himself into France. He could marry Lela and take over her family's business, putting up with her father's constant intrusion in their lives. Or he could gamble on a long-distance courtship with an independent American reporter he had met in Rome and throw away everybody's well-laid plans on a shot at his own.

The American woman had come to Rome in 1960 from the Detroit News to write a story on the preparations for the 1960 Olympics, and he had met her by chance, doing a routine favor for a friend who managed her hotel. Some jewelry had been stolen from her room, and the manager called him instead of the local police to save the hotel from bad publicity. He had obliged and poked around and joked with her in French. Her French was poor, but she spoke no Italian, and he spoke little English. It hadn't seemed to matter that they couldn't understand each other. She was different from the cloistered women he had known—confident, ambitious. She had no family to make demands or tag along behind them. For ten days he showed her Rome, and when she left, the city seemed empty despite the crush of the Olympic Games. They exchanged unsatisfying letters in English and Italian for a year while he went about the business of his life.

That year there were no promotions and no money for investigations. He had to pay informants out of his own pocket. He gave what he could spare to his youngest brother, a medical student in Rome. On Sunday afternoons he rescued his sister from the strict, expensive convent school where she was tucked away. Sunday evenings he could count on a call from Lela, his fiancée, asking him to another boring supper with her aunt, her chaperone while she went to university in Rome. His family or Lela's seemed to tug at him at every turn. His dreams of France withered in dailiness. After a long winter his American reporter reappeared, the papers she'd need to get married in hand and freedom written on her face.

The ceremony had been small and somber. His mother wrote a long letter and never made it to the wedding. She used her absence as her best-held card, counting on the warnings in her letter to occupy her empty place. He was too high-spirited, his mother said, too much the actor, too eager for the game. His impatience and extravagance would be the dragons that could bring him down.

As the flight approached Boston, Bario watched the city coming into view through clouds. Maybe his mother had been right to be concerned. It had been tough for him until this offer from IRS Intelligence. He had used one of his wife's connections for his first introduction at Treasury, but he had got in on his own merits. Being a federal agent wouldn't be so different from a career in the Carabinieri. It would be better. He would have the resources of the U.S. Government to back him up, and he intended to use his new IRS job as the sword against whatever dragons he still carried with him. He had them, he knew. He finally spoke English well enough to quarrel with his self-reliant and competent wife. Even his son could see how his frustrations were spilling over. The boy had once accused him of becoming a monster when he got angry.

He was relieved to get away from his household, but he wasn't just escaping. He was sure he could use his undercover role to work out his problems. Those excesses in him that his mother had so painfully detailed were the material he would use to spring himself onto center stage in Boston.

He had never meant to get back into police work. It was his

father's trade. The Carabinieri Academy had been his father's choice for him. It had the status that his father had required for his sons, and it had been free, no small thing for a man with eight children coming up. Santino Bario—he had been called Santino then—had longed for a film career or an oceanography degree and the privilege of his youngest brother to choose his profession regardless of cost. But it was useless looking back that far. He was grateful for the skill and training he needed to compete in this cold and complicated country that he now called home.

He had convinced the IRS that his Carabinieri training was superb, good enough to truncate most of his special schooling in the States and to win him an immediate top-priority assignment. For once it hadn't hurt to be Italian. He was going to Boston to infiltrate the illegal wagering and racketeering organization of Boston consigliere Gennaro "Jerry" Angiulo, who controlled gambling in the Boston region for the Raymond Patriarca syndicate.

He had been briefed already and had chosen his name, "Sandro," a nickname from home, to play out his role of a young immigrant sponsored by a low-level hood in Detroit, in search of a waiter's job in the North End. He took a taxi into town, checked into his room, and lost no time staking out his little piece of Boston.

The first week he found a job at Stella's restaurant on Fleet Street, where he cultivated the bartender, who introduced him to Frank Angiulo, Jerry's brother. He discovered that he was as much a natural at making friends in the North End of Boston as he had been on the streets of Rome. He fell back on his own techniques, his instincts, and quickly abandoned the low profile that his IRS contacts favored. It had never been his style to hug the edges of the room, to merge with the background and wait for somebody to take his notice. He used his impatience, his openness, to move in on the Angiulos. The IRS could hardly complain when his style worked.

He charmed his way into Jerry Angiulo's inner circle. He had always been likable enough. Even as a kid he liked to stir things up, to make an event out of an evening. When he got into trouble at home, he had always counted on the right attitude to save him. It was the same in Boston. He argued with his IRS contact that he didn't have to become one of Angiulo's thugs to win the big man over. He refused to dress like a hood or speak in some bastardized *dialect, misused for generations. He was playing an Italian; he would show them an Italian. The caricatures who hung around Angiulo were offensive. He hated those petty Mafia hoods. In Detroit, among his wife's Midwestern friends, he was patronized for his accent, his foreign ways, but in the North End of Boston, he was the genuine article and could teach the Angiulos a thing or two. He dressed to please himself. He spoke to please himself. The results pleased the IRS enough to get his contact off his back a little.*

In a matter of months he became a regular at the Old Timer's Club and the Dog House restaurant, headquarters for the Angiulo brothers. There were tense moments, but he was all right. He was sharp, in fact, and it felt good to make such headway. When he didn't understand a particular operation, he simply asked, and the Angiulos accepted his questions. After all, he was a kid straight out of Italy. He wasn't expected to understand all the rules of the American game. He started making payoff rounds and within a year had climbed from waiter to driver to full-fledged member of the Angiulo clan, fronting a grocery store and bookmaking operation of his own. He couldn't resist making something of the grocery store, which amused the Angiulos. If he discovered an old lady who made her own fresh mozzarella, he would convince her to make enough extra to supply his store each week. He carried fresh mozzarella, homemade sausage, and the best ricotta in town. Sandro's became more than just a hole in the wall where Angiulo's clients played their lucky numbers.

He spent sixteen months in Boston. In November 1965, as a result of his investigation, twenty-three members of the Angiulo organization were arrested in the single largest raid in recent IRS history. Treasury agents and police were pelted with eggs and tomatoes as they barricaded the North End and used sledgehammers to break into restaurants, cafés, bars, all fronts for the Angiulos. Each arrest resulted in an indictment, and the IRS was pleased. There was one bad moment near the end when two Angiulo thugs put a gun to his face and accused him of working for the government, but Jerry Angiulo never bought that theory.

At the start of the trials, Bario was assaulted at the airport by Mickey "The Wise Guy" Rocco, an Angiulo cohort, but he stayed cool. Otherwise, it hadn't been so dangerous, he told himself. He grew confident of his ability to think on his feet—but never arrogant. He planned his moves strategically. He did his homework for the trials. During the weeks that followed, he testified without a stammer. "A formidable government witness," they called him in the press. He had star quality, they said. His worst moment came when the defense attorneys pulled out dirty tricks, using a private detective to trail his son. His son was only four. Months had gone by when he couldn't get home to see him.

During the next few years on his various IRS assignments, he began to consider those flights from one city to another as his only time to think, the last few hours in his own name before he set out again as someone else. His year in Boston had earned him a career, a carton of flattering news clippings, money to send home, and a kind of freedom. He liked the challenge and excitement, the absence of routine, but not the stomach pains from too many nights in too many dead-end bars, and least of all, the sense of emptiness when he flew back to Washington for weekend visits. He still couldn't compete with his wife. She was four years older and rooted in her Senate PR job. She outearned him, outclouted him, and outspoke him in her mother tongue. Maybe he was paranoid. Maybe she didn't really look down her nose at him. But he never fitted in with her tightly run ship of a life. When he had a few days or weeks between assignments, he would drive back to Washington and try to find his place. She had bought their house when he was away. She had rightfully defined it as hers. His son looked shyly out of hazel eyes at him as if he were Dick Tracy brought to life. He would visit, argue with his wife, and leave again. He told himself it wasn't what he wanted.

Other undercover assignments followed in Newark, Philadelphia, and Miami, as well as some belated schooling in U.S. tax laws and in the workings of U.S. organized crime. But the next real challenge was deep-cover infiltration of a Mafia organization in New Orleans. In 1968 Sante Bario became Sam Balderi on a driver's license and several credit cards. More sophisticated than Sandro Bartone, the Boston waiter, Sam Balderi was a thirty-two-year-old Italian who became the manager of the Bistro, a favorite late-night spot at the edge of town. For a year, Balderi lived in a small apartment in the French Quarter, hiding his copious case notes behind the metal *panel of the oven door. As top collector for the mob's gambling operation, his notes were so valuable that the gas line to the oven was disconnected for security. The results of Sam Balderi's year in New Orleans were twenty-eight arrests, and trials which would drag into 1976. The day following the IRS arrests, someone set fire to the house where Sam Balderi lived and razed it. Flying back to Washington, Bario could feel the flames in his gut.*

He took Sam Balderi with him from Louisiana to Michigan, where he used a New Orleans connection to infiltrate the Detroit mob. Balderi managed the Georgian Inn restaurant and its nightclub downstairs, the Bachelor's Quarter. The case moved on without a hitch like the ones before it, but the energy to take on a new city, another name, slowly drained out of Bario. He was losing his taste for the game. He wanted to take hold of his own life. In 1969 his mother died. His second son was born that year. He wasn't available for either event. He didn't even learn of his mother's death until weeks after the funeral was over. While he was submerged and out of touch, his life was passing by in distant cities. He couldn't give out cigars to Detroit hoods when his son was born. He couldn't grieve for his mother. At thirty-four he decided to leave the IRS and undercover work. He went back to Washington in time to baptize his second child.

He wanted out of law enforcement. He had a way with people. He could make something of himself in another line of work. He could start his own restaurant, except he didn't have the cash. But, Jesus, he could do anything. He toyed with the idea of applying for a management position at the Washington Hilton. After all, he had run the Bistro in New Orleans. He had spent a year in Detroit, turning the Georgian Inn around. He had brought in a new chef, redecorated, and made clean money for the Detroit mob. He had enjoyed it and was flattered when its new, straight owners decided to keep the menu he had so carefully selected. But his restaurant experience in New Orleans and Detroit meant nothing in D.C., once he moved out of the government. He couldn't even list it on his résumé, which showed long, blank spaces after those first lean years in the States. It was as if the past six years of his life had been wiped out. They existed only in the IRS' secret files. The Sheraton offered him the night shift again, but he couldn't stoop to that. For weeks he wandered the city, pricing efficiency apartments and looking for work before going home to another disagreement with his wife, to his impatience with his kids. He began to lose his sense of himself as the actor at center stage. But he felt restored again when Intertel called.

Intertel was a private, international intelligence organization, hired by businesses to investigate corruption within their own ranks or sabotage by competing companies. Bario had applied as a last resort, when he couldn't face his humiliation any longer. He had quite a reputation, according to the ex-CIA man at Intertel, and they could use a first-rate investigator to assess internal security for the Howard Hughes casinos in Las Vegas. Bario was tempted by the same things that had kept him with the IRS so long—a ready-made life where the lines were clearly drawn, the challenge, the confidence that he could bring a new role off. Yet he hesitated. Intertel was just another step on the same road that he had traveled down with the IRS. It would mean a new name and the same brick wall between his work and his life. But he could do it. He had no doubt that he could do it. It would be so much easier than squeezing himself into some skimpy role in Washington's small world. The assignment would last six months or so, time to consider his real-life options.

He worked four casinos in Las Vegas, climbing from croupier to pit boss in less than a month, getting to know the staff and encouraging any crooked action to come his way. He changed apartments three times, each new complex closer to the strip. It was exciting at first, the off hours, the flash of the casinos. Every apartment was fitted with matching blackout drapes. He sent postcards to his father in Vieste: neon lighting up the city in the middle of the night. He finally stopped gauging daylight time. The days and nights ran into one another. He would get off at six in the morning, have a light supper at the club, and set out at seven for a late night date. There was a girl he dated once, a dancer and suspected leak. When they went for an early morning swim at her private pool, she kicked off her mules, stepped out of a sequined skirt, and neatly set her wig on the poolside table. Her skull was smoother than a ten ball, and she didn't even blink. It was her way of being noticed by the management, she said; it made her wardrobe changes that much quicker. At the eight o'clock show she was a redhead, at midnight she became a *blonde. He was so turned off, he turned around and left her, bald and naked by her kidney-shaped pool. Let Howard Hughes go out and make her.*

It was the loneliness that convinced him to turn down Intertel's offer of a permanent position. Not even Paradise Island could tempt him. He could count on one hand the people he knew well enough in his own name to call after hours on an empty night: his sister in Ohio, his kids, his distant wife. He went back to Washington and took a job with the Senate Commerce Committee. He was expected to take two-hour lunches, to keep a bottle of scotch in the drawer of his desk. Everybody else did. The days were safe and ordinary, the nights were awful. He spent his evenings on an EZ-Boy recliner and his early mornings in silence at the breakfast table. From nine to five it was, Yes, the senator will look at toolmaking companies in northern New Jersey; No, the senator won't be on the floor today. Triple-space the senator's notes on the large-face typewriter when you slip him a page. He missed the freedom of an undercover world.

He admitted he had chosen his work to escape his marriage. He had to accept that his marriage had failed. Never mind that no one in his hometown, let alone his family, had ever been divorced. He wasn't living by Vieste's standards anymore. If he were free of his marriage and could focus on his kids, he would have much more to give them. Face up to his failure, get out of D.C. It had never been his town, with its political swagger. One more time he would go back under cover, but this time when he came out, he would bring his success out with him. If he chose well, he could still become a diplomat. He would travel, go back to Italy sporting a diplomatic passport and a new career. He would look for a posting overseas, and the next time he came out from under cover, he swore he would come out for good.

1

Sante Bario left Washington in 1972 to become a special agent for the Bureau of Narcotics and Dangerous Drugs, traveling between New York and Paris, where he was playing out two roles. In Paris he was Salvatore Bonanno, heir to the famous Jo Attia family of thieves and drug dealers in Paris and Marseilles. It was a sophisticated, stylish case. He assumed Jo Attia's throne after the old man's death by buying a half interest in Attia's Montmartre cabaret and planning complex scams with Attia's aging mistress. For months at a time he lived in Paris, unraveling heroin routes from Marseilles and Madrid into the U.S. through Canada. He learned who placed stolen art and arranged shipments of illegal arms for Attia. At the high point of the case, he dived from the side of a pleasure boat into the Mediterranean to avoid capture by the French police. When he wasn't Salvatore Bonanno in Paris, he went back to New York to be Sam Barone, proving charges by the U.S. attorney's top informant, Robert Leuci, that corruption in the city touched lawyers and bail bondsmen, even a district attorney in Queens, who fixed indictments for a price.

To the small group of prosecutors in Manhattan who knew about his exploits, he was the legendary Sandy Bario, handsome and charming, unlike anybody's image of a narc. Their secretaries at the courthouse raved about him, how he seemed able to play any role without losing himself, how considerate he was, how amusing.

On their coffee breaks, they repeated his stories about growing up in a small resort town in Italy. They were taken by his glamour, his attentions that singled them out and made them special. He sent postcards from Europe and, once, in thanks for late-night typing, delivered a bottle of expensive French wine to the steno pool with an apology for the plastic glasses. That was the same night they overheard him singing Verdi arias with one of the prosecutors working on his case. He sang beautifully. He could have been a movie star, they said.

I was like those secretaries on the edge of Sandy Bario's life in 1972, charmed by him, watching him, wanting to be noticed. We watched each other through what seemed a year of dinner parties, but once he asked me out, it took only weeks to set me up on center stage and change my life.

I had friends in the U.S. attorney's office in New York who used to invite me to their parties. Sandy always came alone, in paper-thin white shirts when nobody wore white shirts, in a dark blue suit as if he weren't going where the rest of us were going. We were studiously casual; he was always formal. I think he knew he'd been invited as the current hot item of the courthouse crowd, the agent who didn't look or act like an agent, who told amazing stories and would be the star witness when his big case went to trial.

I wanted to dislike him. He was a narc when all my friends were smoking marijuana. He was into cops and robbers, low-class stuff. Besides, he was Italian, and my family was Italian—at least my grandparents on both sides had been. I'd get no kick from his tired Mafia stories about crooks who smoked cigars and used bad grammar. In the Virginia suburbs where I grew up, anyone with an Italian name was suspected of having a Mafia connection. Sante Bario was out to reinforce that image. I'd resented him before we ever met.

I expected Sandy to be predictable, boring, but he was a great showstopper. When he came in, the conversation came to life, shifting from politics or complaints about bad judges to vignettes of Paris or Las Vegas. They weren't cop stories either. They never centered on his undercover work. They were character portraits which he acted out. He played the outraged attendant in the morgue where the Paris police had hidden Jo Attia's body wrapped in dirty hospital linen and stolen away by his mistress on the bottom shelf of a hospital cart. Or he played the fussy restaurateur in Montmartre whose dining room was a mock railroad car from the 1930s, complete with fake vibrations that rattled the expensive crystal on the tables. He was best when he talked about Vieste, describing the grottoes and the sea and the kiosk in the square. I saw a young boy in short pants on a high terrace wall, tempted by a row of plum tomatoes ripening in the sun. When the meanest family in town appeared below, he couldn't resist and heaved one at their puffed-up daughter parading in her white communion dress. "Pow!" he said, and I watched the ripe tomato splatter. I didn't know whether to laugh or cry for the girl in her spoiled, starchy dress, but I envied that boy's daring, and every story made me more in awe of the man he had become, a *real* Italian, theatrical and charged. I loved the way he touted his background. The men of my childhood, uncles and grown-up cousins in argyle sweaters whose mission had been to smooth out their rough Italian edges, had moved their backgrounds under cover. I had holiday memories of their gruff voices overwhelming the women's small talk at Thanksgiving dinner, drowning them out with play-by-play descriptions of football games, relaxing in what I considered false ease in their fine houses on tree-lined streets. I wanted them to be at ease enough to show me who they *really* were. My father became less playful and more remote each year as I grew up, absorbed by the construction business and his lifelong work of fitting in. Sandy didn't fit in. I didn't want to fit in either.

Sometimes there weren't any stories. He'd appear at a gathering all dressed up with a bag of groceries in his arms and a smile on his face as he unloaded fresh fennel and arugula, exotic bitter greens he had found in a downtown market. "I could make a little salad," he'd suggest and with the hostess's permission would disappear into her unfamiliar kitchen.

It was New Year's Eve before I realized that Sandy noticed me. It was late, the party almost over. We were sitting on the couch together; he poured a glass of cognac for me. When I couldn't pretend to like it, he covered my hand with his, took the snifter, and sipped from it himself for hours. He asked a lot of questions to keep me on that couch—where I worked and what I did and if I liked New York. That was my first night of sleepless dreams about him. I was sure my answers had been disappointing. I was too ordinary, too young. I hadn't been around enough. Alone in my skinny platform bed by an air-shaft window, I reviewed everything I'd said, hating my tongue-tied, girlish remarks. I should have flirted more, made clever conversation. I was sure I'd blown my only chance. The following morning, he left again for Paris.

He was gone two weeks, returning to another week's solid work preparing for his trial. I didn't expect to see him, but I read about him in the paper when the trial started: "He looks like an Italian film star playing the lead in a private eye movie. But the role Sante Bario has been playing in federal court this week is the real thing." The DA, the bail bondsman, the defense attorney were all convicted. After the trial was over, Sandy called at work and asked me out to lunch. We went to the Hyde Park Hotel, where he kept a "safe" suite and was known by an undercover name. It was an intense, nervous two-hour lunch. I kept trying to invent excuses for being late to work. But the files of book-jacket copy waiting at the vanity press where I worked couldn't compete with my infatuation. Sandy made me feel as if he'd waited years for this lunch. To make it last, we sat at the far end of the bar and drank three coffees. The wall behind the bar was mirrored. It was easier watching his mirror image than watching Sandy himself lean close, stroke my hand, ask if it would bother me to know how much he loved me. "Through all those parties I fell in love with you," he said. I saw in that mirror a thirty-six-year-old adventurer who knew the world, four languages, whom women always fell for. But I couldn't figure out what he saw in me.

He must have made me up the way he made himself up, fooled by my Italian name into thinking I was like him. "Tumolo," he said, meant a measurement for wine. In his voice it sounded musical and lovely, nothing like the mutilations it had gone through in Virginia where I grew up. "Tummilo," "Tamalo," "Tomato" in seventh grade, a name completely lacking grace. I could never show it off, make it over the way my brother did, wearing his own version on his Toyota's license plate—2 Mello. I was never mellow about my name or anything—"Tumultuous Tumolo," I was tagged by my best friend in college. Watching Sandy in that mirror, listening to him describe the woman that he believed I was, I bit my lip to keep from blurting out the failures in my brief adult career—walking away from an exclusive fellowship, turning my back on a Ph.D. because it was too boring, stumbling through jobs and confusing affairs. After three years in New York, I was still at the back desk in a back room writing advertising copy, reworking the same two-inch blurbs for books that didn't matter. How could I expose the real woman behind the image that Sandy Bario was courting? She didn't deserve him. He'd take one look and run away. So I kept her under wraps, determined to become instead that fresh, poised, lively woman that he wanted.

After our first dramatic lunch, Sandy went back to France to tie up his last long-term undercover case. He wouldn't get involved, he said, until he was out from under cover and could come to me in his own name, with more to offer than late-night dates squeezed in between assignments. He called when he was in New York. If he were free long enough, he'd appear at my office and take me to lunch. He was impressive at the office. My friends said he was amazing. My bosses gave me time. We always went to hotels or restaurants where he was known—the Stanhope, the Westbury—or small, intimate restaurants near Sutton Place, where he kept an apartment for another New York case. But I didn't go out with him alone at night until August, when the Jo Attia case was finished.

2

I was twenty-six when Sandy appeared on the landing of my third-floor walk-up on Eighteenth Street with a single red rose and an invitation. He looked out of place in his blue silk suit in the bad light of a hall that smelled like cats, and for a moment I didn't want to ask him into my two tiny, cluttered rooms. They would be too revealing. Too much junk-store kitsch and rumpled blue jeans on the floor of every closet. Even with the prop of a new four-hundred-dollar dress, he'd see right through me. I was sure I couldn't pull the evening off. We were too different: Italian super cop who'd been all over and slow-burning adolescent still waiting for her life to start. He was used to better backdrops than I could manage, but there he was, so I pressed myself against the closet door to let him in. We both laughed, which eased the tension. There wasn't space for two in that cramped corner between closet and front door, grandly called a foyer by the rental agent. I led him into the living-room-and-kitchen combination, pots on one wall, a bricked-up fireplace outlined on the other. He didn't seem to notice the tacky yellow curtains or the artful arrangement on the coffee table of two cut-crystal glasses and a ten-dollar bottle of wine from my corner liquor store. Maybe this is easy after all, maybe I can get away with it, I thought.

"You look beautiful," he said. I knew the dress was beautiful. I'd lived through two hours of anxiety selecting it. With a month's salary bunched in my purse, I'd walked into Place Elegante at Bloomingdale's with a nonchalance suggesting that I shopped there every day. The dress was worth it: wine-colored French silk with long sleeves and a simple V neck, cut low enough to shock my proper mother. I practiced for an hour before Sandy arrived, walking the length of my skinny rooms in that long dress without a bra, trying to look natural. I thought I had mastered the right look, but when he offered the rose, I blushed and backed off from his grand gestures that weren't simply gestures. If he'd offered me a romantic moment, nothing more, I'd have taken it as lightly. But he wasn't offering merely an evening, a dinner and *La Traviata* at the Met. He was setting out with me and said so. The Jo Attia case was over. The Queen's district attorney was convicted. With so much success behind him, Sandy had hired his own lawyer to prepare a formal separation from his wife. For the first time in a long time, he felt free.

If he could start over, maybe I could, too. I didn't want a safe, ordinary life, the life my parents wanted for me. My rebellions had always been so small—runny eggs in bed-and-breakfast rooms in England when I toured alone on the cheap at nineteen, peace marches on the Pentagon grounds when I was twenty. I hadn't even managed to get myself arrested when a brush with the law would have been heroic. There had been a safety net beneath every wild impulse I'd ever followed. If all else failed, my good Italian parents would bail me out. This time I wanted to dive. I wanted to break away. I could be as theatrical as Sandy. I could go out on his limb and match his daring. Only first I had to test him, make sure he was what the newspapers promised—Sante Bario, the real thing, as different from me and the men I knew as Vieste was from Vienna, Virginia.

We set out that night in a rusty Cadillac confiscated from some drug bust and borrowed from his office. I didn't mind when he apologized, saying he had to make a detour through Chinatown before taking me uptown to dinner. I was content beside him on those dirty leather seats with static crackling from the police radio stashed in the glove compartment. I had my private game to occupy me, paring Sandy's convoluted past down to its barest bones to uncover him, at the same time drawing closer to his most complicated parts. I asked him to name all the names he'd ever used and the cities where he'd lived. Too many names, he said, and the fear of the wrong one in the wrong town. I thought I could take him down, bit by bit. He might seem sophisticated, but he was still a narc, and that wasn't so romantic. That was awful, really. It wasn't cool to be a narc—though I had to admit it was far out to be his kind of narc. He might have dived dramatically from a boat in the Mediterranean and won awards for valor, but for nearly ten years he had lived with crooks. He had eaten six-course suppers at their tables and flattered their fat wives. He might even have dated their daughters before he turned the fathers in. He lived by lies. With roses, cognac, and this big date at Lincoln Center, he was deceiving me.

I was a lousy skeptic, too happy to make more than weak stabs at puncturing Sandy. Who was I to criticize? At least he'd taken risks, gone somewhere, lived his life. He looked older than thirty-six. I liked the age in his face. Besides, I wanted to be in that enormous, tacky car parked on a dark corner in Chinatown, watching Sandy slip into a phone booth down the block to meet with his informer. It never occurred to me that he was doing what he said he didn't want to do, stealing time from his work to be with me. I didn't care if he had somehow merged with his job, if being the real thing meant that he was always on, always working. It was enough that he had so much energy and was so handsome, that the evening promised to be original and even had its touch of secrecy and danger. I watched his unlikely informant appear, a small Chinese woman reciting tales of heroin, and I was thrilled to be there. So it was unfashionable to be a narc. So what? He was all the fashion I required.

We went to Le Mistral for dinner. Sandy had reserved a private table in an alcove in the back and earlier that afternoon had ordered specialties that weren't on the menu from the chef himself. There were waiters in white coats discreetly hovering and three kinds of wine. But the dinner was just the evening's setting. He had brought me there to talk about his dream of starting over. He wanted to talk about us, but I wasn't ready to listen. I wanted to be absolutely sure that I could trust him before I plunged. I asked him about Paris instead, and reluctantly he began describing the narrow cobbled streets, the one-room cabaret he "owned" with Carmen, Jo Attia's mistress.

"She was really something," he said. "In her fifties when we met and like anybody's maiden aunt, dressed in dark colors and puffing as she climbed the steep hill to Le Gavroche each morning. She looked harmless, but she was the moving force behind Attia. She cooked up their most complicated schemes and expected to use me just like she'd used Jo. We'd unlock the cabaret together in the mornings and sit at the bar sipping champagne while she'd plan the meetings for the day—whose goods we'd fence, whose we would squeeze out. The more elaborate the scheme, the more she liked it."

He described spending a week in Monte Carlo, watching Carmen in action. She'd decked herself out like a wealthy matron from the provinces, rented the most expensive suite in the best hotel. It took weeks to perfect the charade, but eventually the most exclusive jewelers in town were begging to display their wares in her rooms, graciously offering to leave them overnight while the grande dame made up her mind. She'd left town at 3 A.M. one night, a few hundred thousand richer, and never even warned him.

"She conned you, didn't she?" I asked, watching the candles flicker in his dark eyes. "And why not? That was her game. You weren't worthy of her trust."

He looked hurt for a moment, then smiled. "She needed me. I was her protection. She liked the wheeling and dealing, but she was smart enough to be afraid of the tougher hoods in Jo's crowd. If they pushed her out, there'd be more for them. Attia was dying of throat cancer. He couldn't help her. But I could." He paused, reached across the table for my hand. He had a wonderful smile, flirtatious, worldly, innocent all at once. "You like the thought that she could con me? She tried once, when Jo died. I was in New York, and she sent a telegram to my apartment on Sutton Place, saying to return immediately to Paris. Jo was dead, she was in the hospital. She'd staged a fake assault and robbery at her apartment, had admitted herself with a few scrapes and bruises. She wasn't anybody's fool. She cleaned out the house and checked herself into a place where no one could touch her, in case any of Jo's rivals decided to attack.

"When I got to the hospital, she was in bed with two black eyes and tears running down her face. 'Look what they've done to me,' she said. 'They took everything. I'm ruined.' I gave her one straight look and told her, 'Not with me, Carmen,' and she dropped the act completely. The tears dried. She plumped her pillows up and smiled. *'D'accord,'* she said, and it was over. That's when I knew I had her. She was good. She was very good at plotting her little bits of theater."

"What happened when you left?" I asked. "Was she arrested?"

"No. She wanted to write a book about her life with Jo. We sent a writer in from the CIA, who flipped her. Now she informs for the French police."

He smiled as if that were the perfect ending, but I couldn't leave it. "Didn't you feel badly?"

"Why? She was fine. She still has Le Gavroche. I'll take you there some day. I would love to take you to Paris."

"But you played her game."

"Sure, I played it, as best I knew how. I learned from her. She was shrewd, amusing. She had her style, but she knew all the heroin routes through Europe and the names of the men who ran them. She knew the risks. She took her chances."

The flames of the candles wavered on the table. The classy waiters served dessert and coffee. "If you play the same game, what makes you any better?"

He took my hand again and stroked it. "I'm on the good guys' side, remember? I'm not ashamed of what I do in my work. But this isn't work, and I'm not playing games. I finally have what I've always wanted—you and a real chance of starting over."

"What if I'm not who you think I am?"

"You are. I know you are. You have reservations about my job. Okay, I do, too. I told you I want to make a change. I don't want to play any more Jo Attia cases. But I'm good at what I do because I know who to trust, how to read people. I know you. Oh, I may not know a hundred things about you, but I've watched you, listened to you. You don't want a life where every day's the same, and neither do I. We'll have fun. We'll do crazy things. I'll take a supervisor's job abroad with the Drug Enforcement Administration. We can go to Paris or Rome. Or some place even more exotic if you want."

We were leaning into each other across that table. He touched my face. "Yes, I want to," I said. "I'm a little bit chicken, but I want to."

He looked so pleased. "We're late," he said. "We'll miss the first act, but that's all right. I'll sing it to you in the car. It's too sad a story anyway for this occasion."

We came in on the second act of *La Traviata*, with my long dress rustling down the aisle. Sandy had convinced the usher to seat us during the duet between Violetta and Alfredo's father. Sandy had told the story in the car, tongue in cheek, saying it was too Italian with its big moral sacrifice for Alfredo's little sister, who doesn't even show her face. He smiled, adding it would still make sense to most of the old crones in Vieste that Violetta had to die to play her famous final scene.

"I'm not in the mood for sacrifice," he said, "but we're dressed and have our tickets. We'll make a deal—if you don't think the music beautiful, if it doesn't make me homesick, then we'll leave."

It didn't make him homesick. It put him to sleep. Three kinds of wine and our own love scene across the table at dinner made it hard to pay attention. I thought it was funny to see him nodding off. I giggled, jabbed him in the side. But the audience around us didn't find us so amusing. "Shush!" said a woman down the aisle after my third jab. Sandy sat up and rubbed his eyes. I tried to follow the libretto in the dark. Finally, he whispered in my ear: "I'm not homesick yet. What do you think of the music?"

We left at the end of the second act and ran down the side street where we'd parked the car, then leaned against its hulk to share a cigarette.

"You see how right I am about you," he said. "As a reward for my good judgment, we'll leave this tank right here and walk home. It's against every regulation to take a beautiful woman out in an ugly government car with an official radio that could at any moment send me back to work."

We walked to the East Side and stopped at a fancy bar for a drink. I ordered cognac and forced myself to finish it. It wasn't so bad. I decided I could learn to like it. After walking three more blocks downtown, we hailed a cab, ending up on the front steps of my building. It was almost two in the morning. We'd spent hours in that Third Avenue bar, planning the great escape which would be our life together. Eighteenth Street was empty. I sat on the step above Sandy's, thinking it didn't matter if he were just a fantasy, as long as he continued as the fantasy I wanted. I wasn't convinced I could make myself the touchstone of his new beginning, but it suddenly seemed important to try.

"We could go upstairs," I said, perky and modern. "It's late, the car is all the way uptown. You could stay the night."

He looked back at me, eyes intense and serious. "We don't have to. I don't want you to think I've been sitting here hoping to take you to bed. I've taken enough women to bed. I want more than that from you."

I tried out my old Groucho Marx routine. "But it wouldn't be such a bad start, would it?"

I went to bed with Sandy as another way of testing him. That's what I thought. It seemed daring—I wasn't very smooth about it. The logistics alone were complicated. After so much wine, I wasn't sure I could handle the three flights of stairs, the cardboard walls of my apartment, worst of all the heavy coffee table standing in the way of the pull-out bed. I wanted my big moment without moving furniture or finding space for the sofa's lumpy cushions. I turned on the lamp between the windows, unzipped my dress—one zip and I was almost naked. We'd undone the bed by then. Clean sheets, the summer blanket tucked neatly under. I hoped he wouldn't think me cheap for being well prepared. As I stood with my four-hundred-dollar dress in a heap at my feet, panty hose around my ankles, he reached out for me.

"See," he whispered, "I'm absolutely right about you."

He was everything I'd ever wished for as a girl alone in her room at night, dreaming of her ideal lover.

It was dawn when he fell asleep. The windows turned gray, throwing off more light than the lamp on the desk between them. Sandy lay in the middle of the bed, one arm across his eyes, the other underneath a pillow. He was snoring. I figured if I kissed him gently, he might stop or at least roll over. But I didn't know him well enough to kiss him while he was so deeply sleeping. The kiss seemed like an invasion, or the snoring was. I got up, dragged the sheet with me and tucked it beneath my arms like in the movies. Four steps and I was across the room, bare legs curled under me on the rocking chair. I reached over, turned off the lamp. I would have liked a cigarette but was afraid to get up and look. I didn't want to risk disturbing Sandy. Better to stay where I was with the light crossing the brick wall, touching his face, and spend the time reviewing our evening, tallying up the pros and cons—should I believe in him or not? I remembered his description of Carmen in Paris. What had made her trust him? Maybe he'd slept with her to get his information. I tried to picture Sandy in his white voile shirt, Carmen in stolen jewels. I didn't want to think of them in bed together. I'd never ask him.

Besides, it didn't really matter. I didn't care if Sandy had conned her or a hundred crooks in Boston. I wasn't looking for the morality of his life as much as the drama in it—this man, this night, this high adventure. What I couldn't bear was the snoring, the threat that after the operas, the restaurants, the late-night walks, we might flatten into dailiness.

The sheet slipped off my breasts. I hiked it up again, and the rocker creaked. Sandy stirred, sat up, said my name before he saw me.

"What's wrong?" he asked. "You couldn't sleep?"

I shook my head. "You were snoring."

He smiled guiltily and covered his head with the blanket, muttering, "I'm sorry." When he pulled the blanket off, he reached for me. "I should have warned you. Come, let me apologize."

I gathered up the sheet, made it over to the bed, pounced on him. "I hate snoring."

"So the truth comes out," he said, wrapping the sheet around us both. "I'm not good enough for you, my snoring has finally made up your mind."

He pulled back, took a long steady look, and kissed me.

3

I gave up my apartment in the city three weeks later and moved upstate with him to Piermont, his village on the Hudson, where we'd stay awake all night indulging in midnight walks along the Sparkill Creek, coming home to make love on the wall-to-wall gold carpet. We smoked too many cigarettes and brewed too many cups of thick Italian coffee in his dented Neapolitan pot. We refused to relinquish our long, exclusive lunches even when they threatened my job. I was willing to pay that price for the extravagance of Sandy. I must have deserved some of the pleasure that he gave me. Then why did I continue to punish us with doubts? If I insisted on seeing my life with him as a fantasy, I could at least have lived it completely while it lasted. He was too good, really. He offered everything, and I refused him half. It is difficult forgiving such stinginess of heart.

Sandy was never one for halfway measures. He was absolutely starting over. From his first marriage he took only that copper coffeepot, some photographs, the hand-tailored Parisian clothes he loved. The night we moved my things from Eighteenth Street, he ceremoniously walked me out to the end of the Piermont pier and threw his wedding ring into the lapping water. The next day we bought new wedding bands from Tiffany's, which we consecrated in a glass of Bordeaux wine. We would have to wait almost two years for his divorce to be final, but in the meantime, he asked me to use his name and be his wife. We would make our own marriage, he said, with our own forms to back us up.

The week after I moved in, he rented a car to take me to Virginia and meet my family. He didn't own a car. He hadn't been in one place long enough to need one. He had a government car for use in his work, but he couldn't arrive at my parents' house in a souped-up car from the DEA. That would be too declassé as well as against official regulations. He loaded the backseat of the rental car with the gifts of food he had bought to sweeten his declaration —a whole wheel of Bel Paese, two bottles of Verdicchio, a box of Italian chocolate kisses, and three pounds of cured black olives. He sat on my mother's velvet couch and formally explained his intentions to my father, who fell for him completely. I could see approval on my father's face and in the way he rubbed his chin and moved forward in his chair. My father, who had always been stiff and unapproachable with the boys I had brought home, felt comfortable with Sandy. They discovered that my grandfather's hometown was in Foggia, too, the same province where Vieste was, only in the mountains, far from the Gargano coast. Excitedly, my father recounted how my grandfather had left his mountain town all alone at the age of thirteen, walking all the way to Naples, where he worked for months to earn his passage on a boat. We had gone to Foggia ourselves the year before on a pilgrimage—my mother, my father, and I, up into that tiny mountain town, into the hall of records and on to the idle square where Tumolos were as common as Joneses in Virginia. There were groups of teenaged boys sitting on the crumbling wall of a waterless fountain, notices for the next Communist rally plastered on the sides of buildings. "I understood then why he had to get out," my father said. "I was grateful. But such a nice town, so friendly. We even met some cousins there."

During my father's story, my mother hung back, excused herself, and disappeared into her big yellow kitchen where Sandy's gifts were on the table. I followed her.

"So? What do you think of him?" I asked.

"He's charming and ruggedly handsome. I can see why you're attracted to him." The catch in my mother's throat gave her away.

"But you don't like him."

"I didn't say that. I've just met him. I'm sure I'll like him very much. He seems genuinely in love with you."

"Then why did you leave?"

"You said you aren't staying the night. You have that long drive ahead of you. I thought I'd cook so dinner won't be late."

I grabbed her hand, led her to a chair at the kitchen table.

"This is rude," she said. "He'll know we're in here talking about him."

"Then don't be tricky. Tell me what you really think."

"All right. You're too different. He's from a completely different culture. He's too old-world for you, you're too American for him."

"But that's silly," I said. "He isn't Italian the way your parents were Italian. He's educated, he's lived everywhere."

"Then if you want to live together, why don't you just live together? Why are you wearing a wedding ring?"

Late that night, in a motel room off the New Jersey Turnpike where we finally stopped at 3 A.M., I asked Sandy my mother's question. "She's right," he said. "If we want to be married, we ought to get married. Properly."

That whole week after we got back from Virginia, I felt out of breath from trying to keep up with Sandy. Monday night we went to Staten Island where somebody in his office knew a Ford dealer willing to make deals. Sandy was going to buy me a car—not a VW Beetle as I had suggested, but a proper car, big and white with a tan interior that was supposed to highlight my complexion. What still seemed shaky and private to me, he was impatient to make public. He called my two best friends and invited them to our "wedding party" in a restaurant in Nyack that Friday night. He called his own sponsors, too, an ex-CIA man from Boston and the DEA agent who had hired him in Washington. He made their airline reservations; they would arrive on Friday afternoon. The restaurant was on the riverbank in Nyack. After we picked up the car in Staten Island late Wednesday afternoon, we drove straight to Nyack to plan the menu with the chef and maître d'. It had to be special, Sandy explained; it was our wedding, after all. In the end, he settled for the best they could do, oysters, lobster, dry white wine, and for dessert, champagne and wedding cake with whipped cream frosting.

I couldn't help feeling edgy. Sandy was planning the grand opening event of his new life. He'd spent the week announcing us, giving us substance, loading us down with acceptable IDs. In the peculiar past he carried with him, such credentials were always the starting point, the props he needed to make himself legitimate: a car registered in his own name and the woman he loved to wear his ring and be his wife. He didn't want loose ends, a temporary, casual connection. He'd had enough of those, and they had never changed his life. He had to sanctify us—for my parents, his own father, Vieste. Beneath his sophisticated clothes, he was still the police chief's son in that small, old-fashioned town where form and ceremony mattered. He might stir things up, bend the rules a little, but he never broke the law. He couldn't live with me outside marriage unless he could somehow make a marriage in his mind.

On October 2, 1973, he married me at the Captain's Table in Nyack, New York. From the incongruous group we'd invited, he managed to make a wedding party. The women came in long dresses, the men in dark suits, to sip champagne, to celebrate the necessary toasts, to listen to a short and tender speech from Sandy. When it was over, he was satisfied. He'd dignified us. He had married me in every way he could except on paper.

The only problem left was mine. I couldn't pack myself up and move completely into Sandy's dream. I was too afraid we were making asses of ourselves in that big white car, at that Nyack wedding. I couldn't take his name and use it comfortably, the way I use it now. I let him down, even when I was trying hardest to be exactly what I thought he wanted. I loved his sense of the glitter and show of ceremony, but I couldn't quite convince myself that it was real. He wasn't trying to make us over. He just wanted us to merge the way lovers are supposed to—to match, to fit each other. I wore blue jeans, so he went out and bought blue jeans. I have pictures of him kneeling in our garden in his baggy, badly fitting jeans. He wanted me to be his wife, and so I tried. But a European lover fitted my high-blown image of myself the way a pretend husband couldn't. How could I be his wife when he still had a wife somewhere?

He overestimated my imagination. He didn't know how literal I'd turn out to be. Though I said with a certain cheekiness that I can do this, I'll be this, I wasn't theatrical enough to carry out my role in Sandy's biggest scene.

4

Our first bad moment came one month later, November in Italy.

Sandy had begun to make himself over in his job by joining a regular enforcement group in the DEA's New York office. His plan was to become an "ordinary agent," a regular team player, to prove that he could operate in another setting according to the DEA's administrative rules and regulations. When he had demonstrated that he could function from an office as successfully as he had under cover, we'd leave New York and move into the diplomatic world. The DEA had offices in every major U.S. embassy. Sandy would apply for each vacancy in an attractive foreign city and finally begin a new phase of his career. No more undercover names. He'd use his own name to take his new wife out into the world.

But he soon felt frustrated by the nature of the work—the ineffectual nickel-and-dime showdowns on the street, the hours of surveillance in the middle of the night producing only dead-end, penny-ante dealers who couldn't lead him anywhere. He wanted the big man, the main connection. Almost immediately after his permanent assignment to New York, he switched to a group targeting international heroin traffic. It was a case for that group which gave us our excuse to go to Rome, and from Rome to Vieste.

It was a loaded trip for Sandy. He was taking me to meet his family. But before risking it, he wanted to make sure I'd be properly received. He wrote long, formal letters to his sister in Rome and his father in Vieste, letters proving I was valuable enough to justify his divorce and separation from his children. Especially in the letter to his father, the phrasing and vocabulary mattered. He spent a night on the living-room floor with his Italian dictionary, checking and rechecking every word. My part was to play the worthwhile prize, his family's part was to accept me as Sandy's wife, the symbol of his new beginning. He wrote paragraphs about our Nyack "wedding," translating them for me, asking how they sounded. "Flattering," I said, "but right."

I didn't let him down at first. He didn't know how hard it was to wear his ring and call myself his bride. I wanted to believe he could make it happen, that he had that power. I loved him. I just couldn't match his intensity of purpose.

When we were together in Rome, it was easy. He took me to his old haunts, the bar in the Regina Carlton Hotel where he used to work, the narrow back street where he had his first apartment. We went to Montecitorio to meet his mentor from his early days with the Carabinieri. We went to his old barber for haircuts one afternoon and afterward to a café where he once met his informers. But he hadn't gone to Italy for pleasure. He spent ten days traveling back and forth from his sister's apartment in Rome to Naples, where he was playing a New York buyer in search of heroin. Most of the time he was gone, I did okay. Anna and Ettore, her husband, didn't take Sandy's letter as a joke. They teased but honored him as well. They were kind to me. While Anna taught in the mornings, I played with her children or went for long walks. I even took the metro by myself. I was fine until the children's nurse came to say my husband was calling on the phone, or Anna introduced me to yet another friend as her sister-in-law. Within the week I began chafing at so many introductions as Sandy's wife. I had a passport in my own name in my purse. My own name was good enough for me.

He came back at the end of the week, pleased with the case and more pleased that it was over, eager to celebrate. The next morning was the first of December, misty and cold. We took an early cab downtown, where Sandy ushered me inside the U.S. Embassy on Via Veneto to meet old friends. "This is my wife," he'd say, "my beautiful new wife," each repetition diminishing me.

Afterward we sat under a plastic canopy in the Café de Paris across the street from the embassy, sipping cappuccino beneath a blue electric heater.

"We have the rest of the day," he said. "Our train doesn't leave till midnight. What would you like to do?"

"I don't think I'm going to Vieste," I began, cupping my hands around the coffee cup, unable to look at him. "Not if we have to keep pretending I'm your wife. Your family must realize your divorce isn't final. They know we aren't really married. They know, we know. It's just a stupid game."

I felt the weight of his elbows on the table as he leaned across to me. "Of course we're married. We got married on October 2 in Nyack."

"Let's stop fooling ourselves, can't we? We didn't get married. We had a dinner party and made a lot of silly speeches. We bought rings and pretended, but nothing's changed. When your divorce is final, I'd love to marry you. But now I want to be what we really are. I don't have to use your name to love you. I feel like I'm doing something wrong, that I'm lying. It embarrasses me."

I finally looked up at him, staring hard, slumped forward in his chair with those dark eyes trying to uncover whatever else I might have hidden, and I suddenly wanted to take back everything I'd said. I'd been unfaithful. He'd never believe in me again. I'd ruined the morning, the trip, the entire setting for his new life. I pictured losing him, when I wanted him so much—his intensity, his accent, Rome, Vieste. If I had to be his wife to keep him, surely I could learn to be his wife.

"I thought you were serious," he whispered, "that you understood. I meant everything I said at what you call that dinner party. I don't need a judge to tell me right from wrong, whether or not I'm married. Yes, I'll marry you again to make it legal in the record books. But the real marriage for me was that night in Nyack. I would have never gone through with it if I thought you took it as a game.

"You lied, you conned me." He smiled a hurt and distant smile. "Don't demean yourself by using my name or making the long trip to Vieste. I wanted to take my wife to meet my father. If you aren't my wife, there isn't any point."

He put some splashy lira notes down on the table to cover our bill and got up. I watched him wind around the tables underneath that plastic tent and slip out the flimsy door. I watched his long, beautiful body walk away, distorted through a film of plastic. This is it, I thought. He'll really go. He'll go back to Anna's and wait. No, he wouldn't do that. He wouldn't leave me on Via Veneto with my pocket dictionary in my purse. He'd come back for me, but it would still be over. I could imagine his silence in the taxi, his cold suggestion that I take an early flight back to New York, the drive to the airport in silence. How could I have been so stupid? The Nyack wedding was genuine for Sandy, but I was too American, too middle-class, too suburban to make it real for me. My mother in her granny glasses, in her yellow kitchen, had been wrong. Sandy didn't need a piece of paper to make us right or moral. I did. It was up to me now to decide. I could go on living with my suspicions all the time, doubts and panicky questions in place of love, or I could plunge for real as I had pretended to plunge already.

I couldn't give him up. In three months he had taken me too far. I wanted midnight walks along the Hudson and Saturday adventures in his inflatable raft in the tall reeds of the marshes. I wanted long, intimate lunches with him more than I wanted any job. I couldn't go back to my two rooms on Eighteenth Street when Sandy was offering Rome or Paris. I wanted his arms around me with their own high drama. I might not see how he could pull himself out of a silk hat like a charmed white rabbit and start his life all over again, but I didn't want to miss the chance to watch him try. Whatever little leaps it took to keep up with him, whatever risks, I knew they would be worth it.

We took the train together to Vieste late that night, packed tightly in our first-class car with Christmas travelers and their bags of Christmas presents. There were stars outside the window; in the morning there was snow. I saw Sandy's town jutting from cliffs on the edge of the Adriatic. I met his father, who took me arm in arm through the piazza to the best jewelry store in town, where he pinned a coral brooch on me to prove that I was who I seemed to be, his son's new wife and his new daughter, in the true eyes of the law.

5

After we got back from Italy, we began paying for our whirlwind courtship. American Express and the Bank of America wanted more than our savings accounts could deliver. We tightened our belts and bagged our lunches, but we wouldn't give up our midday meetings. We'd bring two chunks of provolone from home and buy a baguette to split in Central Park, bundled in winter coats on a bench where we fed ourselves the crusts and threw the soft middles to the pigeons. I liked that life on the cheap with Sandy even more than our extravagant nights on the town. We seemed more contained, less dangerous and wild. We tinkered on the weekends, modeling a zoo out of clay for his younger son, trekking down to the Lower East Side or Soho for the day. There were still late-night walks and outings on the river. It was a routine I could understand. We played at being poor the way we'd played at falling in love.

In January I was fired. Too many long lunches and our three-week jaunt to Italy had done my boss in. It was coming, and I wasn't sad to pack up files of manuscript pages typed on company time, but it was still a shock. I'd miss my friends and those surreptitious trips to the Xerox machine to copy another thirty pages of a secret project Sandy and I had started, a thinly disguised novel about Jo Attia and Carmen in Paris. We called her "Marlu" and had written eighty pages.

"Good riddance," Sandy said. "You can finish the book now. They never appreciated you at that job."

"But we need the money. I'll look for something better."

"Is it worth your time? We'll be leaving soon. Maybe you could freelance until we get out."

I cringed when he talked about leaving. The worst prospect of losing my job was losing a place to light every day in the city. I'd have an hour or two to hit the publishing agencies, to make freelance appointments, but then nowhere to go. I regretted the loss of my apartment—not really, I told myself, only a little—though I'd never admit it to Sandy. I loved New York, missed living in Manhattan. But he hated the city. He couldn't separate it from the worst of his job, banging down tenement doors in the Bronx at 2 A.M., sitting for hours at the Hudson docks waiting for a deal that wouldn't happen. He'd never include such seedy nights and even seedier mornings in the scripts he wrote for himself when he was working under cover, but in his new role as team player, he had to go along with other agents' cases whether or not they were badly conceived. He wasn't traveling solo any longer. Calls would come in the middle of the night and drag him out on another pointless chase. He didn't mind the insistence of the phone at 3 A.M. if something came from it, but usually his team was on the losing side. I'd reach for him after one of those late-night calls, but he'd be up and dressing, searching all the closets for his service revolver, hidden so well that it often seemed lost. Once or twice a month he'd come home from work fired up by an overseas vacancy announcement in his briefcase. Bangkok; Ankara; Lima, Peru. I'd roll the names of those foreign cities on my tongue like new exotic foods I was afraid of tasting.

In early February Sandy left the house for Kennedy Airport at midnight on a stakeout for a junior agent's case. Before going he sat on the edge of the bed and kissed me. "Try to sleep. I'll be back late." "I'll wait up," I said. "I don't have any appointments in the city."

It was 6 A.M. when he got home. I was in the kitchen making coffee.

"Have you been up all night?"

I shook my head. "Just since four. A bad dream. In a million years I couldn't have pictured waiting in the kitchen in the dark for my cop to come home."

He took off his overcoat while I stared at him. He'd gone out in a sweater and sports coat. Now he wore only some stranger's tight blue cotton T-shirt.

"What happened to your clothes?"

He shrugged. "I gave them away. You wouldn't have believed this case. Two French Canadians came in from Acapulco. It's freezing, and they didn't have any clothes. Their bags were confiscated. I felt sorry for them. It's a bad case, the charges won't stick. It was a fucking waste of time."

He sat at the table in the narrow dining room. "We have to get out. We have to talk. I can't take this any longer."

We finished the pot of coffee. He grabbed another sweater and we went out for a walk. It was a gray, cold February morning. We walked to the park above town, out onto the top of the Palisades where we could see the river through the bare limbs of the trees.

"I have to move on," he said. "I know I can't get out of this job, not now, not with the divorce and two kids to support, a new wife. I accept that. But I can't take the waste of these cases. These guys, they're out for the little man, those French Canadians with twenty-five grams of cocaine. They don't matter. They aren't part of the real international traffic. Don't you see? I'm going crazy here. I felt sorry for those guys. I was the one to interrogate them because my French was best. I felt like slapping them on the wrist and sending them home. One of them was crying, asked to call his wife. What was the point? DEA dragging out its biggest guns for two dumb kids from Montreal."

We were standing at the edge of the trees. I watched a light go on at the paper mill in town. "What do you want to do then?"

He took my hand, touched my face. Whenever he touched my face like that, I knew how much he loved me. "There's an opening in Rio. It wouldn't be a promotion. It's for a group supervisor, my grade. I want to try for it, Joanne. I was afraid you would hate Ankara, even Lima. But Rio is supposed to be beautiful. Let's try for it. The pettiness here, the stupidity, is killing me. I don't want to see those Canadians go to jail. If I have to do this, the cases at least should be important."

"But what if it's the same in Rio?"

"It won't be," he said, digging his hands into the pockets of his sweater, pacing the line of trees to keep warm. "I'll have more freedom abroad and my own group to supervise. I'll be the one who plans the cases. I can target the sources that I want. Besides, it would be so much better for us, to get away, to start fresh in a city neither of us knows. We can bring my kids down for visits. We could start a family."

He was on a roll, flying, looking through his crystal ball into a future he could manage. No going back, no questions, it had to be the way he saw it. I could almost see it, too, on that gray morning as smoke billowed from the factory below, against the flat, glassy river. Rio, between the mountains and the sea. Just like that, no packing crates or passports or airline reservations.

"Could I go, the way we are now? Your divorce isn't final yet. Would they let me go with you?"

"What do you mean, 'they'? There isn't any 'they.' It's my life, you're my wife. We'd have to wait for your diplomatic passport until the divorce is over, but we'll get you a tourist visa if we have to. We wouldn't leave right away. They have to send me to school first, to learn Portuguese. Maybe the divorce will be settled by the time we go."

"How long?" I asked.

"Three or four months, maybe. Or maybe six months for the language school. I don't know exactly."

He came from behind and wrapped his arms around me. I could smell the anticipation on him. In the cold I could see his breath. "Say yes," he whispered. "Trust me. This is right for us, I know it. I want to live with you in Rio."

I said yes. I couldn't have given any other answer. But it didn't happen, even though he was accepted for the post. He came home one night with the official transfer papers wrapped around a bottle of cheap, undrinkable champagne that we poured down the kitchen drain after our toast. He was so restless, so excited that we drove back to Manhattan that same evening to go to the Forty-second Street library, where he looked up every title he could find on Rio. The next day he came home with presents, a new leather suitcase for me with a photograph album tucked inside the zippered pocket. On each page of the album he had cut and pasted pictures and postcards of Rio. A week later, it was all off. The New York office refused to permit him to move for at least six months. They needed him, they argued. He was too valuable to be let go.

He was duty officer that week, which meant he stayed at the office through the night with the radio dispatcher, checking security on the floors, waiting to hear which cases were breaking, on call in case an emergency arose. He called from the office at eight o'clock in the evening to tell me the bad news. I had never heard him so angry or depressed. "Could I come and see you?" I asked. "Have you had dinner? I could stop and get something."

"It doesn't matter. If you want to."

"Can I get in?"

"I'll let you in. But wait another hour until everybody's gone."

The DEA's New York offices were in a nondescript building at Tenth Avenue and Fifty-seventh Street. I'd only been there once before, in daylight when the halls were crowded and the security devices seemed less obvious. The guard in the lobby rang for Sandy, who came down to meet me. His back was slumped dejectedly. I watched us on closed-circuit TV, winding through the maze of corridors with cameras perched in every corner and funny locks on all the doors. As Sandy put his plastic card into the lock on the top floor, I stared at the miniature screen set high above the doorway. Sandy walked by slowly, and there I was in my camel coat, my chin obscured by the bag of take-out Chinese food. Even depressed, he had much more substance. I saw myself, those healthy cheeks, dark eyes full of false cheer, a face that would not travel well. For me Sandy's six-month sentence in New York was a reprieve.

"Where shall we eat?" I asked. "Or do you have to stay in the radio room?"

He shrugged. "It's okay. The dispatcher can find me. We could sit in the secretaries' lounge. At least it has a decent view."

The view was spectacular. The glass wall looked out on the Hudson midtown docks, on lit ships at harbor. The river was a wide black space between the harbor and the Jersey lights. We sat at a round table in the dark while I arranged cartons of food on paper plates.

"You ordered a lot," he said. "I'm not very hungry."

I set a carton of noodles on the table and looked at him. "I'm sorry about the transfer, Sandy. But it'll be okay. Maybe Rio wasn't right for us. Now you're free to try for Rome."

He pulled out a chair and sat down, staring at the river. "That's a dream. They'd never send me to Europe. I know too much. They'll pick some fool who doesn't know the country or the language, someone who won't make any cases or any waves. They practically told me that I don't belong in Rome, where I might feel divided loyalties. That's something, isn't it? After so many years of government work for them, they still distrust me. Maybe I know the way they work too well. They only trust you in a country when you're ignorant about it. They want to control what you know or don't know. They have their little plans for you. Squeeze yourself into the slot they've mapped out or they make you crazy."

"We'll go to Paris—"

"Forget Paris. Paris is sewn up for the next four years. I should have known they wouldn't let me out. Oh, they'll send me overseas if I want, on the usual assignments. Washington must have some plans for me, that's why they've held me back. I'd bet it isn't really the New York office that stopped the transfer. It's headquarters again with a new pet project. Another couple months as Salvatore Bonanno with some clown in Washington pulling all the strings. But they'll keep me from what I really want. My own cases, goddamn it, my own life."

I didn't know what to say. The smell of our dinner in those open cardboard boxes began to make me sick. I watched the river with him, a barge moving toward the George Washington Bridge. He had his feet on an empty chair, his knees bent. He wouldn't look at me.

"You can have your life," I whispered in the almost dark. "You can get out of DEA and make it happen. I'll help. I'll get a real job. I want to, Sandy."

"You don't understand. I can't get out. I have too many responsibilities, too much invested. I have to see this through on my own terms. I have to make it be what I want, finally. The government owes me that. They owe me something for all the years."

I sat across the table from Sandy, working up the courage to go to him. Finally, I leaned over and wrapped my arms around his neck. He didn't seem to notice. He didn't touch me. Maybe I couldn't understand the years behind him, the peculiar life he'd lived. But I wanted to. I wanted my love to make a difference, to rescue him as his love had rescued me already. Yet there he was, sinking in his chair, lost in the blackness of the river, with a look of fear that shocked me. How selfish I'd been, how relieved not to go to Rio. Maybe my unwillingness had entered him somehow. Maybe it was my fault that New York wouldn't let him go. Too many long lunch hours, too many nights when he'd resented the midnight calls and other agents' cases. If he'd been alone, he would have been eager for the distractions of his work. The more he seemed beyond my reach, the more determined I became. I swore I'd go anywhere he wanted. Six months, and we'd leave New York. Six months, and I'd be ready. He was the one who knew so clearly what he wanted. One of us had to drive us on, to keep us moving. It would have to be him, since it couldn't be me.

II

In March 1975, Sante Bario sat in a briefing room in Washington, D.C., figuring his suspicions must have been right. Somebody at headquarters had held back his transfer to Rio and had been responsible for rejecting his applications to several other foreign posts in the year since Rio had fallen through. Genoa, Costa Rica, London —he'd been more than qualified for each of those posts, but somebody in Washington had shut him out. It had taken a year rather than six months to leave New York, though in some respects he was in a much better position for the waiting. He was finally divorced, free to settle down with the record cleared. He was also more convinced than ever that he was making the right move by getting out of the States and out from under cover.

In the past year things had been happening at the DEA that left a bad taste in his mouth. Though he had no proof, he suspected that Special Operations in Washington had been keeping its thumb on him, nailing him down in New York so he could be pulled out when needed and shuttled off on a pet covert project like the one in Nassau turned out to be. In May 1974—not two months after he'd been squeezed out of the Rio job—he had been notified by Lucien Conein at Special Operations that he'd been tapped as case agent for a top-secret investigation on Paradise Island. Known as Operation Croupier, the project would look into "reliable information" that croupiers in the casinos were involved in drug smuggling. He hadn't been told the source of the information, though it didn't bother him at first. The project seemed reasonable enough. He'd spent several weeks in July 1974 at headquarters for briefings—that was normal procedure. Then Conein took him to Intertel's D.C. office to meet with Robert Peloquin, head of Intertel and a vice president of Resorts International, which owned the casinos. Intertel wanted to supply Bario with a thousand-dollar gambling roll to use while he checked on possible drug-smuggling operations. Peloquin had then said "unofficially" that in return for his support he would appreciate any information that Bario could supply on corrupt Resorts International employees. Conein didn't accept the money, but that had started Bario wondering. Before he left for Paradise Island in August of that year, he'd been authorized to gamble by Conein and hadn't thought too much about it. How was he supposed to justify his time in the casino if he didn't gamble?

He stayed on Paradise Island for twelve days, traveling under the name Salvatore Bonanno, playing a big-time real estate investor and making what contacts he could. A Bahamian senator, impressed by the Bonanno name, befriended him. He got close to some of the croupiers and pit bosses who asked him to their parties. He followed whatever leads he found on drugs, but there weren't many. He spent his evenings at the casino, gambling enough to look legitimate in the Bonanno role. When he got back to the States, he included his six-hundred-dollar gambling loss on his voucher. It was shortly after he'd turned in his report that the problems started. Conein's assistant asked him to delete the gambling expenses from his voucher and wanted to give him six hundred dollars in cash in an envelope. "Where did this come from?" Bario asked, but the man wouldn't answer. He also wanted Bario to change his report of the investigation, leaving out all references to Resorts International and Intertel. Bario refused. He was so pissed off and suspicious that he left a copy of his signed, original report with his father-in-law in case Conein later tried to change it. Maybe Special Operations had kept him from being transferred to Rio because he had once worked briefly for Intertel, which they'd hoped would make him sympathetic to their little schemes. A federal agent had no business investigating corruption within a private company like Resorts International as a side favor to Intertel. He wondered what other connections there might be. Conein was formerly with the CIA. Intertel's investigative staff was thick with former secret agents. He was relieved to be getting out, especially since the Senate hearings had begun on the DEA. He had told the truth to the Senate subcommittee; as a result he had fallen out of favor within certain circles at his agency.

Maybe that's why he'd been transferred to Mexico when he couldn't get any of the posts he'd really wanted. Though it was the DEA's prime foreign target and pivotal to any other Latin American post, Mexico remained a thorn in the DEA's side. The agency couldn't seem to get its Mexico City regional office on the right track. The Mexican narcotics traffic involved Central America, South America, Canada, and Europe. Washington was interested in Mexico. The State Department was concerned and poured millions into Mexico as direct aid. The DEA had earmarked its substantial budget in Mexico for special purposes—payoffs to informants and slots for personnel to sift through the intelligence they bought; money for airplanes, choppers, pilots, the purchase of exotic equipment and deadly herbicides for the eradication of poppy and marijuana fields. But the results of all their efforts and so much cash had been disappointing.

He couldn't get it out of his mind that his three-month temporary tour in Mexico, coming out of the blue at this particular moment, was a kind of punishment for his testimony before the Senate. He'd told the truth to the Senate investigators, told about Intertel's offer of a gambling roll, told how Conein and his assistant Bud Frank had ordered him to "revise" his report, and, now suddenly, after a year of waiting, he was being whisked away. His testimony had embarrassed Special Operations. Conein had been forced to pay the six-hundred-dollar gambling expense out of his own pocket, mumbling that it had all been an unfortunate misunderstanding, implying it was Bario's fault.

After this last briefing, Sante Bario would go to Mexico City as an agent out of favor. His move to Mexico wasn't a promotion, but rather a lateral transfer. Maybe they figured he'd burn out in a trouble spot like Mexico, where the agency had made such little headway in such a long time. So what? Special Operations wasn't the whole agency. He'd work hard. He'd have two good years out of the States to redeem himself. He'd get his promotion. It had been hard for him before. He would gamble on his ability to choose the right cases, to find the best informants, to make himself indispensable to the current regional director. He'd try his damnedest not to make too many waves.

If the DEA expected him to be out of the way in Mexico, he would show the agency that it was wrong. He'd done his homework for these meetings, studied the post reports, the cables, the entire dossier. Though the State Department expert at the podium was covering old ground, Bario forced himself to listen: Mexico produced brown heroin and untold tons of marijuana whose fields were hidden gold mines in the Sierras. More importantly, Mexico was a major transshipment point for cocaine and white heroin smuggled in from South America. But the Mexican Government didn't view narcotics control as a top priority item on its national agenda. The U.S. suspected involvement by Mexican officials in the drug traffic. Moreover, narcotics abuse in Mexico wasn't a national problem. The government didn't care if Indians in the mountains toked on their pipes of peyote as they had for generations when millions in the cities were out of work, crowded into slums without electricity or running water. The U.S. had to persuade the Mexican Government that narcotics interdiction was in its national best interest. The Mexicans saw narcotics control as a means of leverage to get U.S. help in solving more pressing problems, such as overpopulation, so-called U.S. imperialism in the region, issues of international debt—the list went on and on.

The State Department official shuffled his papers into his briefcase, smiled mildly and left. Bario straightened up as the meeting got down to real business. Whatever the attitude of the Mexican Government, the DEA was on the wire to produce in Mexico. So far, the agency had failed to shut down Mexico's middleman role in the cocaine traffic. Congress was on the DEA administrator's back about the huge sums spent in the region and the lack of results. Congressional committeemen were losing patience with new proposals for the agency's expansion. Time was running out. The DEA had to fish or cut bait, make its presence felt or face the consequences. The State Department would like nothing better than to take over the DEA's diplomatic slots and call an end to U.S. narcotics enforcement in the region.

The DEA had to own up to its responsibility for much of the current tension. Regional personnel had been unstable, informants unproductive, the agency unable to make good use of its resources. But the DEA denied responsibility for the host government's lack of cooperation or the difficult topography of the land. The MFJP, Mexico's federal police, had a vested interest in protecting its fiefdoms throughout the republic. Big payoffs were involved. Each division in each state had its own complicated kickback system; the cop on the street took money from local thieves and paid off his immediate boss. Criminals could buy protection at every level. Regional gangs controlled entire states. There were whole regions where the MFJP did not dare to enter. All these problems came with the territory, a fact the U.S. Congress refused to understand. The mountains themselves were a major obstacle. Anything could be hidden in those mountains. Although campesinos lined up in the halls outside the DEA's embassy offices, willing to expose the corruption in their villages for the right price, eager to turn in the local police chief or even the mayor, class feuds ran deep. With such widespread resentment against public officials, the assumption was that the campesinos lied. Along countless miles of coastline on either side of the mountains, small boats slipped in and out of unnamed harbors where there were no roads. The only potential informers were Indians in Mayan villages with a clear view of those boats meeting on the water. Who were they supposed to tell? The DEA was stuck with Mexican officials in the Procuraduría, Mexico's department of justice, who enjoyed repeating their one pat speech: "Mexican drug laws reflect U.S. lawlessness; this is your problem, not ours," they would say with satisfaction.

There were other problems besides the State Department, Congress, the Mexican Government, the lay of the land. Vocal critics in Washington questioned the "propriety" of an American enforcement agency with offices abroad. The agency had to present its arguments delicately and emphasize its advisory role, its technical assistance to the Mexican Government. As the briefing continued, diplomacy gave way to frustration. Bario winced as he listened to special agents from Mexico describe the problems from their perspective on the streets. "The MFJP don't do nothing if we don't push. We make the cases, they go along for the ride."

He tuned out the rest of the meeting to focus on his own strategies for Mexico. He had a lot to accomplish. He would show Special Operations what he could do without their kind of dirty tricks. He'd get his promotion. Leave the marijuana to the eradication program. He'd go for the distributors of brown heroin, the middlemen who brought in coke from South America. He'd make his own connections in the Procuraduría, start at the top if he could. Find out who to trust in the MFJP and go for it.

He didn't need to listen to other agents' complaints to understand the troubles in the region. Another director was on his way out; the staff was constantly changing. In another year, the Mexican Government would switch hands. Luis Echeverría, the current President, was anti-U.S., but he was already losing power. The new "candidate," José López Portillo, would already be putting in his own men to work behind the scenes. It was a decent time to move, if Mexico was the only place they'd send him. Word was that Portillo wanted to cut off graft and wipe out corruption in the system, but that's what politicians always said. Everything he'd read suggested that it wouldn't be easy to clean that system. Corruption filtered down and down and down. He wouldn't count on Portillo, the Procuraduría, or the murky power channels at the DEA. He'd count only on himself. Maybe the DEA would make it tough for him. He'd had it tough before. The meeting broke up. The agents gathered in small groups in the back of the room to smoke or shoot the crap. Bario tried to relax. He'd go down to Mexico for his three-month banishment, come back to the States to get married, and then begin in earnest to make the kind of cases Washington would notice.

6

I wasn't twenty-six anymore when we came down the stairs of my parents' house that July day in 1975, arm in arm through the long living room, the dining room crowded with family and friends, and into the den my father had made out of the porch. Sandy's children stood at his elbow, the younger one looking up with a mixture of fascination and shyness. He was six, and Franco was a tall, adult fourteen. With a little stretch, they might have been mine. I wasn't so young, really. I'd lived two years with Sandy, staying awake nights waiting for him to come home from surveillance, trying to follow his complaints about the bureaucratic politics at the DEA. I should have understood about his job, but he kept his secrets. We never socialized with other agents. He liked to minimize the daily aggravations. He wanted me to see only the glamor of his undercover past. "Come to Paradise Island with me," he'd asked the summer before we got married. "We'll dress up for the casino late at night and go snorkling at noon." A Bahamian senator, impressed by his name, sent us crates of mangoes from his orchard. We'd come back from the casino to make love at 3 A.M., then Sandy would go out again. It was mysterious and lovely. But he never told me anything about the case.

The day after our wedding we left for a month in Europe. On the first of September, we were scheduled to arrive in Mexico to begin our two-year tour. We'd spent two years making up this kind of future. We'd invested countless hours in anticipation.

After Sandy's disappointment over Rio, we needed a destination, a place to hang our new life on, a clean, clear situation to remedy the year's irresolution. We had spent two years being married yet not, leaving New York but never getting out. Planning for the transfer gave us a common past. Going would give us our future.

Sandy's temporary tour in March became a sacrifice we made. It was a wintry March in New York, with rain and wet snow. Once Sandy left, I began hating the cold, messy mornings, the drive downtown in the big white car, the daily hassles of parking, of taking the subway to my job as publicity assistant at a small trade publishing house. I'd accepted the job to fill in time until we moved because it seemed senseless to look for something permanent so soon before our transfer.

"The move" became another presence in our lives, motivating almost all our choices. It began to take on its own life and make us more compelling to each other. Everything would change when we finally got married and split from the States. No more working late for Sandy, no more selling out for me. If I had any leftover reservations, they were dispelled once Sandy was gone. The city, my job, everything about New York became annoying. I didn't mind reading the books at work or writing the releases, but I hated the telephone calls to radio and TV producers in Chicago, L.A., New York, hyping their assistants into believing that this author (and the next) was the hottest item in town and deserved an appearance on————, quickly scanning my index card to fill in the space with the name of their show. I hated selling myself and those inane titles.

Soon I wouldn't have to. I was going "abroad" with Sandy and could not wait. I counted on his daily postcards from Guadalajara, Acapulco, Mérida, Culiacán, stuffing them into my purse to be retrieved at a back desk during lunch, when I'd repeat the names of those cities like a Buddhist chant, ridding my life of New York karma.

Every night while Sandy was in Mexico I'd go to bed at 7 P.M. with State Department memos and the Mexico City post report. I became addicted to that thick, baffling, official-looking volume bound in black plastic, twice as heavy as the New York phone book. There was advice to foreign-service families assigned to outposts in the Yucatán Peninsula—what clothes to pack for living in the tropics, which toys should be brought from home, whether to pack an artificial Christmas tree, the incidence of enfeebling tropical disease. The more arcane the information, the more "foreign" the posting sounded, the more I liked it. Three quarters of the report was devoted to diplomatic life in Mexico City, but most of those sections were disappointingly familiar notes that could have been written about any sprawling, modern city. I skimmed the pages on popular neighborhoods, private schools, the problems of traffic and pollution, trying to find more provocative topics. I read about corruption in the local police, the intricate relations in Mexican families, the likelihood of maids abusing young children or stealing food. I read about contaminated milk and water. I liked especially the section on living at high altitude, its effects and dangers. I liked anything that made Mexico City seem exotic, for my one big fear was that it would turn out to be exactly like New York. This move was supposed to elicit a "sea change" in me and Sandy, to settle any ambiguities between us, to make us over into enduring, heightened selves. Such great expectations couldn't be fulfilled next door. They were otherworldly. I read the State Department's odd directive on responsibility and foreign-service wives, imagining white gloves and calling cards. That, at least, would be a little different. I read Oscar Lewis' *The Children of Sánchez* and thought romantically of poverty. I read *The Honorary Consul* by Graham Greene, embellishing its slower moments with vague, Third World intrigues.

We flew from Rome to Washington on August 31, to find our diplomatic passports in my mother's mailbox. On the flight from Dallas to Mexico City, Sandy kept worrying that it might be dark and gray, that September was still the rainy season. "Damn," he said as we came down quickly through low-lying clouds, "it will be raining." But it wasn't. The final descent was sharp and clear. The mountains came up through clouds circling the city on its high plateau. We came down abruptly to avoid the mountains. I pressed my face against the window, looking beyond abandoned World

War II planes lining the runway to miles of cement walls, pink or sky blue, to corrugated tin roofs, and geraniums blooming in soda-pop cans.

I clutched my diplomatic passport and tried to look official in the customs line. It was disappointing when the Mexican agent didn't even match name and picture, didn't stamp the page. Sandy kissed my cheek and whispered *"bienvenido,"* as we went out through the cordoned exit lined with faces. *"Oyes, Francisco!"* someone shouted. A blonde in heavy makeup blocked the door, issuing orders to her driver while her maid in a shabby sweater marshaled three small children around. Sandy pushed us through and packed our luggage in the taxi van. I sat back and stared while tourists on the seat in front discussed hotels, connections to Acapulco, restaurants in the Zona Rosa, the Pink Zone, where Americans could order salad with impunity. Just outside the airport, when the traffic signal turned, the van was surrounded by street vendors selling Chiclets, Kleenex, marionettes, and flowers. A clown came up to the window, his face painted red, his huge feet dancing. He swallowed the tip of a flaming sword and smiled at us with wide false lips charred with smoke—I loved it.

The van dropped us at the furnished apartment Sandy had rented for his temporary tour. The building was downtown, a few blocks from the embassy. We walked from the corner past young girls in checkered uniforms hosing down the street, past gardeners with hand mowers trimming manicured patches of lawn.

"Don't expect too much of the apartment," Sandy said, unlocking the door to reveal gilt-framed mirrors and a turquoise floor. He put down our bags and opened the drapes on a wall of solid glass. I sat on the couch and stared at blocks of red clay roofs. "But I like it," I said.

I was prepared to like it all—the walk to the embassy, Sandy's description of the cities he had seen so far. "Monterrey is ugly," he explained. "A factory town, so hot I couldn't stand it on the streets. But I'll take you to Veracruz some day. It's dirty but fascinating. The beach is littered with garbage, but the square is beautiful, old French architecture and fresh boiled shrimp for sale on every corner. We'll go to the Yucatán, to the Mayan ruins in Uxmal. The pyramids in all that jungle."

He held tightly to my arm to keep a bus from barreling through us as we crossed a traffic circle. "Wait till you see Tulum," he said. "It's mystic. The pyramid sits high on a cliff overlooking the Caribbean. We can climb the parapets and watch the sea for hours."

Tulum, Uxmal. I practiced their exotic names as we turned the corner to the embassy. There was the famous gold angel, Mexico's monument to independence, on her obelisk in the center of the *glorieta* ("traffic circle"). I had read in a travel guide that when an earthquake toppled her, the people on the street had picked up all the pieces and turned them in, though she was made of real gold and worth a pretty penny.

There was an old woman begging at the embassy gate, a toddler hanging at her skirt. Sandy reached in his pocket for a coin while the Mexican guard at the gate stood watching. "You shouldn't give to them, señor," he said in Spanish. "They rent the babies, to put on a show for the tourists." We went in; he locked the gate behind us.

I had read that this white, square marble building housed the largest U.S. mission in the world. A line of Mexicans formed at a far end of the entrance, circling the opposite side of the block from our approach.

"What are they doing?" I asked Sandy.

"Waiting for visas to go to the States. They sometimes come with blankets and thermoses of coffee, prepared to wait all night."

We walked up the marble steps to the Marine guard's post. I peeked in to see the courtyard below—a fountain, ficus trees, bell chimes sounding. Sandy pointed out his office on the second floor. "My room looks down on the courtyard," he said.

It was strange to hear only Spanish in the elevator, Mexican clerks or secretaries whom I couldn't understand. A frightened *campesino* in sandals stood in the corner, his pass clutched in dirty fingers. He got off at the first floor, peering down both ends of the corridor. The doors closed. I read a handwritten notice under glass on the elevator wall—Embassy Women's Bake Sale Wednesday—and my stomach fell.

The DEA occupied one of four long corridors on the second floor. "This is my wife," Sandy said to the receptionist, who dialed the secret combination on the lock to let us into the interior hall.

The walls were lined with U.S. and Mexican flags, with photographs of poppy fields in bloom, of U.S. helicopters spraying fields of marijuana. At each doorway, Sandy stopped to introduce me. There were agents who had transferred in from Brownsville, Texas, from Panama, and from Europe. The regional director was an older man, who shook my hand, calling me "young lady." "Show her your tie," somebody shouted from a room across the hall, and all the agents laughed. The regional director hesitated and blushed a little, but Sandy encouraged him. "It's okay," he said, "she can take it," hoping to show what good sports we'd be, what good team players.

"It's a joke, you understand," said the regional director, yanking his necktie up and down until its design spread out to spell "Fuck You" in orange letters.

Farther down the hall was a glass enclosure where the secretaries sat, but the corridors belonged to men in cowboy boots and leisure suits. I was relieved when we ended up in Sandy's office.

He had my picture on his desk and dried opium poppies in a vase. I reached over and fingered one. It looked carved from wood, its round bulb lined and rippled.

"That's where the opium gum is," Sandy said. "They drain it from the pod when the flower's dead."

I sat on a vinyl chair and took off my shoes.

"Maybe it was too much for one day, all those introductions. I should've waited till tomorrow to bring you by. It'll get better. These guys aren't so bad, once you get to know them."

I looked up at Sandy, made a face. "You don't really think so. Except at our wedding, you've never introduced me to any agents."

He shook his head. "How could I? When I know you're such a snob. So you won't like them. We'll find other friends."

"I could join the embassy women's group and bake a cake for Wednesday."

"You'll get a job."

"Where? All the memos say wives can't work on a diplomatic passport."

"You'll teach. They let you teach. Or you can work at the embassy."

"If I can pass the typing test."

"You don't have to get a job tomorrow. With our living allowance, we can afford it. You can write. We'll find a beautiful house with a room made for writing, with windows onto the garden."

The telephone rang; he grabbed for it. I could hear his secretary —somebody from Oaxaca on the phone. I sat with my shoes off, listening. He shrugged, mouthed "I'm sorry," then went back to Spanish. I finally slipped into my shoes and out the door. I should have known it would be like this, I thought, our first day in Mexico. I managed to avoid the agents in the hall. A woman passed with a plastic shopping bag, and I smiled. One of the agent's wives, I figured.

So that was it. We had started. I was on my own. I wasn't going to be one of those wives with a plastic shopping bag who hung around the commissary and zipped upstairs to say hello. I stopped at the top of the embassy entrance, looked out on Paseo de la Reforma. I'd start by learning Spanish. The post report had listed classes offered in the city. I'd find my way back to the apartment and call them up today.

7

By the end of September the rains had stopped and we had found a place to live. We didn't want a big house behind high walls with shards of broken glass cemented on top to scare away intruders. We looked down on the stuffy kind of life they offered in the popular diplomatic neighborhoods of Polanco, Lomas de Chapultepec, or Tecamachalco. Instead, we found a quiet, private street—a *"privada,"* it was called—in colonial San Angel where the stone and stucco houses were simple and unpretentious. We were warned against San Angel, a forty-minute drive from the embassy when there was no traffic on the Periférico. Usually the traffic was bad, the pollution worse. But on the Sunday when we found our house, the sky was blue, the mountains were clear and awe-inspiring south of the city.

San Angel had once been a small village, half a day's carriage ride from the Federal District. It was the kind of Mexico we wanted—quaint, pretty, impractical. What we found there was a large top-floor apartment in a two-family house with a big terrace, pegged wooden floors, a stone fireplace with carved columns. We were given a hard-sell tour by the current tenants, a Canadian couple who were anxious to move across the dirt road on the same private street, into a larger house with a garden for their dogs. Sara and Paul became our first friends in Mexico. I think we finally chose the house on Las Flores as much for them as for the balconies off every room or the giant water bottles built into the stucco walls, tinting the sunlight green. Sara and Paul showed us the burros who lived in the empty lot next door, the rooster who'd wake us in the mornings. They told us the *privada* had Mexicans, Peruvians, Swiss, a Canadian or two. We'd be the only Americans. "That's exactly how we want it," Sandy said.

We took the house the same day. While Paul went to find the landlord, Sara made coffee. We drank it on the terrace as Sandy planned his garden of pots for the terrace wall: bougainvillea, yuccas, giant fuchsias, *copas de oro*. When Paul returned, we learned he was head of the Mexican region for a Canadian hotel firm and that he and Sara had lived in Mexico four years. "You'll love it," he promised, "the climate, the *ambiente*, if not always the natives." He was shrewd enough to wait until we'd signed the lease before showing us the great chinks in the stone walls, admitting how cold the house would be.

By the time our things arrived, we'd made more friends in the neighborhood. We'd even found a family we liked with the DEA, an intelligence analyst and his tall, blond Connecticut wife. Polly in her wraparound skirt and Dan with his Tiparillo stopped by as we unpacked. We introduced them to Sara and Paul, overseeing the movers. Our Peruvian and Dutch neighbors downstairs appeared with Chilean wine and flowers. It was like Christmas in October to have our own belongings again, to be sitting on the floor drinking wine with people we liked.

We slept that night on a mattress in an empty bedroom. Through the high windows on one wall we could see the cupola of a neighbor's house, the white new moon hanging above it. We made love slowly. Sandy fell asleep and didn't snore, but I was awake for hours listening to the unfamiliar sounds of the house. The wine hadn't settled well; my stomach was uneasy. I couldn't be pregnant already, I thought, counting the weeks from that night outside of Naples on our honeymoon when Sandy said it was all right, that it would be wonderful to make a child. The fig trees in the villa's garden had been heavy with fruit. After making love we'd gone out to sit on the garden wall. We'd eaten figs from the lowest branches, watching the lights weave along the mountains on the coast, hoping I was pregnant. That had been in August. But now in October I wasn't ready. It was too soon.

8

Sandy was elated when Sara's doctor confirmed my pregnancy. His workload was staggering, but he cleared an evening for us. We met in the DEA parking lot behind the embassy and walked the few blocks to the restaurant he'd chosen, Les Moustaches. There were white enamel tables in its interior garden, soft green lights in the ficus trees. The waiters served lime ice between the courses.

"When will the baby come?" Sandy asked. His eyes were very bright.

"Late June, the doctor says. So it couldn't have happened in Naples."

"It doesn't matter. Late June is fine. By then things at the office will have settled down. The chaos is just temporary, until the new agents arrive."

"So you keep saying, but they never tell you when. I hate the hours you've been keeping. We haven't had a free weekend since we moved to Las Flores."

"We will, I promise. Now I can call in late and blame it on your pregnancy. We can take a weekend off and go to Cuernavaca. We'll take Thanksgiving if you want."

I wanted it badly, but it didn't happen.

Thanksgiving week found us where we always were. I spent my mornings at the bilingual school in a northern suburb where I taught seventh grade. Sandy would leave the house at six-fifteen each morning. At seven I'd climb into our orange Volkswagen, a trade-in for the big white car, and stop three times along the Periférico to be sick among the succulents that grew wild on the shoulder of the road. The days were gray, cool, polluted. The clouds above the mountains trapped the dirty air and guaranteed a dreary yellow sky by afternoon. I'd wipe my face with tissues and look up into the dense clouds, knowing the evening would be awful, too. I would be lonely; Sandy would be working.

Either I'd be late for my first class or a group of students would be waiting for me outside my office door to say I talked too fast, to say they hadn't understood the history lesson. Pretty little girls with made-up eyes, boys in pressed gray slacks who whispered slurs in their quick Spanish behind my back. I didn't understand the jokes in the teachers' lounge at lunch or the headmistress' expectation that I'd gladly raise a low grade for a boy whose father "mattered" in the government.

Thanksgiving came and went. Friday morning Sandy was back at work; I was driving on the Periférico again. We saw too little of each other. I couldn't fill so many late afternoons and every evening. Spanish lessons in the Pink Zone, afternoon tea at Sara's, or when Sara wasn't home, a drop-in visit with Polly, who was American, at least. I'd play board games with her kids and complain about teaching and my confusion in the streets. Even mundane chores seemed overwhelming. I couldn't explain to the laundry clerk that I needed a zipper fixed. The markets smelled. The chickens were strung up by their necks above the stalls, stained feathers shuddering in a foul-smelling breeze. I hated the neat piles of unfamiliar fruits and vegetables—black *zapotes, tejocotes, chayotes*. The smell of cilantro covered everything as I pushed through the maids and beggars at the door. I didn't want to teach. I didn't want to do the grocery shopping.

Friday afternoon I called Sara's obstetrician. "Something must be wrong," I said, "the markets make me want to cry."

"A mild depression common in first pregnancies, compounded by the change of culture," he rattled off. "I'll prescribe a mild tranquilizer. Go to bed, get some sleep, and in the morning you'll feel better."

I didn't want his tranquilizers or to go to bed alone. If Sandy and I couldn't go to Cuernavaca, we deserved to be together for the weekend. On Saturday we'd make love all day and afterward eat turkey sandwiches out on the terrace. But Sandy wasn't home on Saturday. He spent the day at the embassy planning for his Monday meeting with a distributor of Mexican brown heroin. When he got home late Saturday evening, I was in bed under the quilt, pretending to sleep. Sunday morning he brought in a tray of coffee in his favorite dented pot, but I rolled away from him, covered my head with pillows, and refused to speak. I didn't know whether I was angry or just embarrassed at wanting him so badly. He left Monday morning at 5 A.M. for the town of Iguala in the mountains of Guerrero.

I heard his car back out the drive and watched him through a slit in the drapes. Now you've gone and done it, Tumolo. I called the school and left a message in poor Spanish with the maid, saying I wouldn't make it in that morning. Because I hadn't spoken to him, I didn't know what time Sandy would be back, but I was sure it wouldn't be later than ten that evening. I'd take a bath, dress, and work up my courage to go to the *mercado*. If I could find fresh basil, I'd make pesto. We could eat outside. I'd stick candles in the soil of the hanging pots. We could wear three sweaters each if it got too cold.

But Sandy didn't come home. The candles swayed in the wind for hours until they all burned down.

He always called if he was going to be late, but by 7 A.M. the phone hadn't rung. He never said he was going to stay away all night. If he'd known, he would have told me when he brought in the coffee tray on Sunday morning. He could have excused himself on any pretext or slipped a note to one of his agents on the street: Call my wife, she's pregnant, you know. I called the school again and asked to speak with the *patrona*. "I'm sorry," I whimpered, "but I can't come in. I'm not well, and my husband isn't home."

I dressed in the cold house, out of sorts, worried. My stomach felt as if it were in the car already, bumping over the ruts in the road. I couldn't go to school, but I couldn't hang around the house all morning either—I'd go crazy. I stared at the telephone, willing it to ring. I thought of calling the embassy and asking Sandy's secretary, Excuse me, Marta, do you know where Sandy is and when he's coming home? I couldn't. She'd think I was like the other agents' wives, set down in their cute little stucco rooms, safe and left out of everything important. There was an envelope on the telephone table that I'd ignored all week, addressed to Mrs. Sante Bario in royal-blue ink. I tore it open and read the invitation. "You are cordially invited to a coffee," it said. There were faint pencil lines beneath the carefully penned name and address of a DEA wife. A coffee, like a tea. I hadn't been to a tea since applying to college in 1964.

We were eight women in a cold room, balancing egg salad sandwiches, carrot cake, and china cups on our laps. A maid in a black uniform circulated, cleaning ashtrays, pouring coffee. I tried to match these women with the agents I'd met or heard about from Sandy. Which belonged to the alcoholic who spent his mornings in the Jorongo Bar? Who lived with the deputy director's inside man, recently arrested in a barroom brawl in Acapulco? The regional director's wife wiped the corner of her mouth with a linen napkin while describing those dear little papier-mâché clowns made in Jalisco—"What's the cheapest place to buy them in the city?" On the couch two women discussed the births of their children out of the country. "My husband was working both times," a blonde announced with contempt. "But luckily, we were in Panama, with a clean, American hospital on base."

There were lace doilies on the serving plate that the maid passed around, antimacassars on the arms of the chairs. There was even a painting on black velvet.

The deputy's wife caught my eye, came warily across the room in her high heels. We'd met a month ago when she and her husband invited us for drinks. Sandy had chided me for acting badly, calling her husband down for his war stories about shoot-ups, for his gun collection under glass. I asked him outright: Did the deputy always welcome new agents and their wives with horror stories? In the car driving home, Sandy shook his head and laughed.

The wife was about my age, though she had three children twelve and under. I hoped she wouldn't remember our first meeting. "I'm glad you came," she said. "Are you settling in?"

I nodded and tried to look settled.

"Good, then you're ready to come along on one of our shopping trips. Next Wednesday the embassy women are going to Toluca."

"I'd love to, but I teach, you see."

She smiled painfully and hiked herself up to return to her place across the room. This coffee made the sherry parties of my graduate-school days seem like Mardi Gras. Which woman called the office every morning, sure that she was being followed? In two years, or less, would I be like them? Was I like them already? I wanted to shock them, to stand and say my piece on marijuana. Educated people in New York, in California, snorted coke and didn't go crazy. But what would Sandy think if I opened my big mouth and caused a scandal? I carried around my own policeman who pasted on a wan smile, who set my plate aside and spoke for me: "I *am* sorry, but I'd better go. It's morning sickness, I'm afraid."

It worked. Like a charm. The women were solicitous. They ushered me out to my car with knowing glances at my womb and much commiseration. Saved for another day. Sure of an invitation to return.

Sandy was waiting on the terrace when I got home. He was tired, in need of a shower and shave, but he'd set a bottle of wine and two glasses on the table to prove he cared.

"Hello," he said sheepishly. "Are you very angry?"

I sat at the table and tried not to cry. "You could have called, at least. I was sure they'd shot you. You didn't say you'd be gone all night."

"I didn't know. I couldn't have said much anyway. You weren't speaking, if you'll remember." He sat beside me, took my hand. "I couldn't call, Joanne. I was with the dealer all night. I was never alone. There were DEA and MFJP agents on my tail the whole time. While I waited for the dealer, one was sitting at the next table drinking beer. Another followed us in his phony taxi. I couldn't exactly tell the dealer that I had to stop to report in to my wife. Look at me. Please. Don't be angry. Have some wine."

"I'm not supposed to. I'm pregnant, remember?"

"You're beautiful pregnant and all dressed up. How was school?"

"I haven't been for two days. It's not a real school, you know. It's a baby-sitting service for rich kids, where they learn a little

English on the side. I went to a DEA coffee this morning, to make you feel guilty."

He laughed. "You needn't have. I felt guilty already. I purposely didn't shave so you'd feel sorry for me, dirty and covered with chigger bites."

"I don't feel one bit sorry. You deserve them. The case went well, I guess?"

"It was a good case," he said, sipping his wine. "We got two kilos of brown heroin, and the lab. I talked the dealer into showing me the lab, to check the purity of his stuff, and we got them all in one blow. The region really needs this case. But you should have seen that town. It was a real dust bowl, with old 1950s Fords parked on the *zócalo*. You couldn't even tell the color of the cars for all the dirt. I still have a film of it on my teeth and in my clothes. You should have seen what we ate for supper. This guy takes me to the best *cantina* in town, he says—tortilla soup and refried beans, rancid with bacon grease. My poor stomach. I didn't even have any Mylanta with me. He insisted that I go in his car or he wouldn't take me to the lab. I could see the agents going crazy when I left my car. He drove like a maniac, the agents lost us. I knew DEA would shit a brick. I had the money. They're never supposed to lose contact with the money, but I wanted the lab so badly I could taste it."

He smiled: "It was funny, Joanne. You would have appreciated some of the moments. I told this guy about my stomach, how a European isn't used to such *picante* food. Then I doubled over, faking one of my worst attacks. The guy got nervous, pulled over. There he is, wringing his hands while I'm practically writhing on the seat. I saw the unmarked car with the MFJP go past, and I miraculously got better. We got the lab, this guy, his sidekicks, and the dope."

"You could have said you had to call your doctor. You could have made up some excuse to let me know you were okay."

He stood up and mugged for me, dirt on his jacket, on his hands, in the creases of his eyes. "Do I look all right to you?"

"But I'm serious."

"So am I. We needed this case, Joanne. The more I do now, the better off I'll be when the new director arrives. I don't want to do street work forever. I want to be a supervisor, I want my promotion. But I have to show I've earned it."

"That's what you said in New York. That's why we left. It was supposed to be different here, you promised. You weren't going to do street work or play any undercover roles. You were supposed to be a diplomat."

He dropped my hand and stood up. "Jesus, give me a little time, can't you? We just arrived."

"But I'm lonely. I want—"

He turned and looked at me, with cypress trees behind him. "I know what you want. Can't you see I'm trying?"

9

He traveled to cities I'd never heard of that fall: Chetumal, Chilpancingo. He blacked out once on a DEA flight from Mexico City to Mérida, from Mérida to Chetumal. It wasn't the pilot's fault in that tinny, unpressurized craft, above those mountains. They were flying in dense cloud cover, high above the Sierra. The pilot was forced to keep climbing to clear the mountaintops he couldn't see. Afterward Sandy incorporated the story in his bag of tricks—how they'd taken turns on the only oxygen aboard until the climb became so steep that the pilot had to claim the mask to save them while Sandy almost turned to stone. It was all in a day's work, another adventure, another magical escape—except for headaches plaguing Sandy for the following six months, and those he never talked about.

Autumn went by. I changed jobs, found another private school closer to San Angel where I taught fifth grade. In December we threw a Christmas party for the DEA, ending up with six drunken agents at 4 A.M. and wine stains on the whitewashed walls. In January a city bus drove me off the road while I was driving home from school. I swerved, sideswiped another car. Hands trembling on the wheel, I pulled over, got out with my insurance papers, my embassy carnet, but before I could try my Spanish on the other driver, he was yelling at me, *"Ándale, ándale pues, señora,"* pointing to the traffic cop behind us. I thought I was supposed to fetch the cop and tell him it was all my fault. I started down the block. The driver jumped out of his car, joined by rubberneckers on the curb who quickly pushed me back into my car, picked up its front end, and pointed me in the opposite direction. I locked the windows, the doors. I thought of screaming. How was I to know that they were only helping me escape? The last thing they wanted was a cop to come over. I made it back to Sandy's office and dissolved in tears.

"What a baby, what a dumb broad," I wept. "I'll never figure out this country."

"Look, it's okay," said Sandy. "It's because you're pregnant, because your Spanish isn't that good yet, because the cops are crooks. It's not your fault. It'll be all right, I promise."

But it wasn't all right, everything went wrong. Because we wouldn't have a maid and I was out of the house all day, we were always running out of cooking gas. The delivery man would ring the bell and leave. The house was cold; the DEA wives were boring. If Sandy was late, I'd visit Sara in the evenings, stiffening my back to be more like her—cool, unruffled, fitting in. Sara was pregnant, too, which didn't seem to throw her. It must have been her resilient, Anglo-Canadian stock, or maybe because she was a nurse.

"You're too American," she used to tell me. "You should get a maid, relax, and take Mexico the way it comes."

When I couldn't measure up to Sara's standards, I'd run a hot bath after Spanish classes. Turn on the electric heater, shut the door for fifteen minutes so the bathroom would steam up. Roll down my stockings, step out of my maternity jumper. That bulging, funny body in the mirror couldn't be me. I wouldn't call Sandy—on principle, the way I refused to have a maid. I never stopped to see him after shopping at the commissary. I'd wait for him to call and invite me to lunch, but they weren't like our lunches in New York. We'd eat downstairs in the embassy, standing in the cafeteria line, Sandy asking *"¿Qué es esto?"* looking for something that wouldn't start his stomach turning over. I'd lecture myself: Don't nag, don't ask him if he's going to be late. I talked to myself in the bathtub in the afternoons: I want this man, this child, this house—then why can't I be happy?

The bathroom floor is cold on the bottom of my feet. My belly floats and changes shape. Deep inside me somebody opens and closes the fingers of his hands. He's like a crab walking on wet sand. I haven't any notion how to be his mother. I'm not up to this, I can't do it. Soon even Sandy will see through me. He'd said he wanted me because I was so open. What's left to want when I'm shut down?

10

February 1976, a Tuesday morning in class with my fifth graders. Umberto Hernandez leaned back on his elbows, crossed and uncrossed his legs in dark blue trousers, lisped through his social studies lesson—until he was interrupted by a soft knock at the door. The California nun who ran the school stepped in and the children tripped on American textbooks spread out on the floor as they rose to their feet to perform like little parrots—"Good morning, Sister"—setting my progressive teeth on edge. The recitations, curtsies, bows, and pin-dropping order in the halls were daily reminders that ours was a covertly Catholic school, though Catholic schools were outlawed by the government. There were no prayers, the nuns couldn't wear their habits, but the style was familiar. The mother superior lowered her eyes, the children fidgeted from foot to foot, waiting for permission to sit down.

"There's a call for you in the teacher's room," Sister said with mild disapproval.

It was Sandy at the embassy, excited: The new agents were finally starting to arrive. The new deputy director was Jacques Kiere, an old friend from Paris, Sandy's contact when he was working deep cover on Carmen. He'd come to Mexico with the new administrative officer for a briefing before their permanent transfers.

"You'll like him," Sandy said. "I want to bring them home for dinner." He asked me to call Tikio, our new houseboy, and told me to buy him a white guayabera and flowers for the table. Our bad luck was about to turn around.

Tikio worked Tuesdays at another agent's house. I called him through the embassy operator and stumbled in Spanish through Sandy's request. *"Si, señora, puedo ir,"* Tikio shyly answered. After morning classes I drove an extra forty minutes to the flower vendors at the cemetery on the back road to Toluca where, Sara said, the flowers were fresh and the prices fair. I'd never gone alone before—the haggling scared me—but this occasion buoyed me up. Dazzled by the thought of free weekends, of Sandy mine without distractions, I put down the VW's top and enjoyed the winding road, the narrow bridge, the edge of the barranca. Tin-roofed barrios dotted the hills with cement lean-tos, with children and dogs raising clouds of dust. The worst of the slums couldn't blot out the beauty of those hills.

The cemetery rose up after a final bend in the road: domed mausoleums through cypress trees. The flower stalls formed a wall around the entranceway. I especially liked the white wildflowers that smelled like candy. I bought two bunches, a dozen carnations, and black-eyed Susans, all for a dollar and a half.

Tikio wore his new white shirt and timidly served cocktails in the *sala.* I sat on the floor in front of the fire in a rose-colored Mexican dress that Sandy had bought in San Miguel de Allende and that draped loosely on my belly. Jacques and Sandy were talking about old times in Paris. Jacques was Belgian by birth, in his late forties. His face was creased. He looked a little like Robert Mitchum. I wanted to like him for Sandy's sake, and so I listened to their good old times, sneaky meets in Left Bank cafés where Sandy turned in his reports. On slow days, he'd drive to Jacques' house for dinner, and Jacques' wife would cook Italian meals and the children would amuse him with anecdotes from school. But even with Sandy's memories, I didn't like Jacques Kiere very much.

Our skinny dining room table shone. The wildflower blossoms were already dropping on the tabletop like snow. I'd prepared what I hoped was a delicate meal, shrimp soup with avocado, *langosta,* fresh raspberries and cream. I'd cleaned the kitchen before Tikio arrived. I'd tweezed my eyebrows. If I were very good and tried my hardest, I might be able to entice these men to give up their last few months at home and move down sooner. We sipped champagne from the commissary; the baby moved inside.

"You wouldn't recognize my kids," Jacques Kiere said as we sat down at the table. "We're only bringing two on this tour. We lost the oldest on our last transfer, we'll lose one now."

Sandy was encouraging and warm. "They'll like it here, though not as much as Paris."

Kiere shrugged. "What do teenagers know about Paris?"

They spent fifteen minutes comparing Paris and Mexico City. The administrative officer clucked at the jokes that crossed the table while I watched Tikio take the salad plates away. I had more to do with him than with these guests or the dinner conversation: chemical sprays on poppies, field work in Monterrey, a French informant whom Sandy hoped would help him make big cases. They talked about the new regional director who had recently arrived. A Mexican-American with a Ph.D., uncovered by a computer search for the ideal candidate to work closely with the MFJP, to follow the new guidelines expected when Portillo took over. The DEA was supposed to take on an "advisory" role. The MFJP were expected to make their own arrests. Sandy was so involved in the conversation that he ignored his dinner. I wanted to call out, "Sandy, pay attention to me," hating myself for being such a baby. I couldn't see any big deal about these men. Jacques Kiere dragged out old war stories, same as the old deputy director had. Cops and robbers stories, some of them played out in the presence of his kids. I could understand why he'd lost a child with every move. But Sandy was focusing considerable attention on Jacques Kiere. He wanted Jacques to appreciate the potentials of the region, to agree with him on the kind of cases to be made. It was as if Sandy had everything at stake.

We had brandy after dinner in front of the fire. At midnight they left. The buses had already stopped running. We offered to drive Tikio back to his barranca. There were scattered lights on the mountains on the highway to Toluca. The lights high above the Pemex station turned the sky mauve. My ears began popping as we climbed above eleven thousand feet.

Tikio lived behind a factory, down the steep side of a hill where there were no lights. Sandy tipped him generously and left the headlights on as he disappeared in darkness. "Did you know," Sandy asked, "that he lives in one room with seven other members of his family? None of them knows his own last name."

Driving home there was nothing to say. I was feeling guilty about the three cognacs I'd drunk—what might they do to the baby? We went silently down Reforma, past palms and blacked-out cactuses. The Periférico at 2 A.M. was pink streetlamps on an empty road. I wished that Sandy weren't quite so beautiful in profile.

"Let's keep driving," I say softly, "over the mountains, through Cuernavaca and Iguala, to the sea."

No response.

"Remember that newspaper story in New York? About the driver who dropped his last fare on lower Broadway and just kept going? All the way to Miami in a cloud of snow?"

He shakes his head and still won't speak.

"Never mind," I whisper. "Home it is. Straight home, no detours to the beach." My lips tingle from the brandy.

In the darkness of a tunnel, Sandy's voice is deep. "You didn't like them. You don't like anything about this life."

"That's not true—"

"It is. I can't seem to please you."

Is he right? Am I a spoiled brat who needs propping up at every moment? I loved the weekend we took in San Miguel when we first arrived, toucans in the garden and window shopping before we bought the dress I'm wearing. Two whole days together without a single phone call or an urgent breakfast meeting at the embassy. We had two days of slow, lingering breakfasts on the balcony watching the town below us—clay roofs and courtyard gardens. I wasn't unhappy then. We were in love, and I want it again for more than brief moments. I want those long nights back when we talked about the baby, what he'd be like, how we'd love him. I'd cut Sandy's hair with blunt nail scissors. He gave me a back massage. His time and care—is that too much to ask?

I don't want to argue. "Please, Sandy, let's not fight." The pink lights recede again. The mouth of the second tunnel is purple in the late-night smog. I want New York again, my body as it used to be. In the distance double chains of small white lights climb the mountainside. If I close my eyes, I can pretend they're rising above the George Washington Bridge.

11

Spring came. Political posters were plastered on every available wall in the city. The Periférico was solid with them—one party, one candidate, López Portillo. Everybody knew the election was a hoax. Army trucks would take the *campesinos* to the weekly rallies, to the polling place where they wouldn't have to waste their energies on making choices.

The election would take place in July, when we were in the States. I was going there to have my baby. I would leave in May, eight months pregnant, and Sandy would follow in early June. He had signed up for a training course at the University of Maryland as an excuse to leave Mexico for more than a week. We would stay at my parents' together after his two-week course was over. As the time to leave grew closer, I began to feel foolish about going. But I wanted childbirth in my own language, in the U.S.A. My Mexican doctor could speak English, but the labor nurses couldn't. What if I needed to tell them something? What if it really began to hurt? Sandy didn't seem to mind missing Mexico's elections. "The politics here remind me of Italy," he'd say. "Nothing ever changes."

I felt as little interest in embassy politics as in who became the next President of Mexico. Who cared about the regional director, the office squabbles between the DEA's intelligence and enforcement divisions, the intense competition between the DEA and the State Department? Maybe Portillo would improve the lives of his people, maybe the embassy infighting would eventually stop; but neither would change my life. I'd married Sandy, not his job.

But the DEA infighting did not die down. In spite of myself, I began to recognize the issues. Since diplomats entering foreign countries were admitted under quotas, and only a certain number of diplomatic passports were issued by Mexico, a diminishing allotment in an agency meant an erosion of power. Take away three from agriculture, add them to narcotics, and the power balance shifts.

When we arrived, the DEA was struggling to win the numbers game. By 1976 the DEA's numbers in Mexico were moving up. There were temporary personnel to help spray paraquat on marijuana fields, but more importantly, DEA-Washington had requested and received several new diplomatic slots for agents. Now, to hold on to its advantages, all DEA had to do was produce. The Mexican election would prove crucial. Supposedly, Portillo would be more receptive to U.S. narcotics aims. That spring, months before Portillo was elected, rumors were flying about the new Attorney General and the man he would choose as the new head of the MFJP, Raoul Mendioleya, a retired general. Mexican and embassy politics began competing in importance with the coming of our baby.

"Let's not talk about it anymore," I complained one Saturday morning during breakfast on our terrace. "Let's call Jacques and tell him not to come over. We could go to the hardware store and buy paint for the baby's room. We could go look at material for curtains."

"I can't, Joanne. I thought you'd be pleased that I invited Jacques here for coffee instead of meeting him at the office. The new Attorney General and Mendioleya are important to us. If I'm going to be gone when they take office, I have to prepare now, to find out everything I can about them."

"So State Department won't try to squeeze you out, I suppose? Or so DEA can look smart to Congress? Politics again. You'd think DEA and State were working for different countries."

"It sometimes seems that way." Someone in Sandy's office had gotten hold of a State Department cable laying out all its arguments against the DEA's role abroad to persuade the ambassador and Washington to close the Mexico office. The State Department had always resented the DEA's presence overseas, Sandy explained. The DEA took up our embassy space and used up diplomatic slots on former cops who didn't know the meaning of diplomacy. The State Department complained that DEA agents were the only diplomatic personnel who didn't take foreign-service exams, that none of them knew the meaning of diplomacy. "You can see their point if you look at some of the staff we have abroad," Sandy said, "but it freaks out headquarters, as you can imagine." Now State had formed its own narcotics unit, Narcotics Assistance, they called it, hoping to take over more of the DEA's role. They were paying the Mexican Government to stop the farmers from planting marijuana and opium poppies, but the money was getting used up along the way. They'd sent in trained foreign-service officers who were smoother than most DEA agents, who knew the language and worked through more traditional channels. "There's a kind of race going on, Joanne, to get in tight with Oscar Flores Sánchez, the new Attorney General. Mendioleya is his old boyhood friend, they say. Flores supposedly talked him out of a comfortable retirement to take over the MFJP. He's considered a tough old man who'll run the federal police himself. He's important, Joanne. I want to get to know him."

I wanted another cup of coffee but didn't take it after thinking of the baby. "I thought you didn't care about politics," I said.

He stood up and started to take the tray away. "I've got a lot of work to do here. There are people in Washington who might like to see me fail."

The end of his comment drifted off as he went into the house. I followed him. "What did you say?"

He was getting ready for Jacques, putting more water on to boil, measuring fresh coffee. "Nothing, really. I have to pay attention to the politics, that's all. Now the new regional director's here. The new agents have started coming in. More are due while we're away. Washington has high expectations for the region, but so far, we haven't raised our production level. Congress used to wring its hands about the opium coming in from Turkey. Now they're panicked about cocaine from South America. We don't have much leverage in Colombia or Bolivia, where the real sources are, but we have hopes for Mexico, where most of the coke is shipped before entering the States. According to the rumors, Mendioleya is a straight shooter who wants to work with us. He's already wealthy. He doesn't need to be corrupt. In fact, he wants to clean up the MFJP as best he can. He isn't taking the job with ambitions for something better, ambitions that would compromise him. He's just doing a favor for his old friend Oscar Flores. I'm going to try to get next to him, Joanne. If we trust each other, I can work directly with him and make the kind of cases that the region needs. We couldn't have even hoped for that under Echeverría. He was so vocally anti-U.S."

He took down three clean cups and saucers and put on a small pan of milk to boil. He liked to heat the milk before serving it with coffee. He took out some cat's tongues and arranged them on a plate. Why did this business he was in have to be so complicated? He didn't belong in the business of narcotics. Why couldn't he have chosen something simple, that I could do with him? I wasn't used to feeling so ignorant. I'd always been the smart kid, the one who caught on quickly.

"I've bored you into silence," he said.

"No. Awed me is more like it. I don't like to think of your job as being so compelling or so hard. I hoped you could do it with one hand behind your back. I wish I understood it better."

"No, you don't. It's not the agent in me that interests you. I could give you a brief history of narcotics interdiction in Mexico and put you straight to sleep."

"Try me."

"There isn't time. Jacques will be here any second."

"You should take away one of the cups and saucers. I'm not going to hang around while you and Jacques are meeting."

"You might learn something about my job."

"Maybe, but it wouldn't be something that I'd like."

I did hang around a little while, though, long enough to nibble through one cookie while Sandy and Jacques talked about the changes the region could expect. Although Luis Echeverría had been unsympathetic to U.S. narcotics goals, DEA agents had enjoyed great latitude in some respects during his administration— they carried guns and took an active role in arrests. The MFJP, however, never really cooperated. Corruption within the federal police was the rule rather than the exception. The low salaries paid to even high-level officers was seen as tacit approval for widespread graft. Because the police were often paid off by narcotics dealers, it would be hard to implement many changes in the field, no matter how sincere General Mendioleya was about cooperating. There would be entire states that even the general himself couldn't penetrate—Jalisco, Sinaloa. They were like privately owned fiefdoms.

Sandy poured more coffee; Jacques lit another cigarette. They couldn't count on much help from the new regional director in spurring on the general. It was hard not to think that headquarters was trying to sabotage the region at the same time that it put the pressure on. The new director may have looked on paper like the right choice to compete with State Department types—he had the right degrees, the right ethnic name, and a command of Spanish. Sandy gave him six months on the outside before there was outright rebellion in the region. He implemented every regulation according to the book until it was impossible to make a decent case. Instead of bailing Sandy out from some of his enormous work load, the regional director had made more work, took up unnecessary time with meetings, caused a lineup of younger agents outside Sandy's door.

"Then you haven't heard?" Jacques Kiere said dramatically. "In June I'm taking over."

"So that's why you wanted to meet this morning!"

"I thought you should be the first to know."

"What are we doing drinking coffee? I'll go get a bottle of champagne."

I followed Sandy into the kitchen, on the pretext of helping. "Are you happy?"

"You don't know? This is it, Joanne!" he beamed. "Jacques knows his way around the street. He's not a pansy or a cowboy. After Paris he was head of intelligence at the El Paso center. He knows me. He knows what I can do. There's finally someone I can work with here."

Jacques understood Sandy's style and would give him the leeway he needed to produce important class-1 cases. They both agreed, informants were the key. They couldn't risk an agent in deep cover in Mexico—it was too dangerous, too hard to monitor his moves with so much corruption in the system. The trick was to put in the right informants and develop long-running, hard-hitting cases that followed the cocaine from its South American source through distribution in Mexico and into the States. Sandy envisioned elegant, multinational cases, the source in one country, the dealer in Mexico, the buyer in California or New York—all would be nabbed in Mexico, where the regional office and Jacques would get the credit.

By April Sandy had come up with two good informants. One was a Mexican lawyer named Alfredo Campos whom Sandy had enlisted while he was under investigation by the DEA in Monterrey. Already imprisoned once in Mexico for importing contraband from the States, Campos didn't want to go to jail again. He'd inform on his clients, convict them, then defend them. He ratted at every stage of the game. Campos was the lowest kind of informant, perhaps, but he knew the dealers.

To find the sources Sandy had already begun developing a French informant, an ex-dealer named Claude Picault whom Jacques Kiere had recruited in France in 1971. Both agreed it was an odd coincidence that Kiere should know Picault. He had started working for the DEA in France to avoid arrest, and after several cases in Paris had been sent to Montreal, where he worked with both the DEA and the Royal Canadian Mounted Police. When things in Canada and New York got too hot for him, Picault had traveled to Mexico City with a hundred thousand dollars in cash, proceeds from a recent narcotics case. The money had been seized in a routine search at the Mexican border and confiscated from him. His first dealings with the DEA in Mexico, long before Sandy arrived, concerned his money. He had asked a DEA agent to plead for him with the Mexican Government, and the money was returned. Afterward he'd been eager to work with the DEA in Mexico, but no agents in the Mexican region spoke French, and Picault was unwilling to work in any other language. When Sandy came down to Mexico in 1975, he'd been working on a case in Montreal with the same RCMP agents who had worked with Claude. It was through them that he and Picault met. The RCMP agents warned Sandy that Picault had his problems—he needed undue attention, a lot of time and coddling, but in the months that Sandy had begun to work with him, Picault had produced a heroin case in Acapulco and a good case in Jalisco, which was one of the hardest states to crack. With Jacques in the captain's seat and two good informants working, things were finally moving into place.

12

I was intrigued the first time Claude Picault appeared uninvited at our front door. I'd heard about him from the two Canadian agents who came to dinner at our house in the early fall and recounted some of their experiences with him. They had stashed him in a safe house outside Montreal after a big case. He was living with a girlfriend who was pregnant, and the agents would get frantic calls in the middle of the night, false labor alerts or urgent requests for bread and chocolate. After the girl gave birth to Claude's child, the agents were asked to buy her nursing bras and formula. They put up with those calls because Claude produced big cases. If Sandy took him on—as he should, they urged—he'd be getting his own calls soon.

Although Sandy had spoken enthusiastically to me about the cases he had worked with Claude since September, he wasn't eager to invite him into our house that afternoon. He seemed surprised to see Claude, and for a moment, I was afraid they'd go outside to talk and I'd be cheated. I had never met an informant before.

"Ask him in," I said. I remembered our first date, when I had watched Sandy and his female informer meeting by a phone booth in Chinatown. It had been dark then, and I was in the car, but Claude in his sweater and leather clogs was real-life stuff. We had only been in Mexico a few months, and I relished the excitement of having a European con man in our stucco living room, talking with Sandy in rapid French. Yet the reality of Claude was disappointing. He didn't look like a gangster from the twilight world of informers and narcotics. He was more like a short, balding European tourist, very clean-shaven and smelling of cologne. I searched for signs of the kind of life he'd lived and found them in his heavy gold jewelry, in the way he dropped his eyes and wouldn't look at me. But the only real clue to his past was a pronounced limp in one leg which Sandy later called a "souvenir" from a Paris shoot-out.

For the first fifteen minutes of Claude's visit, I sat on the floor across from him and listened. He was a nervous talker who gestured a lot. His stiff leg seemed to give him trouble. He couldn't get comfortable until he had stretched it out on the ottoman, in the process turning over his satchel on the floor. He said he had stopped by to check on last-minute details for his latest case before his afternoon flight to Paris on the Concorde.

"I don't remember giving you this address," Sandy casually remarked. I could understand his French with its thick Italian accent, but it was harder to follow Claude's reply. He spoke too fast, too colloquially. I thought he said he had gotten the number from another agent when he tried calling Sandy at the office. But that seemed unlikely. No one at the embassy would reveal a residential telephone number or address. It was strictly against regulations. When Sandy didn't ask any further questions, I figured I must have misunderstood Claude.

The rest of the conversation floated by. I grew bored and restless. I had to concentrate so hard to follow them that my head began to ache. Claude seemed to sense that I was losing interest and turned to say in halting Spanish, "I could bring you something back from France. Some perfume. What do you like? I can get it at the airport, duty-free."

He had caught me off guard, but Sandy was quick to answer. "*Merci*, Claude. But that's not necessary."

There was something blurry, intangible about Claude that kept slipping by me. I didn't realize he was setting the tone for his long relationship with Sandy. Even then, at the very beginning, he tried to buy his way into our lives.

The next time I saw Claude was at a party he and his girlfriend gave in their temporary flat in Mexico City. They were between cities, preparing to move to Guadalajara from Acapulco, and stuck unhappily in the Federal District for a month or two. Claude hated it. He said it reminded him of New York, cold and dirty. Since he wasn't working then, giving parties was the only way to amuse himself. It was the first of many parties given by Claude. The DEA agents hugged the edges of the room while the other guests were dancing. There was a professor from the French lycée in Mexico City, a librarian from the French bookstore, an attaché from the French Embassy. A beautiful turbaned woman in a long black dress danced with a gaunt teenaged boy in pleated pants. I wondered how Claude had met them. There were endless trays of food—pâté and sausages, real French cheese smuggled through customs on Claude's last trip from Europe—as well as a steady supply of champagne. But the party was boring. Claude tried too hard, was too willing to play the fool.

He was so busy celebrating the success of his third case with Sandy that he didn't seem to notice when his girl disappeared to the bedroom with one of his French friends. He opened a new bottle of champagne and pitched drunkenly against the table, the champagne splashing on the terra cotta floor. Though he was stuck in Mexico City, he was in the money again—thanks to the DEA. He had made a follow-up case against the same French trafficker he had fingered already in Acapulco. He had gone to see him in jail and won his confidence again. They had nailed two dealers in the prison traffic, but for Claude the real coup had been conning the same man twice, which proved in his own eyes how truly talented he was. Clearly, the flush days wouldn't last long. It was expensive keeping such high-class friends, not to mention his dark-haired girl —*"la flor de Acapulco,"* she was called.

Sandy whispered in my ear that Claude's French friends believed he was a member of the French press corps. He had shown them his impeccable phony credentials. Only the French Embassy attaché was convinced he knew the "real" story, that Claude was a special consular officer and a probable spy for the U.S.A. Another of Claude's many calling cards had passed around the French Embassy, introducing him by his legal name—

RENÉ DE KERCADIO
Conseiller Spécial et Chargé de Mission

Près les Ambassades et Consulats des États
Unis d'Amérique à Mexico, Montréal, et Paris.

I was shocked when Sandy pulled this card out of his wallet. What did the embassy think of such a fraud? Sandy put his arm around me and said I was naïve. Security had probably produced the card itself. Claude was eager to pass high-level information to anybody for the right price. The CIA must have known that he was in the country.

"Do you know for sure?" I asked.

Sandy shrugged. "Look around you. Does this look like a group put together by a stool?"

As I scanned the group, Claude's girlfriend stole out of the bedroom, her long black hair tangled from an hour on the sheets.

The French guests were still dancing when we left that night. Claude had weaved to the door with us and tried to kiss me on both cheeks. It was 2 A.M. when we got home, and the telephone was ringing. It was Claude, appalled and very sorry for himself. He'd been robbed by one of his own guests, those high-class people. A case of champagne, his jewelry and the girl's, seven bottles of their best perfume. "I bet she staged the heist herself," I speculated. "For effect—like Carmen, to protect herself."

By spring we had lived through two of Claude's parties, and I had vowed never to attend another. But when Sandy called from the office in April to see if I wanted to take a weekend with him in Guadalajara, I couldn't resist—even though I knew it would mean seeing Claude. "Come with me," Sandy said. "We'll have a great time. It will be our treat to ourselves before you leave for the States to wait for the baby. We'll make up for the weekend in Cuernavaca we never had."

"But you'll have to work," I said.

"Not much. Claude's nervous about a case we've got down there and wants to introduce me to the dealer, but that's only for an afternoon. We'll have the rest of the time to ourselves. We'll go out to the market in Tlaquepaque and buy you another Mama Carlota dress. It will be your last maternity dress, something you can take in after you've had the baby."

"I'm not so sure. Maybe I'll never have this baby. Could you get used to it if I stayed like this?"

"If you go to Guadalajara with me, I'll get used to it, I promise."

I had tea with Sara on Friday afternoon. She and Paul were always traveling through Mexico. "You'll love Guadalajara," she said. "You should take the overnight train so you can see something of the country the next day." But we didn't have time to take the train. We flew down early Saturday morning.

It was beautiful as we deplaned, much warmer than Mexico City, without any smog in sight. Sandy carried our overnight bag on his shoulder. "You'll see," he promised, "This weekend is exactly what we need. We'll swim in the pool and bake in the sun."

But he didn't know that Claude had other plans for us. On the small lawn outside the terminal, a mariachi band was tuning up. It stopped as we approached and made straight for us. We tried sidestepping the musicians, looking over our shoulders for the unfortunate targets of the serenade, but whichever way we moved, the band followed. A camera on a tripod was set up on the sidewalk. The photographer called our names and took our picture. "Look," Sandy said, "isn't that Claude behind him?" It was Claude indeed, half hidden behind the camera with a satisfied expression on his smooth, tanned face. Sandy couldn't get to him. The skinny, worn musicians had surrounded us by then and were cranking out their numbers. The trumpet player was the worst. His mustache twitched; the baubles on his tight black pants jangled up and down. People leaving the airport made a wide circle around us. When the last song finally ended, Claude jumped forward, tipped the bandleader, and limped up for *abrazos* all around. I was afraid Sandy would start shouting, but Claude didn't give him time.

"I had to abandon my car," he sputtered in his fast French. "I left it on the bridge outside town. They won't have the parts here, they never do. So we'll have to take a taxi. *Lo siento mucho*, but that's how it goes. I'll drop you at your hotel, and we'll make plans for later in the day."

"No no, Claude," Sandy managed to get in. "We'll get our own cab. How did you know what flight we were taking? I didn't give you the time or number."

"There's a flight every hour. We just waited, the band and I."

"It was unnecessary. Completely unnecessary," Sandy said.

"Ah, but I wanted to welcome you. I had a sign made, but I left it in the damn car."

"No signs, Claude. And no more bands. Do you understand?"

The three of us walked awkwardly to the curb. Sandy hailed a cab and made curt arrangements. "We haven't had breakfast, which we want to do. *Alone,* Claude. You and I can meet at our hotel at four. Just call from the desk and I'll meet you in the lobby."

Hurt by the brush-off, Claude stood on the sidewalk and pouted as we got into our cab. He leaned his head through my open window. *"Bienvenido a Guadalajara,"* he said sadly.

The cab drove off and Sandy put his arm around me. "I'm sorry. I had no idea he'd be at the airport. I purposely didn't say what time I was coming in, but he's amazing. You can never tell what he'll pull next. I should never have mentioned that you were traveling with me. He did it for you, to make a good impression. He thinks you don't like him."

"It was an awful show," I said, "but he looked so hurt."

Sandy cocked his head and looked at me. "Don't tell me you're feeling sorry for Claude? Now you see. That's how he operates. Imagine what it's like for me. He tugs at you. He acts so fucking needy. He's a real pain in the ass, but he means well, I suppose. He's lonely. I always end up feeling sorry for his empty life. Every woman he meets is after money, and he lets them get away with it. He thought we'd be pleased. I'll try to smooth it over when I meet him later."

When we registered at the desk, the clerk told Sandy that our party would be waiting in the garden for lunch at two o'clock. Sandy turned to me and shook his head. There was a huge bouquet of flowers on the dresser in our room, with a note from Claude addressed to "Señora Bonanno." We had registered in that name. Sandy was to play Salvatore Bonanno when he met Claude later.

"Please don't apologize again," I said.

Sandy fingered the orchids, the roses. "What should we do about lunch?"

"I guess we'll have to go. I'll excuse myself as soon as we finish eating. I can say I'm tired from the baby."

"I'm sure his girlfriend will be with him."

I shrugged. "I've met her before."

We were led to a table set for four under a canopy in the hotel garden. Claude and the girl were already seated. He could have passed for a tourist from Miami with his bronze tan and his expensive summer shoes, somebody rich who knew his way around. He wore a white guayabera; a flat gold chain glittered on his neck. The girl's peasant blouse was pulled down off her shoulders. We made small talk while the waiters served shrimp and champagne. One of them accidently bumped Sandy on the arm, and I was surprised by his tense annoyance. He was ill at ease, as if he couldn't wait to get Claude alone and clear up whatever problems there were with the case. He didn't want this social afternoon in the carefully planted shade. He didn't even look at me during the meal, though once he reached for my hand beneath the table.

Pregnant as I was, I felt confident. It was easy to be gracious. In my improved Spanish I asked the girl about her son who was living with her sister in another city. I was pleased when I understood every word she said. Claude ordered a rich dessert which none of us touched, but it was pleasant enough to look out on the sunny lawn. There were peacocks strutting in a fenced yard and hundreds of flowers. Over coffee Sandy and Claude conversed in French. I heard them talk about the dealer—*le mec*, they called him. The Man. It was time to excuse myself and go upstairs.

The hotel room was stuffy. I opened the sliding door to the balcony with its view of the garden. I could see the table, set off to one side. The girl was bored and played with her hair and with the flatware on the tablecloth. Perhaps because he and Claude were finally working, Sandy seemed more relaxed. He sat back, legs crossed, a cigarette in one hand. Claude leaned into him, oily and ingratiating. I still didn't like him. But Sandy could handle him, I was sure. He disagreed with Claude about some point and showed his disapproval with quick, clean moves. When Claude nodded, I felt satisfied. It was good to see Sandy in control. It was also good to feel the baby kick so low, reminding me that it was almost time. I turned from the garden, closed the sliding door, and lay down on the bed.

In the evening Sandy would meet with Claude and the target of their investigation. Sandy would play the money man, Salvatore Bonanno, chief of Claude's organization. What would it be like to be Mrs. Bonanno? I could try it out and see, dress up in one of my Mexican tents, put an orchid in my hair, and stroll into the lobby during their meeting. Mrs. Bonanno might do that, might make grand and vulgar gestures. But probably not. More likely, she would do what I intended to do—stay in the room alone, waiting for Salvatore Bonanno to come home, making up her weak excuses that really such a life wasn't so bad.

Admit it, I told myself. The weekend would be a loss. Sandy's time would be monopolized by Claude. He had engineered it skillfully. I couldn't compete with his mariachi band, his perfectly appointed lunch in the shade, his drug dealer waiting in the lobby. Claude was more conniving than any wife could be. I turned on my side, trying to focus more clearly on the reasons that I hated him. "So fucking needy," Sandy had said, but I couldn't understand the basis of his need. What did he really want from Sandy? Because he was a double dealer, he feared for his life. He wanted Sandy to protect him. But that wasn't all of it. He claimed to have come from a prominent French family. Then why had he picked such a disreputable career? How had he gotten the gunshot wound that made him limp? Why had the RCMP dumped him on Sandy? He seemed to have won their trust in spite of his calls in the middle of the night, but they weren't working with him anymore. He'd told Sandy that he liked Guadalajara, where the drug traffic was controlled in political circles. He liked cultivating big shots—with money, I supposed. He liked their power. He claimed good friends who believed he was straight—doctors, reporters, TV personalities. I couldn't imagine what anyone saw in him or in his lavish, boring parties.

Why had he picked us to clutch on to? He called the house when Sandy wasn't home, when he couldn't reach him through the embassy switchboard, and tried to get me to give him the number of Sandy's direct line. He stopped by our house unexpectedly when it was hard to throw him out. He wanted something, something big. But he belonged to the DEA and Sandy. I couldn't let him be my problem.

Sandy came back from lunch to find me reading on the bed.

"Did you sleep?"

I shook my head and turned my cheek when he leaned down to kiss me. "Did you settle things with Claude?"

"The meet is set for ten o'clock. Tomorrow we'll be free, I promise."

"Was this trip as urgent as he said?"

Sandy sat on the edge of the bed. "With Claude it's always urgent. Supposedly, the buyer is trying to back out. I'll know more tonight."

I was propped on the pillows with my book on my stomach. I opened it and laid it against my chin, half hoping the words I was about to say would be too garbled to understand. Since we'd moved to Mexico and Claude had come into Sandy's life, there had been one underlying question: "Will it always be like this?"

Sandy took the book away and pressed his palm on the side of my face, gently patting back my hair. I suddenly remembered being small, maybe five or six, waking up in my room in the apartment where we lived. It was summer. My mother was vacuuming the floral carpet in the hall. The radio was playing. She liked to sing to the radio. I used to know the words to all her songs. My mother and Frank Sinatra crooning, "A Foggy Day in London Town."

"No, it won't be, I promise," Sandy said. He was right, of course. In less than a month I would fly to Washington to have our baby. He kept caressing my face. "Claude wanted to drive us out to Tlaquepaque tomorrow morning, but I said absolutely not. After tonight, we're on our own. He's so impossible, the waste of his life, the show he's always giving. I told him to end it with the girl. She wants to set herself up in Cancún. He should give her the money and write her off. Then he could begin to save his rewards. He can't work Mexico forever. Sooner than he thinks, he'll be burned here, too."

"Shhh," I tried to say. I closed my eyes. How old could my mother have been with her vacuum cleaner and Frank Sinatra? My brother wasn't born yet. She still wore her hair long, chestnut brown, brushing her shoulders. I used to wake to the smell of the summer lawn and the radio blaring. She was young, my mother. She couldn't have been more than thirty-two. I couldn't sleep with

Sandy's hand on my face like that, with Claude's bouquet of orchids on the table, when in a month I would have a child of my own. I sat up and took Sandy's hand away. "Come with me to Washington," I said.

"You mean fly up with you? I've considered it. We could change your reservation to Saturday morning."

"No, I mean stay with me until the baby comes."

"For two months? How? I have this case—"

"It's not your place to save Claude. This is the life he's chosen. Who cares if he keeps his girl or not, if he wastes his money? He isn't your responsibility."

"But the cases are. He entangles his life with each investigation. If something goes wrong with his girl, he drags his feet, he cancels meetings. After you left, we convinced her to look around the shops, and he got started—how he needs to make this case to get her off his back. He's offered new sources if DEA would put him on retainer. He's met somebody else. A proper kind of girl, he says —she's nineteen, for Chrisake. He wants more money to win her family over. When I finally got him back on the subject of this case, he admitted to stalling the dealer until he could arrange to end it with the first girl and move her to Cancún. Some crap about how the two women had met. I exploded. I told him we can't advance him another cent, that he'd better move his ass, that this case better go the way I've planned it. I should drop him now, on the spot. But how? I can't go in here myself and make these sources. We don't have anybody else."

"You should drop him. He isn't worth the trouble. He isn't worth missing out on your own life."

"But you don't understand, this is my life. Or part of it. This is how I make my living. And Claude is part of it for now."

At nine-thirty that night I lie in bed watching Sandy dress. Neither of us is talking. I can't produce for him what Claude produces. I don't even mention Mrs. Bonanno's cameo appearance in the lobby—though he might have liked the goof. It would have been the kind of moment he enjoyed when we were living in New York. Not now, though. I'll order tea and stay in bed. Sandy comes and sits by me again, placing his hands on my stomach and waiting, though the baby doesn't move.

"Try to rest," he says from the door. "A nap would be good. I'll turn off the light."

The room goes dark. Sandy goes away. My enormous womb is a disease I've been sent to bed to cure. If I'm good, he'll take me for a walk when he gets back, a treat for good behavior. I remember that, too—paper dolls from my father after work when I had the mumps. My pregnancy is like the mumps to Sandy.

Outside this dark room the tourists are enjoying their vacations. There are floor shows in the nightclubs. Claude's soon-to-be former girlfriend is no doubt wearing sequins on her dress. It isn't fair. I hear music coming from the garden, real music instead of a radio playing some depressing tune. Maybe it's Claude's mariachi band from the afternoon. I recognize *"Sin Ti"* and *"María Elena,"* and even know the words. I push the sheet down, sit up in Sandy's cotton nightshirt. From behind the curtains at the sliding glass doors, I see colored lights strung around the garden. The tablecloths have been lifted from the tables. The gringos in Guadalajara are having fun.

Well, why not? What harm could it do? There will be other nights like this with Sandy's job. I'll have to learn to use them. I haven't got the mumps. I'm not a child. I don't want to stay alone in the dark.

I pull out my caftan with long pink ribbons down the front, with plenty of room for the baby. I put a flower in my hair. It really could be funny, strolling through the lobby with my ribbons trailing. I could compete with Claude. He makes productions. I don't. He's splashy and gets himself noticed. If I don't botch it, Sandy won't mind. It's the kind of nervy thing he likes.

The elevator is solid brass. The shops are heavy with pottery, with papier-mâché clowns. Ten feet from the main archway I pretend to look in the windows of the shops while scouting the scene in the lobby. There's the registration desk, French doors leading to the garden, and off to one side, Claude, Sandy, and their source in dark plush chairs. I'd have to go for the farthest door, that way they couldn't miss me. Thinking about it makes my stomach flutter. How will Claude react? Do I pretend that I don't know them or walk right up, Señora Bonanno with a flower in her hair? No, I'll breeze through and disappear into the garden, a ghost of myself for Sandy.

Halfway into the room, I consider backing out. I don't want to blow Sandy's meeting with the dealer, to catch him off guard. As if I could. He's a pro, remember. Both he and Claude are pros at orchestrating scenes like this. Chin up, shoulders back. Sandy lights a cigarette and glances over. I don't stare or give myself away, but he has absolutely noticed. How queer—my knees are shaking. It's titillating. It's satisfying to understand at last why Sandy's in it, for these same jitters, this fear, for heightened moments all the time. Not five feet away from him, I have an urge to raise the stakes somehow, to do something, to stumble, maybe fake a faint. My mouth goes dry. No, no, that would be all wrong. Too clumsy and obvious. I line myself up with the pretty French doors. I could reach out for him now, tug lightly at his coat sleeve, but that's not the gesture he's expecting. The small beaded bag hanging from my shoulder bumps against my side when I take another step. That's it, exactly right, and I relax my shoulder, let it slide. It drops on the deep-blue carpet like a stone in water, touching Sandy with its rippling effect. He stands. I've stopped to watch him. He easily extricates himself from Claude and the dealer. He's looking at me as he leans down to pick up the purse from the floor. He's beside me, flattening his tie inside his jacket. He's mine for that one moment and smiles, eye-to-eye.

It's cool in the garden. The colored lights are calling. I dismiss the tourists at their tables as a bore and rise above them, over Claude and Jacques and the DEA. Wherever Sandy's going, I am, too—long pink ribbons sailing.

13

May went by in a blur of calls to Mexico from my mother's house in Virginia, in the flatness of waiting. I rang up a hundred-dollar phone bill in three weeks and read four books on childbirth without feeling any wiser. Pant or blow during transition?—I couldn't remember which meant what. The longer I stayed in Washington, the richer the texture of Mexico seemed. I missed Sara and Polly, the bougainvillea, the sweet-potato man who pushed his cart and blew his long, sad whistle down our private street. As summer came in hot and early, I even missed the thick stucco walls of our apartment, the drafts through the chinks of stone I'd complained about for months. I was convinced our baby would never come.

Sandy arrived the first of June like one of those cleansing breaths described in all my childbirth guides, ready to rip through his two-week management course at the University of Maryland, impatient to move me into his dormitory room. "We'll be alone," he said. "You'll cause a stir in the cafeteria. It's what we need to take us to your due date."

I wasn't so sure. The room was small. The single beds were narrow. "We'd better push them together," I suggested, "unless you think they're bolted down."

"We don't need both beds. We've been apart a month, remember?" But he'd changed his mind by morning, with bags beneath his eyes from trying to fit himself around my ninth-month womb.

In between his classes I forced him to help me practice the exercises from my books. We lay on the grass beneath the heavy summer trees. "Contract you left big toe and button your lip," he'd tease.

By the second week, I didn't find him funny.

"This isn't a joke. This is really going to happen, you know."

"I'm ready. Just tell me what to do."

"I'm not supposed to have to tell you. You're supposed to know. Besides, you're the one who's already had children."

"Secondhand, in absentia. You're the one who's reading all the books."

"They're not enough. We need those classes—if your stupid management course ever ends."

"Just relax. It can't be that bad. Think of my mother. She did it eight times without going to one class."

We beat Sandy's mother by two Lamaze sessions, which weren't enough. On the way to the hospital he started to panic. "I don't remember anything. I won't do you any good." In the labor room he whispered in my ear, patted a wet washcloth on my lips, and couldn't believe it could be so hard. In the delivery room, in his green surgical mask and paper boots, he kept repeating, "Look, his head! Oh my God, my God." I'd never seen him so happy. He held our new son David and said: "How could I be a father of two and never know this?"

We had a week together at my parents' before Sandy left for Mexico. I had to stay, to wait for the baby's diplomatic passport to come through.

"It doesn't seem fair," I argued. "We should at least be able to fly home together."

"I can't wait, Joanne. Jacques didn't want to give me time for that management course. He only did it for you and the baby. Claude's lying low in Cuernavaca, waiting for me to start his next case, probably getting restless. The new deputy is in and needs help. Mexico's had its elections now. There isn't time to wait. Besides, David's passport shouldn't take long."

"But you never take any time off. You deserve a vacation."

"When you come home, I promise. We'll take the baby for a week in Cuernavaca."

"Sure, in Cuernavaca, where you can work with Claude."

Time for a dirty look between us before the phone in my mother's kitchen rang. I held the baby close to my chest and answered it. The international operator spoke with an accent when she asked for Mr. Bario. It would be Jacques, I figured. But I was wrong.

"Oui, Claude. Comment ça va?" Sandy asked.

14

I cried all the way to Mexico—because the baby wouldn't nurse on the flight, because he was so small, because the blanket I'd modestly draped across my shoulder kept slipping down, all the time telling myself it was useless to cry, that there wasn't such a thing as mother's instinct, anyway. But the crying came and went for weeks. David didn't sleep, we didn't sleep. Sandy would get up and bring him to our bed at 2, at 4, at 6 A.M. After a month of never knowing what was wrong, Sandy said, "That's it. Feudal or not, we're hiring a maid."

Her name was Concha, a sullen, sloe-eyed woman who rarely smiled and was too shy to talk. Every time she'd whisper "señora," I'd look around for the adult she was addressing. I couldn't imagine how we'd ever make a team. She wanted to eat her breakfast at the counter in the kitchen. I wanted her at the table with me. I felt guilty that she lived in the servant's quarters, a cold concrete box on our roof, up steep outdoor iron stairs that meant she got wet every time it rained. I went up there once in tears at dawn when Sandy was away, to see if she might know what could be bothering the baby. She had a view of Popocatépetl, the volcano, through her hanging laundry. She refused our offer of the extra bedroom down the hall; she wanted uniforms to wear; she waxed the wide pegged floors each morning. I hardly let her pick the baby up. He was mine. It was my job to learn to know him, his mouth always open like a letter *O*, his pink, scaling fingers. I used to lie on the daybed with him, across the room from the unused typewriter and a stack of new bond paper, staring at him, amazed every morning that he was still alive.

Sandy was gone by seven and usually called by noon. "Leave the baby with Concha and come downtown for lunch. I can take half an hour, you could go shopping."

"It's so far, and David needs to nurse so often. I'd better not."

"I don't like it," he'd press. "You aren't getting out enough. You're not teaching anymore, and I'm not home. Maybe we should move. We could take a house closer to the embassy where there are other diplomatic families."

"That isn't what we wanted."

"Things change. We didn't know the office would be like this, and we didn't have a baby. I could save an hour each way commuting. It might make every difference if we moved."

We had to move or take a trip or buy another dress in Tlaquepaque. We couldn't change ourselves or Sandy's job, but we had to do something. Sandy was the one who had promised to take charge and make our choices. He had gotten to know me better in time. I wasn't just the pretty girl with the Italian name—his wife. Once I was his wife, he realized being legally married wasn't the solution. Still, we didn't move right away. Instead, we went to Cuernavaca for a weekend.

We stayed in a small hotel owned by a Swiss couple in their fifties who felt close to Sandy because he was European. They were missing their only son who was back in Switzerland for his military service. We were in Cuernavaca to find a new safe hiding place for Claude.

The dining room was slow on a Sunday afternoon. The owner and chef, René, hung around our table. He leaned one arm on the back of Claude's chair and confided his fears to Sandy. His wife had been ill for months. Both of them were growing older. Maybe their son wouldn't return to Mexico at all. He sounded happy in Switzerland. René was considering selling out. His wife sat at an empty table next to us cradling David on her lap, singing him a nursery rhyme in French. She stopped to say to me in Spanish that our baby was too thin. "How old is he?" she asked. "Three months," I answered, incredulous that he had lived so long with such an inexperienced mother. She reminisced: When her own son was an infant and wouldn't take the breast, she fed him from an eyedropper, milliliters at a time. Did that mean she had noticed how impatient I was, how annoyed at Claude for showing up on our two-day vacation?

We were supposed to scout the city for a place for Claude. He wasn't supposed to know about it. He wasn't supposed to come along. Just because he was between cases, between apartments, between women yet again, didn't mean Sandy had to bail him out. Sandy sipped his milk and smiled at René. He looked happy, enjoying the easy conversation after the tension between Claude and me.

Friday afternoon, an hour before we left on the drive to Cuernavaca, Claude had called. I should have told Concha not to pass the phone. I should have put my foot down once I'd overheard Sandy's half of their conversation. *"Oui,* Claude, yes. We're leaving now. I think I know the perfect place, a small hotel with maisonettes, a swimming pool. You and the owner share a name. Château René, it's called." Claude, sitting at my side on the glassed-in porch at Château René, was looking petulant, refusing to speak. What a jerk, I thought. This is his life, what he's chosen, hiding out in Cuernavaca after every case. Sandy hasn't saved him. He's still despondent. He's bored, that's all. I watched him staring through the picture window at the garden below. The weekend guests had all returned to Mexico City. A waiter cleared the dishes from an outdoor table. The gardener cleared the debris of children from the small fish pond.

The long dinner had begun to drag for me as well. Everyone was ready to go home but Sandy. He liked planning cases, liked this middle-aged Swiss couple. Though he was aware of Claude's mood, he still encouraged René to go on. He asked about the hotel's expenses, the business it brought in. They discussed the menu and what René substituted for those ingredients he couldn't find in Mexico. Sandy's face was sunburned from the day before, from our long walks before Claude arrived when our marriage had almost been rescued. Over coffee and dessert I thought of asking him again, Will it always be like this?

René and his wife finally left. Sandy held David on his lap and let him suck on his little finger.

"You should buy this place," he said to Claude.

"What for?" Claude asked, frowning.

"Because you can't be in this business forever. Do you really want to start all over after Mexico, another country, another city where you'll throw your money away? You could invest it now. Find a manager until you're through with DEA, until you're burned completely, then come back here and make a home. The waiters speak French. René will come to know you. He'd make a deal. You wouldn't even have to change the hotel's name. You could have a long, simple life."

Claude flinched, lifted his stiff leg, and set it on the empty chair between them. "You can say that. When you're done in Mexico, you'll go home to the States where you're safe, where you have a family. There's nothing for me in Cuernavaca, nothing but rich old Americans waiting to die."

"It's only an hour from Mexico City. You have friends there."

"And enemies, too. What happens when they get out of jail? A Frenchman with a limp can't hide in Cuernavaca."

"You can get your leg fixed. It's about time. Go to Houston if you don't trust the doctors here."

Claude finished his beer and shook his head. "It can't be fixed. I've tried." He gestured toward me and David, tossing us away with a flick of his wrist. "You'll go back to the States, I know that. When you leave, I'll be finished here. I won't work for DEA without you. The rest of them don't understand me. So you'll go, I'll be finished, that will be that."

My head ached from trying to follow their conversation. I kissed David's cheek, brushed my hand against his fine, new hair, and dreamed that Claude would soon disappear, disenchanted by his slow life in Cuernavaca, bored by Sandy's projections. After all, it's Sandy who would have liked to own Château René, Sandy who wanted to escape. He felt sorry for Claude's undercover life as though it were his own. But I'm not sorry for Claude. I hate him for showing up in Cuernavaca, for hanging on Sandy like a spoiled kid. There must be something else about him, though I can't name it. Really, what else has he done wrong? He doesn't lean on Sandy any more than I do.

15

After Christmas we moved to a small house on the edge of a barranca, closer to the embassy and next door to another DEA agent whose wife, Sandy hoped, would be company for me. From our bedroom window, tile roofs on the street below, brittle trees. We were so high up we could see lines of yellow smoke rising from the bonfires of burning tires in the *vecindades* on New Year's Eve.

They were celebrating 1977, the year Sandy had set for his promotion—if he could only get his informants to produce. Claude wasn't enough. Claude was a pain in the ass with his money troubles, his moodiness, his love affairs. Claude had become intractable. He had no new names, no good sources. The DEA had found a possible buyer for a case in Montreal, another in France, deals that could have made the Mexican region look good, but Claude could give them no suppliers at a time when Jacques Kiere had come down hard on the recruitment of new sources. There had been little improvement in morale since Kiere took over. The intelligence and enforcement divisions in the office had almost come to blows. Kiere couldn't handle the friction. Biased by his previous post at the El Paso Intelligence Center, he sided with intelligence too often. He had responded to pressure by the intelligence division, which wanted to locate and control its own major sources, though street agents traditionally recruited and debriefed the region's informants, and intelligence agents never worked the streets.

It looked like enforcement would now have to prove itself to Jacques Kiere, too.

So the telephone calls from Licenciado Alfredo Campos started coming in. Campos could supply the names, and Claude could work the cases. Campos came up with the kind of information that Jacques was clamoring for. Campos knew judges, cops, politicians throughout Mexico. They'd lean on him for the Bolivian or Colombian sources and let Claude do what he did best, draw in the traffickers once their names were known.

"You need to realize," Sandy would say to me, "that these calls at home are really best for us. The sooner we get the region working, the sooner I'll have more time for you and David. The sooner I make management, the sooner I can let the informants go, turn them over to the younger agents, and just come home."

One more call, one more conversation at 6 A.M., and he might get Claude to work again, get Kiere off his back, and headquarters, too. He had pushed hard to form a good relationship with the Mexican feds. General Mendioleya was finally in charge, and the general liked him. Sandy promised me I'd meet the general soon. Then I'd be more optimistic. He liked the diplomatic aspects of his job. He liked this crusty old general. If it worked with Campos, if Claude had good sources to dig his teeth into, Mexico could give us what we'd wanted from the start. It would be tricky, working Claude and Campos side by side without either guessing who the other was, but it was the only way to do it. Knowing Claude, he was bound to get jealous, jumpy, difficult again.

It worked beautifully, for a time. Campos, the crooked lawyer, was anxious to prove he was more valuable outside than in jail. He promised hard facts about his trafficking clients, and he came through. But the more Sandy learned about Campos, the more uncomfortable he became about relying on him. By his own admission Campos had functioned as an attorney only by bribing judges and other officials. He had never tried a case in court. He used the same payoff techniques to report to the DEA. He called in daily, giving the DEA a complete account of his clients' activities. When he had enough on them, he would set them up for an enforcement action. But he didn't report solely on his clients. He also supplied information on corrupt judges and other high officials in the Mexican Attorney General's office. He obtained records for the DEA by bribing officials, and the DEA would later reimburse him for the payoffs. The top-secret cables which came back to Jacques Kiere from Washington practically buzzed with excitement at the information Campos was producing. In fact, the level of excitement and its implications were disturbing. The CIA began focusing its attention on Campos. The DEA and the CIA clung to him as a potential card up their sleeves, as possible leverage against the Mexican Government's attempt to take over the expensive eradication program. Promoted by the DEA as "technical assistance," the eradication program was a costly big-time operation. Its staff was separate from the enforcement or intelligence groups. Its operation was self-contained and, Sandy suspected, questionable. The DEA brought in airplanes and helicopters which carried paraquat and machinery—who knew what else. It was the kind of operation that could have been a perfect front for the CIA, or for Lucien Conein's Special Operations group which the Senate had shown to have such a tight relationship with the CIA and Intertel. Sandy didn't trust Conein, and after his testimony before the Senate, he was sure that Conein's group would have sacrificed him for their own ends. Though the connections he could make between the CIA or Conein and the eradication program were tenuous at best, he didn't like to follow them. The DEA's interest in Campos made him nervous.

The DEA didn't want to lose control of the eradication program. If possible, the agency would use Campos' allegations about corruption in the Attorney General's office to prove that the Mexicans couldn't be trusted to run the program themselves. Beyond that, Campos' reports might be used to protect the DEA from the coup the State Department was trying its best to bring off. The State Department was working even harder behind the scenes to terminate the DEA's enforcement role in Mexico. It argued that if the DEA had any legitimate business in Mexico, it was solely liaison with the general's men. Fine, Sandy thought. He believed his job would be clearer then, but headquarters was paranoiac. Campos was their ace in the hole; they counted on his daily news, even when Sandy warned them in his cables that he couldn't be trusted. They had already caught Campos in fabrications. Like Claude, like every informant off the street, Campos had a vested interest in padding his reports. The juicier they were, the safer he remained with the U.S. Government, the more the DEA would pay him. The records Campos supposedly bought from his contacts in the Attorney General's office with money proffered by the DEA were the right kind of weapons for the DEA's battle with State to keep its frontline foreign stations open. Campos' list of names—filed, coded, secretly numbered—was the DEA's only wild card. On Washington's command that winter, a meeting was called in the embassy bubble room with State's narcotics unit and the ambassador himself. The DEA's safes were unlocked, its files opened. We have hard evidence, the DEA charged, to prove that the Mexican authorities can't be trusted. Our source, a reliable, practicing attorney, has documents to prove that judges, government and police officials are central figures in Mexico's narcotics traffic. How can the State Department justify our removal in light of such intelligence? The DEA implied that the State Department didn't understand the business of narcotics.

Licenciado Campos had made a lucrative decision when he appeared at Sante Bario's door to meet with General Mendioleya's golden boy. So Sandy feared. He knew the word had passed through Mexico that he and the general had gotten close. The general had begun to trust him and would investigate whichever names he suggested. Campos had worked his way into a world of potentially fat fees. Sandy pictured him at lunch, at a large round table with his clients all about him, traffickers every one. He had only to pick and choose which story to retell the DEA for profit, which man to finger, which associates to uncover high up in the government. Campos would catch his clients coming and going— when one became the target of a joint DEA-MFJP investigation and ended up in jail, Campos was the ideal choice to defend that man in court. He'd merely pay a bribe, buy his client's freedom, and the client would become a source again. The same money paid to Campos as a reward might well be used by the Licenciado to buy his client out of jail that night. No doubt about it, Campos was distasteful, the worst kind of informant the DEA had. It wouldn't have been so intolerable, however, if he were reporting solely on his drug-dealing clients. It was the political information, the fact that so much might end up riding on a sleazy source like Campos, that made Sandy truly wince.

By spring I had grown sick of their names, of their voices on the telephone—Campos the formally polite one, Claude usually frenetic. Sandy's promotion came through that spring, but nothing changed. If the informants missed a day's call, the general would ring at 6 A.M. to set up another breakfast meeting at the Procuraduría. There were social obligations which took up any slack, an official dinner at our house for the general and his wife, a reception for congressional VIPs on their way to Acapulco. In the summer Jacques gave a party for a Congressman Mann, which made Sandy particularly nervous. The men were huddled on the couches set up near a large bay window. The women were on straight chairs spread out around the room. I sat as close to Sandy as I could manage, watching him shift uncomfortably on the edge of his plushy seat as Jacques performed for the DEA abroad. He had an important audience that night—the congressman, the acting ambassador, the head of State's narcotics assistance. To demonstrate how well the DEA spent its budget in Mexico, Jacques suggested that a high-ranking official of Mexico's justice department himself was a preselected class-1 narcotics violator—thanks to information purchased by Alfredo Campos. I couldn't hear the entire conversation. Why, I wondered, did Sandy look so scared? Driving home, he admitted things he'd never said before, that the DEA had no real business in Mexico. They didn't know for sure if anyone in the Attorney General's office had ever dealt narcotics. The DEA had begun walking too fine a line for Sandy. The agency was taking credit for cases made by the MFJP. The DEA used Campos' allegations about corruption in the Attorney General's office as an excuse for its lack of productivity. Sandy said he'd have to make much better cases to validate the kind of work he did.

"Don't take them all so seriously," I urged when we got home. "It's just politics. Politicians always speculate."

He'd unbuttoned his shirt and sat on the bed, using a shoe horn on his good black loafers. His shirttail rode up, and I saw his bare back. He'd gotten very thin. His ribs were showing. "I shouldn't have had that scotch tonight," he muttered. "I've got to be more careful."

It was his ulcer acting up again, but I refused to be impressed. He takes every move by the DEA too much to heart. If he suffers from his stomach, it's his own fault. Loosen up, I want to say. Give up the long hours, the silly chase after General Mendioleya. Stop worrying about Campos, and especially, stop worrying about Claude. "All you have to do," I finally suggest, "is call the congressman tomorrow. Let him meet Campos, and then he'll see the truth. Invite him to have lunch with Claude. Both of them are obvious crooks."

Sandy disappears into the bathroom. I hear the medicine chest open and shut. He's after his Mylanta. I hang up my dress, flip through the drawers looking for a flannel nightgown. This house is even colder than the one on Las Flores. Sandy comes out in his underwear, climbs into his side of the bed. The lights go off.

"Am I being too hard?" I want to know. "Did you like that party? Do you believe in the likes of Claude?"

He sighs and turns over.

"It's all political bullshit, isn't it?"

His voice is thick with his back to me. "What do you want from me, Joanne? Like it or not, it's part of my job."

For half an hour, we lie side by side pretending to sleep. Then Sandy turns his lamp on, sits up and lights a cigarette.

"I'll try to explain it one more time. I know you resent the informants calling. So do I. I know you don't like them. Would you rather that I blow some kind of whistle to the congressman and go back to doing what I used to do? I could get lost in Mexico the way I did in France. I could make my own sources and know I had the evidence to prove my cases. It's this or that. If I did deep cover here, I wouldn't have any protection. I wouldn't want to be in Claude's place. Much as I think he's a snake in the grass, I wouldn't want to be Alfredo Campos. Maybe he lies to save his life. Maybe this entire business stinks. But it's the only one I know."

"You shouldn't smoke," I whisper, "if your stomach's acting up."

"You have to trust me," Sandy says. "If I can get through this year with my promotion, maybe I can finally get out."

Like Sandy, I don't have too many choices. I lie in bed in the dark, laying them out. I could leave him, take our baby and go back to my mother's, where I don't want to be. Or I could stop thinking about the DEA, about Campos and Claude and Jacques Kiere—if I knew how to stop. I could accept Sandy's job and his informants. I could be nice to Jacques Kiere, to Claude, to every creepy agent. I could learn, if it killed me, to be a good wife.

I tried to see Claude—Claude Hernandez, Claude Pichambert, Richard Hernandez, René de Kercadio—not as an intrusion in our lives, but as a challenge to me in my new role as Sandy's good wife. Maybe Sandy knew things that I didn't know; maybe he had reason to believe Campos was the sleazier informant. But for me, the worst aspect of our life in Mexico was Claude. It was Claude who always tried to come between us.

In August I had to see him again. Or I suppose I didn't *have* to see him, but Sandy asked me to. Claude was living in Acapulco, courting his new nineteen-year-old girlfriend and making cases. He was giving himself a birthday party, and we were both invited. It would have been easy to beg out. I could have used David as my excuse, but Sandy had to check on the progress of a new case. "Stay home if you'd like," he said to me at first. But saying no wasn't good enough for Claude.

He called the house and asked for me. *"Dejé el niño con la muchacha y venga.* [Leave the baby with the maid and come.]"

He was even more direct with Sandy: "She thinks she's too good to meet my friends. If we were true *hermanos,* you'd convince her. Are we friends or not?" He went on to say that I'd turned down every invitation to meet Sulena, his new girl. Both he and the girl were frankly offended.

When he hung up, Sandy looked at me and said, "I would appreciate it if you'd come."

The party was at the house of Sulena's mother in Acapulco. There were ten tables set out in the garden. The mother wouldn't show her face. She disliked Claude, he confided to us, though she didn't hate his money. With appropriate gifts to prove his intentions she had allowed him to come and court her daughter. She even went so far as to invite her relatives to this affair, though she had them placed at a good distance from Claude's table, where Sandy, Sulena, and I were seated. Very early on, the party was already depressing. On one side of the garden wall a long banquet table offered Claude's favorite treats. A band was playing. Local celebrities from the TV station where Sulena worked mingled with her prep-school friends. Their shoes echoed on the dance platform. A handsome boy no older than eighteen grabbed the microphone and sang into it, embarrassing his friends who were lined up at the table. Plates piled high with disrespect for Claude, they wound their ways to their separate tables, snickering behind Sulena's back. She was tense beside me, aware of them. One stopped behind her chair, reached beneath her thick dark hair, and put his hand on the nape of her neck. She looked up at him, her eyes hard and ironic. Claude floated around the crowd, oblivious. He'd drunk too much, everyone had. Sulena's school friends monopolized the microphone onstage, finding themselves uproariously funny. One of them limped onto the platform, hammed his way through a Spanish love song with a French accent, and everybody laughed. Claude laughed hardest of all. Another yanked the microphone away, called Sulena through it, inviting her to dance. Claude took a slug from his champagne bottle, moved onstage, hummed an off-key verse of "The Star-Spangled Banner"—"*A mi hermano, Sandí,*" he slurred. Sulena's face went blank at our darkened table. Before the verse was finished, Sandy took my hand and snuck us back to our hotel room.

I was a good wife and didn't say a word. We went straight to sleep. The next morning on the flight back to Mexico City, we had nothing much to say.

16

That Christmas we bought a tree imported from the United States for forty dollars. A few days before Christmas Eve, Jacques and his wife stopped by, along with Ron Garibotto and his wife who lived next door. Ron was with the intelligence division of the DEA. He and Sandy competed for Jacques' attention, which wasn't very pleasant. The living room was crowded with the six of us and the decorated tree, but Ron stayed on for fear of missing some important politicking. It was 1 A.M. when they finally left. Concha slipped downstairs to bed. Sandy poked the dying fire.

He kept his back to me. "I want to move," he said. "We need a bigger place with some privacy. The yard here is a hole in the ground and isn't safe for David."

We'd been through it before. Sandy didn't like living so close to Ron, his rival at the office. But I hated the idea of moving. We hadn't spent a year yet in our second house. Sandy had some kind of moving fetish. He was ready to change houses as often as my mother used to move our furniture around. She'd push the couch to another wall, rearrange the chairs and pictures. I'd kept quiet about it when I was ten, but I wasn't keeping quiet any longer. "I don't think it's worth the trouble. Our tour is almost over."

"Your usual song. Can't wait to get us out of Mexico," Sandy said belligerently. "My promotion may mean we'll have to extend another year. We might as well be living in a decent place."

"Why do you have to pick a fight about it?"

"Because you're unhappy. It's my fault, it's my job, it's because of me we're here, but you won't let me do a thing about it."

Those were our conversations by Christmastime 1977. We made arrangements, discussed Sandy's latest travel plans, argued whether to move or not. He left for work before I got up. He'd come home late and spend his evenings on the telephone. I'd lie in bed and listen. My Spanish had improved a lot, although I couldn't follow every point. I understood that Campos was planning a South American trip, to find a potential dealer in Bolivia where the real dope was. Claude was looking for a buyer. He didn't know about Campos, though he knew there was some DEA informant making a Bolivian connection. I didn't care about the details. Half-understood telephone conversations had become the backdrop of my life. They discouraged me. I wanted to blame the informants, the buyers, even the crooked Bolivian Government for the undoing of my marriage. I could leave, I'd think, go to New York and find a studio apartment. I could put David's crib behind a movable room divider. I could find a job and decent day care. But all our belongings were in Mexico—David's bed, his high chair and stroller. It was too hard, too complicated for me, though I recognized that hundreds of other women must have done it. Foreign-service wives in Bangladesh or Turkey must have sometimes left their husbands. The government would have to ship me home. "Reason for transfer?" it would say on the travel order, and some bureaucrat would write down the failure of our marriage. I didn't have the nerve to strike out on my own in New York with an eighteen-month-old child, but I could have gone to Washington instead. Washington was safe, though it would mean I'd have to tell my parents. Franco, Sandy's eldest boy, would eventually learn about it, too. He was sixteen, nearly seventeen. He had been eleven when we met, and how he had believed in us. The thought of my parents and Franco settled it somehow. I couldn't go. It didn't matter that everything was awful.

There was a New Year's Eve party at Jacques Kiere's house. His son's band was playing in the dining room. We had to step over a jumble of electric cords to reach the bar set up in the kitchen. Everybody from the office was invited. Even General Mendioleya showed up, his slick bald head hidden beneath a midnight-blue beret. While Sandy took his arm and led him to a corner of the living room, I slipped into the den where Sandy's secretary Marta found me.

"I hoped we'd get a chance to talk tonight," she said. "I'm worried about Sandy."

Caught off guard, I stared up at her from the couch, taking in her jewelry, her carefully applied makeup. I never expected to hear anyone from the DEA say to me what she was saying. "Oh, Marta, will you sit and talk?"

"He never lets up anymore, Joanne. He doesn't go out for lunch. He stays at his desk eating crackers and drinking Mylanta. He yells at the junior agents. He's impossible with me. He tries to do everything himself, as though he doesn't trust us. He must have lost twenty pounds in the past few months. Have you tried to talk to him? He looks so awful."

"I can't talk to him. He says I'm nagging. He says I hate it here, and it's his fault. He just won't listen. Marta, he gets up every night when he thinks I'm sleeping. He must have bad dreams or else it's his stomach. When he does sleep, he talks aloud, sometimes in Italian, sometimes in French. I can't make it out, but it's clear he's sleeping. I don't know what to do."

"You should talk to Jacques."

"I couldn't. Sandy would be furious."

"But if it's for his health? I don't think he can keep this up much longer. What if he has a heart attack or something?"

No, I couldn't talk to Jacques. I couldn't. I was amazed I'd said so much to Marta, private things, married business that Sandy would never forgive me for. Besides, not at a party when Jacques was host. But when? I couldn't imagine calling him at home, making up some feeble excuse to Sandy, and going to Jacques to rat on my husband. Jacques came into the den. Marta got up and excused herself. Jacques was easy and approachable in his cardigan sweater and that laid-back smile that must have taken years of practice. I didn't know him very well. We'd met occasionally as couples at the Loma Linda restaurant. He would tease his wife about the hot sauce she was eating or make offhand remarks to Sandy about work. He wasn't remotely like a friend, yet he turned that smile on me, crinkling his eyes.

"They're beginning to dance in the other room. You ought to find Sandy."

I shrugged. "He's with the general, I'm sure."

"And you're hiding out here to escape the music? I could make them turn the amplifiers down."

"No, I'm fine. It's a good party."

I had convinced him. He was turning to go. If Marta hadn't brought up the question of Sandy's health, I'd have gone on nursing my hurt feelings privately, badgering him when we were alone. I'd begun to believe that I was merely jealous of his job, jealous of Claude and the time he took. But if Marta saw the changes, too, then they must be real. He *had* lost weight. Why hadn't that seemed significant to me? What were the nightmares about? Why was his ulcer getting worse each day? It wasn't just me, my unreal expectations for our marriage, my stubborn unwillingness to leave David with our maid. It wasn't all and only me.

"Jacques? Do you think I could talk to you a minute?"

He came back into the room with that smile again. "Of course. Do you want another drink first or one of those little roast beef sandwiches?"

"No. I'm not hungry. I really need to talk to you. I know this isn't the best moment with the party going on, but it's important."

He seemed hesitant to close the door—what would his guests think of us in the den together? "We could go sit at the top of the stairs," he said.

I would have preferred the privacy of the den, with the door closed. But I nodded and tried to match his smile with a trembling one of my own. As we walked up the wide staircase, I glanced at the band, at the dancers in the hall. Sandy wasn't anywhere in sight.

We sat at the top of the stairs. Jacques put his drink down on the carpet. I wished he hadn't chosen such a public spot, though no one was around. His son was singing an old Beatles song downstairs.

"I never thought I'd do anything like this," I said, "I mean, take my worries to my husband's boss. It doesn't seem like the right thing to do, but you've known Sandy for a long time now. I don't know what to do about him."

I paused, hoping Jacques would move in and make it easy for me. I wanted him to say it was all right to squeal like this, but I should have known he couldn't. It wasn't part of his policeman's code. He looked uncomfortable and played with the ice cubes in his glass of scotch.

"He's pushing too hard, Jacques. He's not sleeping well. His ulcer is bad. Haven't you noticed?"

"Well," he said, using that smile to put me off. "We've all been pushing. He must have told you this is a crucial time for the region. I guess it's been hard on all the wives. But I can't say I've noticed too much out of the ordinary. He's impatient, Sandy, but he's always been temperamental. That hot Italian blood of his, I guess. Then, too, he's managing a group now. That's a new role for him. He's taking a little time to adjust. Sure, I've seen that. He hasn't gotten the kind of guidance he's deserved. It's hard for him to delegate responsibility. He's accustomed to sitting on a case himself. Sure, it makes him tense."

This time his artful smile was meant to reassure as well as shut me up. I was breaking the rules by complaining. The wives of cops were supposed to be as stiff-upper-lipped as the cops themselves, and before he was a federal agent, Jacques Kiere was a cop. He wasn't quite old enough to be my father, but he was older than Sandy, who was ten years older than I. As nicely as he could, he was teaching me a lesson. Not only was I a second wife, a new wife, I was also the younger woman, a wise-ass college type who had to learn her place.

"I'm sorry for coming to you like this," I said, trying to sound humble without backing off. "But this isn't just some small adjustment. I'm really worried, Jacques. And Marta's worried, too. He doesn't eat, doesn't sleep. He spends all his time at the embassy or on the phone or meeting with informants. His ulcer could perforate if he doesn't slow down."

"Now let's not exaggerate, Joanne. I've known Sandy a little longer than you have. Actually, for about eight years. He's a hardworking, single-minded agent. He's always worked hard. Maybe you're just not used to the demands of his job. He's riding several cases. In a couple of months he'll be able to ease off. He would do that on his own. But if it makes you feel any better, I'll speak to him. I'll encourage him to take some time for lunch. Maybe that's all he needs, to get his stomach back on a normal schedule."

I sat on the top step hugging my knees while Jacques finished his drink and stood up. Before going he leaned down and patted the top of my head. He hadn't been persuaded that Sandy had changed. If anyone had changed in Mexico, it had been me. In the space of our tour, I'd gone from girlfriend to wife to interfering mother.

17

New Year's morning I slept late and Sandy got up with David as he always did on weekends. He'd take him downstairs and make his breakfast. If it wasn't too cold, they would go for a walk to the fountain at the bottom of our street, La Fuente de la Plazuela. David would walk along the fountain wall, and Sandy would hold his hand. Sometimes I'd watch them from the guest room terrace. I liked seeing them together. Even when he was angry or impatient with me, Sandy always took time with David. He seemed to relax when they were together. He could accept David's rhythms more easily than mine.

When I got up, they were in our back "hole" of a garden. I watched them from the kitchen window as I made fresh coffee. Small legs splayed and wobbling, David stood with his shovel while Sandy dug in the flower beds. I took a tray of coffee out to the back terrace.

"Do you want some?" I called down to him.

"I'd better not," he said without looking up.

"I could make you some camomile tea."

"I had two cups already."

It seemed the morning was going to be a continuation of our late night. We had been silent in the car driving home from Jacques'. I had stayed in the den throughout most of the party. "You couldn't make an exception to your snootiness even on New

Year's Eve," Sandy had said. The morning sky was grim and yellow, like his mood. I watched him take David's hand and circle the walled-in square of grass. He had been right to criticize the garden. It was like a deep pit. Perhaps I had been selfish in refusing to move. Sandy liked to garden. He worked hard and deserved to have the pretty, open space he wanted.

"Do we have any plans for the day?" I asked, taking my cup of coffee down the stone steps into the yard. David toddled over and sat beside me on the bottom step.

"Not really. Jacques called earlier and asked me to stop by. You and David can come if you'd like, but I'm sure it's business."

I felt my stomach drop. What if Jacques were calling Sandy in for a heart-to-heart in response to our little talk last night? I hoped not. I'd expected Jacques to wait for an opportune moment at the embassy, to pop his head into Sandy's office while Sandy was popping his Mylanta at noon and casually remark that he was pushing too hard. I couldn't believe he would call Sandy to his house on New Year's Day to make a big production of my confidence—"Your wife says you're in pretty bad shape." No, he wouldn't.

"Do you know what he wants?" I asked, taking David on my lap for protection.

"Who knows? He was buddying up with the general last night. Maybe they've got something on together."

"But on New Year's Day?"

Sandy frowned and spread his palms out. "Hey, what do you want from me? He's the regional director."

"I wasn't complaining. Just curious." I sounded as defensive as I felt. Carrying David upstairs in one arm, I spilled coffee with the other. It was going to be another bad day.

Sandy called up a quick good-bye while I was changing David's diaper. I put the baby down and went to the window to watch him get into his green government car. His face was drawn, his jacket baggy. Well, there wasn't anything to do about it. I'd already made my move by approaching Jacques. I'd have to wait it out. I took David downstairs for some juice. "What shall we do?" I asked him. "Bye-bye, outside," he said, but I didn't feel like going out. We went back upstairs and sat together in the rocking chair. I read

Goodnight, Moon to him, hoping he would take a nap, but he wasn't sleepy.

Finally, I relented on the idea of a walk. I got his stroller out and pushed him slowly to the top of our street where the watchman, Don José, was burning coal in the brazier in his hut.

I tapped at his narrow door and waited. Smoke from the coals curled out an open window, carrying the smell of tortillas burning. The weathered, wrinkled old man came out, nodding and bowing. *"Buenas tardes, señora."*

"Have you eaten this morning, Señor Don José?" I asked, never sure if the "Señor" part was right.

"Si, tortillas, señora. Gracias."

"I have some *carne asada* in the house," I added.

"Si, señora." More scrapes and bows. *"Muchas gracias."*

"After I take the baby for a walk."

He thanked me again, nodded some more, and disappeared inside. I could never quite figure out his job. He was too old to protect anybody. He didn't have a gun. There wasn't a telephone inside his hut. If he ever ran for help, his legs would give out. He just sat in that little brick *casita*, no bigger than a phone booth, freezing through the nights. I had probably offered my bit of charity to him to make my own new year better.

David chattered, pointing at every passing car, smiling at the maids sweeping their driveways. We walked five blocks and turned around. He still didn't look very sleepy.

I walked him up and down in his room and patted his back in the crib. He would seem to be sleeping and I'd try creeping out of the room, but he always bolted upright, grabbed the crib posts and demanded to come "down." I heard Sandy's car and his key in the door long before David fell asleep.

Sandy wasn't in either the living or dining rooms. He wasn't in the kitchen. I took the meat out of the refrigerator for Don José and put it in the oven to heat. Through the kitchen window I saw Sandy sitting on the back steps.

"That didn't take too long," I called to him.

He didn't answer.

I sat on the step behind him, reached out to touch his bony back, but he pulled away.

"What's wrong?" I asked, already knowing.

He didn't turn around, didn't raise his voice. "What the fuck did you think you were saying to Jacques? What the fuck right have you to say that I'm not well?"

I reached out again, he leaned away from me. "I'm sorry. I didn't know what else to do. I've been so worried, and then last night, Marta said how worried she was, too."

"Marta?"

"Yes, at the party. She said everything I've been saying, that you look awful, that you're not eating, that you're working too hard. She thought we had to do something since you won't listen. You could crack up, you could have a heart attack, your stomach could start bleeding. . . ."

"Shit," he said, tossing his cigarette over the wall into Ron and Kathy's garden. He got up, stepped over me, and went into the house. The glass door thudded shut behind him.

I didn't move. I looked up, across the garden wall into Ron's house. The curtains were all drawn. We could move. We ought to move, really. There wasn't enough privacy. It was like living in a fishbowl, with the threat that Ron and Kathy would hear every fight. The garden was a piece of shit. There were too many stairs for a toddling baby. What had ever made us think this house was right?

I got up and went into the empty living room. Another vomit-colored gold rug, thin and patchy, the same color as the rug in Piermont. Hadn't we noticed it? Cold brick floor on the staircase. He wasn't in the kitchen or the dining room. He was lying on our bed, turned away from me. I closed the door in case we started screaming, so we wouldn't wake up David.

"I'm really sorry. I didn't think Jacques would call you on anything. I just thought he could mention it in passing, and if you thought *he* was concerned, then it would be easier to listen. I love you, Sandy. I didn't mean to upset you."

His voice was cold and steely even when it was muffled by the pillow. "What the hell did you think you were doing, talking to my secretary behind my back? That's the way you love me?"

I put a knee down on the mattress. "I would have never said anything. She came to me. She brought it up."

"That excuses it. Because she's a big-mouthed bitch, you go along with her, encourage her to stab me in the back? How do you think it looks to Jacques? How does it look for my promotion? My wife goes up to my supervisor and says that I'm a basket case, that I'm not eating right. For Chrisake, you think I'm a child? You think I don't know my limits or what I'm doing?"

It was worse when he was looking at me. His brows furrowed, a knot of anger between his eyes. He had come to hate me in so little time. "I'm really sorry. I didn't mean it to be like this. We can't talk anymore. You think I don't know how often you get up at night. I hear you in the bathroom, hear you talking in your sleep. What was I supposed to do, just watch you fall apart?"

"Fuck you. I'm not falling apart. I'm a little tense, all right. I've got a lot riding on this year, on the cases of the next few months. The whole region has a lot riding. So I've been hard to talk to, what about you? All you want to talk about is how much you hate Mexico, hate my job, hate Claude and Campos and even Jacques."

"I don't hate Mexico."

"That's news to me. You're always talking about getting out, going home, making plans for the next trip to see your parents. Maybe this whole thing is a mistake, our great marriage."

"You want me to go?"

He turned away again. "I don't know. Sometimes I do."

"I don't want to leave you, Sandy. I just want to start talking again."

"You have a peculiar way to show it."

I lay down beside him on the bed, shoulder-to-shoulder. There were patches of mold on the ceiling, on the whitewashed cement. There was the dampness and the yellow sky. I started crying. "Maybe you're right. Maybe it's over and there's nothing more to say."

18

In January Sandy found a house. The perfect house in Lomas Chapultepec, the rich gringo neighborhood we had rejected when we first arrived. It was a stucco colonial on Montañas Rocallosas, with a sunny front garden for Sandy and big rooms that looked out on trees and garden walls. We would be closer to the embassy, to the American bookstore, to the supermarket. A new house would make every difference, Sandy said. Though it was a little rundown, he had great plans for it. He'd pull out the dilapidated fence and cart in flowers from Xochimilco. He'd trim the rubber trees to give the living room more light. He'd patch the cement in the portico wall. I had to see it, I had to try one more time. Climb up on the roof with me, he asked, bringing over a ladder. He had already pulled out weeds between the tiles. He took me up on the roof as if the view had been personally ordered to transform our lives. We wobbled on the terra-cotta tiles, watching the city spread out in layers like a rich, slightly spoiled dessert.

I was tired of starting over. I wasn't convinced we could. But it was hard to imagine going home as a failure after so much strutting, so much hype. I had decided to lie to my parents by saying I had come for a short visit with David while Sandy dug in for his big Bolivian case. Although I wouldn't admit the truth to my parents, I did tell Sandy I wasn't sure I would be coming back.

I left for Washington a week after we had found the new house, and Sandy took charge of every detail of the move. He and Concha packed the boxes. He and the *mozo* from our old neighborhood painted the house on weeknights and Saturdays. Sandy called almost daily with a progress report—the rugs had been cleaned, the furnace repaired. "You'll have to come back, won't you?"

It was winter in Virginia. I didn't want to shop or go visiting with my mother. I wanted to go home to my new house and Sandy. I finally wrote a long letter and sent him a chocolate bottle of champagne that melted in the mail. I'm coming back, the letter said.

Three weeks later we were together in the Rocallosas house. The first night we buried ourselves beneath layers of quilts in the coral bedroom. "We'll be better now, you'll see," Sandy said. I couldn't help thinking how familiar it sounded. "I'm getting used to my promotion. I'm learning how to handle my men. Both Claude and Campos are working now. Pretty soon I'll turn them both over to new controlling agents." He reached for me beneath the quilts. David murmured from the other room. "I hope he doesn't wake up," Sandy said. "We need this night alone."

About a month later I had a funny dream which I told to Sandy in the morning. "It was so weird. You had this round bald spot the size of a quarter on the back of your head."

We laughed about it—until we realized it hadn't been a dream. It took a month for Sandy's hair to begin falling out in patches, a good month with no fights, though we rarely slept together anymore. He kept his problems at the office from me. I'd drive down to the embassy to meet him almost every day for lunch. I'd taken a free-lance job working on a video production for the U.S. Information Agency. It was to be an in-service film for families about to be transferred to Mexico. Sandy and I were chosen as the ideal couple to star in the film—we looked that happy to everyone around us. I began believing we had turned the final corner, that we'd be fine. Then Sandy's hair began falling out for real. It upset him so much that he had to let down a little with me. He stopped hiding his ulcer pains, the voices he had heard at night for months. The voices terrified him.

The embassy nurse didn't know what the problem with his hair could be. She sent him to San Antonio to see a doctor. The dermatologist in Texas diagnosed alopecia nervosa, a condition caused by stress. It had no known cure, though he shot Sandy up with cortisone to slow the process. But eventually, Sandy might go completely bald.

"You want your hair to grow back?" the dermatologist had said. "You had better quit your job."

"That's it," I said to Sandy when he got home. "It's time to get out."

"How? Where will I go? I never told you, but I tried to quit last year. When I made that trip to headquarters, I looked up everybody I could think of. I even went to the Senate investigator who had interviewed me during the hearings on DEA to see if he had something. I wrote to IBM Security. I called the fucking Sheraton Hotel. I've wanted out, Joanne. I haven't liked what's been happening here."

"Tell me. What is it?"

But he grew vague. "It's everything. You know, Mexico, DEA, Claude and Campos. There's so much, I could never lay it out for you. I never told you about the tortures, did I? We go in for an arrest when the MFJP are there, and they're using cattle prods on the defendants. What could I do? I never told you. I just walked away."

"Tell me, Sandy, please," I begged, but that's all he would say.

I had been right. Something was wrong and had been wrong for almost a year. Maybe it wasn't really his job, and that was why he couldn't tell me. What if the stress he was under came from me and from our marriage? His hair wouldn't fall out if it were just his job. He'd had guns pointed at his head; he'd jumped from boats to save his skin. They had burned his apartment down in New Orleans to try to stop him. His hair hadn't fallen out then. The real change in his life wasn't his job. It was our marriage. Tufts of hair in the sink, on the hand-painted tiles, strange voices whispering in his ears at night—if that was the price he'd been paying to stay with me, he had paid too much. I had been impossible. I was selfish and demanding. I wished he would come clean and tell me just how terrible I was. If he could only let it out, his hair would grow back in, the voices would stop, we could touch each other in bed again.

"It's okay," I said to Concha the morning after Sandy saw the dermatologist. "I'll cook the señor's breakfast." I cooked bland, medicinal meals to make Sandy well again: papaya juice, oatmeal with skimmed milk, boiled potatoes and plain baked snapper.

When he came home late at night, I made camomile tea and suffered through it with him, listening dutifully to his sporadic stories about his Bolivian case, Campos in Santa Cruz in January on a tip from a trafficker in a Mexican prison. Añez-Vaca, Asaf y Bala, Vierzon from France—I never successfully sorted out their names. The big meeting had taken place in Mexico in February, when I was in Washington. "How is it going?" I'd ask. "Okay," he'd answer in a way that seemed to me understandably distracted.

I was trying so hard to be good, to be therapeutic for him, but he wasn't any better. Night after night he had nothing much to say. I'd set the table with fresh flowers, linen napkins, long tapered candles in his favorite holders. "How was work, how is the case?" He'd take another bite of his dry lamb chop: "Coming slowly."

In the spring Polly planned a weekend at a cottage in Valle de Bravo, three couples and their kids, horseback riding in the mornings, hikes about the dry lake bed in the afternoons. "You must come," she urged. "It would be good for Sandy."

Valle was a town in the hills with colonial chalets. Ours was high and rustic, rooms spread out through narrow corridors, the front veranda overlooking a waterfall of wildflowers. Orange, fuchsia, lilac bougainvillea, a fireplace in every room, and Sandy's silence at the long plank dinner table.

"What's wrong?" I'd ask in our room at night. "Have I done something? Are you sorry we came?"

"Jesus Christ," through his teeth. "Just leave me alone."

He'd grab David and lift him onto the front of his saddle, carry him off at a gallop, fields beyond the rest of us. On the last day's hike, he climbed the path along the steep mountain stream much faster than the rest of us and didn't stop when we did to dangle our feet in the shallow water. There was a dead tree that had fallen across the stream at the top of the mountain. "My God, what's come over Sandy?" someone said. We all looked up to see him, a balding tightrope walker in baggy jeans, crossing the dead tree trunk fifty feet above the water, with David balanced in one arm.

He went slowly, one foot in front of the other, while we held our breaths. "He's going crazy," I whispered, hoping somebody would hear. That was the night we started fighting.

"You have to tell me what's wrong. Is it work? Your stomach? You've shut me out completely these past weeks. I've been trying as hard as I know how, but it's gotten worse than it was before I left. I know you hate it that your hair's falling out—"

"Shut up, would you? Get off my case."

"Maybe it's me, maybe you don't really want this marriage. I'll leave. I could take David to my mother's."

"That's what you've always wanted, isn't it? So do it. Stop threatening and go."

What about the Sandy I knew in New York? What about all those long nights, those walks, those captivating stories? I would have left if I had only known how. Maybe he had been conning me then, and there was nothing wrong. This was the real man, patchy hair, bony back and all.

III

Jesus, he was losing control of it before it even happened. He couldn't believe it. This, the main case, the only case that mattered, the kind of case he'd imagined when Claude and Campos were recruited. He'd been right to manage it alone, paying for it with the cold shoulder at weekly meetings, with disciplinary memos from the deputy director, but they'd see when the case came through, when he got it back on track and rolling, that he was right to handle these informants on his own. They needed him, he was the only one to make it play, and when it did, it could carry the whole region. So he had closed his junior agents out, so he should have assigned the informants over. There was time for that. This case was special, his baby, his tune, Campos in Bolivia with the source, Claude working on the buyers. They would bring in France, Montreal, on this one, and all the meetings would be scheduled to go down in Mexico so the region would get every credit. With this one case he would secure Jacques Kiere's reputation as the region's most competent regional director and help headquarters demonstrate to the State Department that the DEA was crucial to narcotics control in Mexico. Victor Hugo Añez-Vaca, Campos' supplier in Santa Cruz, bragged that he had access to limitless amounts of cocaine. Let him produce them, and for every load they would find a different buyer. Bario had brought Claude in for this last case, and then he'd end it with him. This was their final dance, their tour de force, and by God, he'd have it working like a charm.

The first of January, 1978, he had sent Alfredo Campos to Santa Cruz on a tip from a trafficker in a Mexican prison, Lorgia Añez-Pereira, a Bolivian who had told Campos about his son, Victor Hugo Añez-Vaca, a big-time dealer in Santa Cruz. During the meeting with Añez-Vaca in Bolivia, Campos had mentioned an Italian narcotics boss named Salvatore Bonanno, in the market for cocaine in Mexico. Añez-Vaca was willing to deal, but not in Mexico, he said, not after what had happened to his father. Campos called Bario from Bolivia for advice on how to persuade Añez-Vaca to sell the cocaine in Mexico. Bario gave Campos his next move: Tell Añez-Vaca to come to Mexico, to make a visit to his father. He would carry no drugs, just appear for a meeting with Bonanno and his associate, Claude Picault, to prove how easy Mexico could be. Añez-Vaca agreed to meet Bonanno in the María Isabel Sheraton Hotel, directly across from the U.S. Embassy in Mexico City.

Like a charm, like a goddamned charm at Sanborn's restaurant, Añez-Vaca shows up and spills his guts. He could supply fifty to a hundred kilos of pure powder, but would never risk transportation or delivery from Santa Cruz to Mexico. He would transfer the merchandise in Bolivia and let them sweat out the transportation.

It was easy for Bario to stay cool, to act the top Bonanno. He'd told Añez-Vaca that he had anticipated his fears, given his old man's time in jail, but there was no way he would deal in Santa Cruz. Besides, the Mexican authorities could be had. He would work out the details and demonstrate the security of the route to Añez-Vaca. Bario had ordered espresso and asked the waiter to hold the cinnamon on top. Añez-Vaca was sitting on the edge of his seat by the time the coffee came, but Bario took his time thinking. He didn't want to lose Añez-Vaca or to agree to deal in Santa Cruz. The Bolivian Government was uncooperative. Mexico needed this contract.

Bario ignored the junior agents planted in the restaurant on surveillance, ignored the warning in his gut, and sipped his coffee.

Añez-Pereira was still moving drugs through the prison traffic. More importantly, he was a link to the "godfather" of Mexican dealers, Jorge Asaf y Bala, whom Añez-Pereira had befriended in the prison. They worked together. Añez-Pereira had told Asaf y Bala about Campos, a powerful attorney with strong connections. Both were interested in placing large quantities of coke. If Campos succeeded in convincing the elder Añez that delivery in Mexico was safe, the old man would convince his son, and the DEA could bring stronger charges against Asaf y Bala, to assure that he was put away for life.

The case was ambitious and well within his reach, but Bario had to play his cards exactly right. He had to make the potential traffic so big, so alluring, that Añez-Vaca would not back down. It was to "pad" the show that he had brought in Claude, as well as to hook one of Claude's mecs, his good buddy Bernard Vierzon, listed in the DEA's files as one of the last class-1 violators working the European markets. Vierzon was the frosting on the cake. While Campos worked Añez-Vaca, Claude would tap Vierzon to make a test run and prove the routes. They'd move the powder into Mexico through Panama—the Panamanian Government and DEA-Panama had given their okay. When Añez-Vaca arrived in Mexico City with Claude, Vierzon, and a small sample, the MFJP would let them ride for delivery to Bonanno. The first bust would come with the first big load, when they would take Vierzon. They would hold out with Añez-Vaca until he had brought in a second, maybe even a third load to be delivered to Asaf y Bala in the prison and to a potential buyer from Montreal.

The meeting ended on an up note. Bario pushed his chair back, saying, "Then you agree to make a practice run and see?" Añez-Vaca nodded. The agents on surveillance in the street took photographs as the three men walked along Reforma. Bario made sure that Añez-Vaca was on the curbside for the camera, but otherwise wasn't paying much attention. He was considering the potentials of this case, the names he would target. Through Añez-Vaca and his father, he now had access to the most powerful dealers in Mexico's narcotics traffic, Jorge Asaf y Bala, his brother Alfredo, and Jorge Favela Escoboso, all currently doing time with Añez-Pereira. Each would become a target, with Añez-Vaca's coke as bait and Claude in the wings to promenade the buyers. As the convicted traffickers began to trust Campos, they would doubtless drop new names along the way. The prison traffic was a lucrative business. The traffickers' suites were carpeted, furnished with color TVs and private bars. Their mail was hand-delivered, their tailors personally escorted in on Tuesdays. Prison partnerships were profitable and lasting. It was time the DEA cashed in on them.

Sure, there were potential problems. There were always problems. It had to be tricky working two difficult informants on the same case yet keeping them apart. It would have been cleaner to move in an agent to keep tabs on suppliers and stools, to let the agent place electronic devices, but the DEA would never approve an agent under cover in Bolivia, unprotected. They were stuck with Claude and Campos. Information would come secondhand. There were only so many questions the controlling agent could ask without tainting evidence or jeopardizing the entire operation.

Campos or Claude could lie; he might never know. Those were the rules he had to work with. When the agent of record depended on a stool, it never smelled exactly right.

He had heard all the horror stories, read all the documented cases —the stool who reported to his controlling agent that he was about to finger a coke lab where the dealers were delivering twenty kilos of processed powder. The informant got a fat reward for a full-fledged lab, knowing all along the coke would be delivered raw. So to earn the big payoff, he planted the equipment, processed the coke himself while the source hung around waiting for his money. Presto, the DEA agents arrived during the processing, bagged the supplier, seized the phony lab. The stool got his money, the traffickers went to jail for operating a lab in process, all of it a lie. Unless an agent worked a case himself, gathered his own evidence, was his own witness, an informant could manipulate a case to suit his needs. Bario hated to see so much ride on the word of his informants. At least he had worked Claude long enough to know his games. He could live with Claude. He wasn't convinced he could live with Campos. But he'd made his bed, was living in cramped quarters with both of them now.

Jesus, it was taking so long to get them rolling. Mid-January already in Mexico City, the air still thick and grim from the bonfires of rubber tires on New Year's Eve. The pollution stung his eyes so badly he kept a bottle of Visine with the stash of Mylanta in his desk. He needed the Añez-Vaca case. It was high-anxiety time at the DEA. An agent working with State's narcotics unit had found another classified memo to the ambassador, kicking the DEA in the tail again. A Xerox of the memo had hit all the agents' desks. The memo had Jacques Kiere wired. He had come in, closed the door to Bario's office. The worst was coming down. Rumors were flying and it looked like they were true this time.

"We've got to stall a week or more," Bario told Jacques. "With a little more time, we can turn them on their ear. This Añez case should have the ambassador eating from your hand."

"Can I count on it?"

"Tomorrow Claude leaves for Santa Cruz with Vierzon. I've got a call in to the general right now to plan Claude's arrival with the sample."

It was carnival in Santa Cruz. Claude and Vierzon checked into a hotel in the heart of the city, went out carousing and got drunk. They were supposed to have been on their best behavior, to show Añez-Vaca they were cool. This was, after all, Añez-Vaca's town. He didn't want any foreign dealers blowing his cover. He had already called Campos to complain. He was nervous as hell and, finally, Campos had flown down to hold his hand. Campos' flight to Bolivia had given Bario his first bad moment of the case. Jesus, the idea of both informants in Santa Cruz together was dangerous. They were bound to meet. Perhaps they would realize they both worked for him. There was always the possibility that they would double-deal behind his back. Claude would get paranoid, or Campos would get jealous. He was playing it too close. He'd never intended Campos to fly down. The telephone calls from Campos hit him where it hurt—his stomach was eating at him again. Campos complained about Vierzon's style and the Frenchman with the limp. Añez grew more cautious, was stalling out on his commitment to fly up with the sample. When Campos finally got back to Mexico, he called the office with a warning: If the DEA couldn't find some way to pull in the reins on Vierzon, Añez would back out. Then he asked Bario a crucial question: "Is he your man, the cripple from France with Vierzon?"

For four nights it was saltines and peanut butter as Bario waited at his desk for Claude's next call, for another evening conversation with the general. But he hung around. His family was away. He was restless, waiting for news from Claude, and had left several messages at his Santa Cruz hotel. Time to get tough with Claude again before he and Vierzon blew Añez out of the water. Whenever Claude stopped calling, it meant trouble. He had already had plenty of time to get his hooks into Vierzon.

At six sharp Bario's secretary poked her head inside the door. "Unless you've got any other emergencies, I'm going," she announced. "You should, too. I could call Concha and tell her to start your supper."

"Never mind, Marta, just mind your business."

"I promised Joanne I'd keep an eye on you. Crackers again—how many times is that this week?"

"Go home to your kids. I'll take care of myself."

He watched her at the door, manicured hands packing up her purse. He had half a mind to fire her. He couldn't trust her anymore, chatting up his wife behind his back, telling tales. He'd already withdrawn his recommendation for her promotion. She'd turned out to be another high-handed bitch, intruding in his affairs. He couldn't get that New Year's party out of his mind. He'd called her on it once, would have to soon again. But he didn't have the energy to mess with her now.

After she left, he closed the door. He was usually an open-door man, not that it did him any good. His agents were pissed at him, didn't trust him. He knew he held them in too tight, but he didn't know how to let go with the whole fucking place like a pressure cooker. He'd had too much on his mind these days.

The six o'clock bells chimed in the courtyard, Christmas carols. Christ, it was the end of January, time to change the record. He walked to the window, raised the blinds. He had a good view, looked down on the burnt leaves on the top branches of the ficus trees. The gardeners were overzealous with their feedings. Still, he couldn't complain about the view. He hadn't done so badly in Mexico. He'd been promoted to grade 14, equivalent to a colonel in the military, his brother's rank in the Carabinieri. But Mexico was taking its toll. His ulcer, for one thing. He'd never get used to the garbage these people put in their stomachs. He was thinner, rough around the edges. He could see the loss of sleep in the lines around his eyes, never mind what had happened to his hair. He wouldn't think about his hair or the voices at night.

If his marriage was shot, he'd get out of Mexico, hit the road again. He'd get to Rome, alone if he had to, on temporary duty, on the street again. He had to accept the fact that the DEA would never send him to Italy with diplomatic status. The bureaucrats in Washington would treat him like a second-class citizen forever. Politics and discrimination, that's all there was. They'd send out any agent who applied with an Italian name, just as long as he was born in Brooklyn and spoke only English. They'd pay thousands to train him and send him blind. He'd show them they were wrong. Make them take notice—look what Bario accomplished on a straight diplomatic tour, no deep cover. He'd give them Añez and Bolivia, though it meant late nights waiting on Claude, losing his wife.

General Mendioleya called at seven-thirty, finished up the details on the airport surveillance team. They'd let the sample ride until Vierzon was on his flight to France.

Bario closed the box of crackers, took a long swig of Mylanta. One step at a time, and he wouldn't lose it, couldn't lose it now. He locked his file cabinet, his desk. Let Claude reach him at home—if he called at all. Once it got smoothed out, once Vierzon was fried and Añez was cooking the real load, he'd call Joanne, beg her to come home. He had the new house ready. He missed his son. In the meantime, lights out, the drive home, the wait for Claude.

The house looked dark from Montañas Rocallosas. Concha was either in the kitchen or waiting in her room. She'd have his supper ready. He'd be stuck with her sullen face. He decided to take his meal on a tray, move the TV upstairs, and watch dubbed American cops and robbers till Claude called.

The call from Santa Cruz came at nine o'clock. He had to yell so Claude could hear him, but it was set. They had the sample, would move it the next day. The Añez-Vaca case was rolling.

19

Throughout the spring we pretended that we were better again. Maybe this is what it's like, I told myself, to live with someone as intense as Sandy. Life had become an emotional seesaw. Sandy didn't talk casework, informants, or embassy politics, and I stopped asking him to see a marriage counselor with me. The calls from Claude and Campos kept coming in, but we ignored whatever implications they had for our "free time." We didn't want as much time anymore. Spending time together had become too painful. Though our unexamined truce was largely successful, Sandy's hair continued to fall out. He started wearing hats wherever he went and gave up going to dinner parties. Our arguments tapered off—they weren't as frequent or as vicious, but they didn't stop completely. We couldn't predict what might set us off, but at least we didn't fight about his job any longer. I had finally accepted it. That summer we signed up for another two-year tour in Mexico with very little discussion between us. I didn't even blink when he said the paperwork for our new tour was done. The logic was that with two more years behind him, Sandy would be in better shape for an opening in Europe when one came up. Two more years in Mexico. We smiled at each other, considerate and careful.

We were entitled to home leave before the new tour started and rented a cottage at the beach in Delaware. Sandy's children and my parents came with us. We went clamming in the bay, learned to play bridge, took long walks at night. Sandy was always the last to go to bed. I'd find him asleep on the couch in the mornings. Ours was a guarded peace. If there were times that he turned on me, I'd tell myself it was okay, that he was only crazy.

"Things are better, really they are," we convinced ourselves when we got back to Mexico in August.

By September 15 the rainy season was declared officially over, by presidential decree. The storms that came in October were aberrations. The hailstones that slashed the rubber trees and buried the manicured lawns like snow were never acknowledged in the newspapers or on television. The government allowed only sunlight, perfect days, hordes of tourists streaming in.

The first weekend in October 1978, there was no rain. When I woke up, the coral bedroom was filled with morning sun. David was playing on the floor in his pajamas. Concha was out front sweeping the walk. I listened to David's truck roll back and forth on the bare floor, to the sound of Concha's broom. I half expected to hear Sandy in the shower, only Sandy wasn't home. The milkman whistled. *"Dé me dos litros,"* Concha called. He flirted with her.

I was still groggy when the telephone rang. It was one of the agent's wives, but I couldn't place her voice: "So if you decide to go, we'd be glad to keep the baby."

She finally realized I didn't understand and passed the receiver to her husband. "We're sorry, Joanne. We were sure you knew. Sandy was arrested last night in San Antonio."

I was sitting up by the time they rang off. What could that peculiar call have meant? Something to do with Claude's urgent call to Sandy yesterday, with Sandy's change of plans. A new case, somebody's goof, and the local police had gotten involved. Probably Sandy had been arrested in the role of Salvatore Bonanno. It had happened before, in Boston when he was under cover. He'd hung the framed arrest warrant on the bathroom wall as a joke in Piermont. Alias Sandro, real name unknown. Still, the agent on the telephone didn't sound amused. The DEA must have screwed up; the arrest would cause unnecessary complications. They hated that, hated the exposure unless it was produced by their own PR department. "Federal agents confiscated 150 lbs. of marijuana in a well-planned raid last night in South Miami"—that was the kind of press release the DEA sent out. I put on my bathrobe, got out of bed.

The floor was cold, the room, too, in spite of the sunny morning. I went out on the terrace, wanting the warm bricks on the soles of my feet. The leaves on the potted plants were torn and brown from the heavy hailstorms of the past few weeks. The milkman was long gone, the walk swept, the fallen leaves and needles piled neatly on the curb. David followed me out, tugged on my robe: "Apple juice now, please, Mommy."

Sandy would have called if anything was wrong. It was just some dumb mistake. That agent and his wife had a flair for melodrama. I picked up David and went downstairs.

"Buenos días, señora. Hola, niño."

David put out his arms, and Concha took him. I watched him play with her hair, pulled back from her face with a string of orange yarn. She rolled up his pajama sleeves. *"Dormiste bien?"* she asked. *"Sí,"* he answered gravely, but he said *sí* or *no* to everything.

"No ha llamado nadie, Concha?"

"No, señora."

I sifted through my last conversation with Sandy from the embassy the day before: "I know you wanted to go to that party, but Claude called. He's just back from Europe, from Canada and Vermont. You know Claude, he's upset, it's urgent, the usual business. I told him I had to go to San Antonio on Monday for a doctor's appointment so I couldn't meet him at the embassy. He wants to meet in San Antonio instead. How do you feel about it? Maybe you could come, do some Christmas shopping? The girl is with him. She's seeing a doctor in Texas, more problems with her pregnancy."

It had to be a mistake. Sandy would have never asked me along if he'd suspected any problems. It would be all right. It was only Claude, stirring up some kind of trouble.

Particulars of Sandy's old Boston case came back slowly. There the arrest had been planned, to solidify Sandy's connections with the mob. He was doubted in the North End. Someone had pointed a gun to his head and asked point-blank if he was a fed.

The arrest was proof that he was with them. Had he gone to jail back then? I couldn't remember. There was a box in the garage filled with clippings that might tell the story.

I wondered if I should call the office. Somebody might be working early Saturday morning. No, I decided, it was better not to call. Sandy would get in touch when he had gotten the problem straightened out. I went back into the kitchen. David was seated happily at his feeding table eating scrambled egg. Concha was at the sink washing out the frying pan. The coffee was ready. I poured a cup and stared out the window. The maid next door was hanging out her wash already. Despite the presidential weather decree, it would soon cloud over. It was October—7. The rainy season had ended three weeks ago.

The telephone rang in the hall. It was Jacques Kiere. "I want to come over with my wife," he said.

My stomach knotted up. I packed Concha off with David in his stroller. "Take him down the street to see the ducks," I suggested. I was standing at the gate in my bathrobe watching them go off when the Kieres arrived.

They stood solemnly on the opposite side of the gate. Their expressions seemed unreal. They're playacting, I thought. I had never liked Jacques Kiere's wife, who called everybody "babe." She wore no makeup that morning. Her long, angular face was sallow and filled with high purpose. I opened the gate for them, wondering what time it was—it couldn't have been later than nine o'clock. They had come with bad news, I could feel it. I accepted Jacques' perfunctory kiss on the cheek, thinking I'd back off if she tried to hug me.

We sat in the living room, the two women on the couch and Jacques on the chintz side chair. Mrs. K. started the conversation. "How could Sandy get involved in anything like this?" she asked, waving one arm toward the fireplace, the paintings on the wall, the air. "It will be such a scandal. The press, the embassy. Think how the agency will look, think of Jacques."

He leaned forward in his deep chair, knees high, hands clasped earnestly together.

"You don't believe this, Jacques?" I asked.

He lit a cigarette, turning it between his thumb and forefinger. He looked at his wife, then away.

"Tell me, do you believe this?"

"It's true, it must be," he began. "Sandy was arrested last night at the elevator on the sixteenth floor of the Hilton Hotel in San Antonio. One-thirty in the morning. He took a bribe, Joanne. How could he? But he did, they found him with the money. The evidence is substantial. I know I haven't any right to advise you here, but when he calls, tell him it's no use fighting. Lawyers, court costs, the whole bit. They've set a bond for him—I don't think I should be the one to tell you what it is. You'll be tempted to try to raise the money. But you have to try to be sensible, Joanne. You have to be the one to talk him out of fighting. Think of yourself, think of his kids."

"I don't believe I'm hearing this. I don't believe you're saying this to me. How could you, Jacques? Sandy would never take a bribe. Who from, what for?"

"From Claude," Jacques said softly. "I can't tell you anymore. They found him with the money. On his person, when they stopped him at the elevator."

"Who stopped him?"

"DEA, Inspection."

I suddenly felt better. So that was it, another internal DEA screwup. Nothing to worry about, nothing to fear. Kiere was all wired up by some bureaucratic goof. He'd chosen sides, that's all. I wasn't to believe anything he said.

"Where is he?" I asked.

"In a county courthouse fifty miles from San Antonio. There's been no arraignment yet. Kerr County, the Kerr County Jail, I think."

They must have left soon after. There wasn't any more to say. Mrs. K. clucked, shook her head to show her disapproval. They were a united front at the gate: "Anything we can do for you or David, apart from Sandy, let us know, you hear. . . ."

By the time I locked them out, the telephone was ringing. I ran to answer it, noting there was no more sunlight on the drive. The day was clouding over early. It wasn't even ten o'clock.

Polly's voice on the telephone: "Dan just found out. We're worried about you. Shall I come over?"

If Polly knew, it must be true. I wanted her to come. With her there nothing too terrible could happen. With her there the morning would take root, would somehow become like any other morning. She was like that, Polly, my blond, blue-eyed, safest friend. She and Dan had had their own bureaucratic mix-ups with the DEA. He'd applied for an extension of his tour. No one understood why he'd been turned down. Even as we spoke, the movers were at her house, packing them out.

"Yes, come, soon, Polly. Now, if you can."

The day turned into a slapstick filmstrip of trips back and forth from the front gate. Agents from the office would arrive on condolence visits, guarding every word they said. The embassy lawyer would be summoned by Polly. Nothing would be ordinary anymore. At one-thirty this morning, while I was sleeping, our world had been transformed as we had never imagined it could be. I remembered hearing about the Indian farmer in Oaxaca. He had been plowing his little plot of land one day as he had for twenty years, when suddenly the familiar pull of metal in the hard red clay had caused a rumbling. Or seemed to cause it. The wooden handle of the plow had quivered for an instant in his hand, his only warning. Then his hectare, his mule, his entire village had been blown away. His wife, husking corn two kilometers away, was the only member of the family who survived to tell the story.

The bell rang: Polly. The clouds had moved off for a moment; sunlight had reclaimed the garden. There were lilies blooming that had weathered the hailstorms. I could smell the bark on the jacarandas outside the gate. I didn't look at Polly as I walked down the drive. I wanted to be lost in that front garden. The ivy had recently been clipped; new shoots were sprouting. I wanted to lie in the freshly cut grass, my face in the sun. I wanted to sleep the afternoon away.

Polly stood outside the gate in her wraparound skirt. Was it right to let her in? Look at her, so neat, so safe, her hair expertly cut, her small gold earrings gleaming. She belonged on the other side of that gate. I wanted to join her, hide myself behind her, a small, sloppy girl in a bathrobe, with bare feet.

We sat in the living room. I watched her—how perfect she was, how clean. She was like the garden, already out of reach. She was so organized, on the telephone to the lawyer at the embassy, a personal friend of hers, someone I could count on. It was amazing, really, how efficient she was, as if Sandy's arrest were a manageable thing, like a leak in a bathroom sink or a bit of plaster peeling. She had her feet planted on the ground; I was off somewhere and couldn't touch her. Recently in the news, they'd reported the death of a CIA agent, not suicide but murder. The report took thirty seconds of the anchor's time, then on to the news of the rest of the world: OPEC countries fiddling with the price of oil, local teams winning and losing games. But think of the woman whose husband was murdered. She isn't part of normal time. Think how she locks the house like a tomb. Every fifteen minutes she tiptoes down the hall to check the children. The room, the sound of their breathing, the way the youngest kicks his covers off—so ordinary, so unchanged, like Polly in her country sweater, innocently playing with the telephone wire. The children recede, the rooms back off, that woman cannot reach them. She knows she's alone, scattered —like the farmer in Oaxaca, blown away.

At noon a deputy sheriff at that unknown county jail called and said, "Mrs. Bario?" "Yes." "Hold on, please." Sandy's voice came on through water—distant, muffled, thin: "Joanne?" My own echoed, "Yes, Sandy, I'm here. How are you? Are you all right?" A long time passed, and he didn't answer. I was calm, someone I didn't even know. Polly's friend, the lawyer from the embassy, was sitting in the living room. I was suddenly aware of him as I heard my own voice echo in the hall.

"Then you know?" Sandy said, a question, flat.

"A little, but I don't understand. I want to come to you. I could fly up tonight or tomorrow morning if I can't get a flight."

His voice rippled. "All right. But not alone. Bring someone with you. Polly would come, ask Polly."

As though ours were any conversation: "I'm not sure. Her packers are in. But I'll ask her, I'll see."

"I don't want you to come alone."

"Don't worry. Have you seen anyone? Do you have a lawyer?"

"The sheriff called somebody, a kid from Kerrville. Don't worry, though. It's not important."

"What do you mean?"

He seemed to be falling asleep, drifting off on an ocean wave.

"Don't worry. You'll see."

There was static on the line. If I whispered, would the echo carry?

"Sandy?"—my voice underwater, lapping. I wished I could cover my head with my woolly robe or tuck the receiver up my sleeve. I whisper secretly: "What is this? What's happening?"

With my eyes closed I can almost see the deputy standing at Sandy's shoulder. I invent a sterile, misty green room where the telephone might be. Sandy's voice breaks when he tries to whisper. It's hard to make his deep voice go so low. It must be that; it can't be that he's crying.

"Not now, Joanne, please not now. Besides, you know already. It's Claude."

20

The embassy lawyer, Polly's friend, had moved out of the living room and was standing in a far corner of the dining room, pretending to study a Mexican painting on the stucco wall. He seemed as embarrassed as I was. We'd met perhaps twice before at Polly's dinner parties, and there we were, intimate and awful. The day couldn't decide to rain. The sun came in at times through the casement windows, then disappeared again. It flooded the lawyer's pale, baby face with light. He seemed so innocent when I was already tainted by the day. How shabby it must seem, my life and Sandy's coming undone while the sun came out and went away, streaks of sun on the eggshell carpets. I wondered what he made of us. Did he think this was an administrative error as Polly did? Had he been briefed by the DEA already? He was embassy counsel, after all. A lawyer, who would think in terms of innocence or guilt. Or maybe he was hedging. It could be true. It had happened in other places, other times. An agent goes bad, takes a bribe from whomever for whatever greedy reason.

He turned from the painting with reluctance.

"I didn't find out very much," I apologized. "I'm afraid I didn't ask very many questions."

He followed me back into the living room. "Until this begins to sort itself out, don't push. Your husband needs a good lawyer. That should be your first priority. Let the rest fall into place. I know it's hard to believe that this is really happening, but you must trust Sandy. It's an obvious mistake on the DEA's part. They're not well thought of at the embassy, you know."

When I turned to face him on the couch, I must have looked at him with love. "I'm going to fly up tomorrow. I'll find a good lawyer first thing."

"Do you know anyone in Texas?"

I shook my head.

"I'll make some calls. I know a few people who might help."

"But I don't want to put you in a difficult position."

"You're not. I'm a friend, you're a member of the embassy community. You have a right to some legal counsel, especially until you get back to the States."

He left then, promising to call with the name of the best criminal lawyer in Texas and to find out if the bond had been set or if Sandy would be released on his own recognizance. That would be the reasonable thing. At worst, it might cost five thousand dollars. I'd get the money, pay the bond. Sandy would be free. I walked out to the gate with him. He was like Polly. He made me feel safe.

For the first time all morning the house was quiet. Concha and David had returned. I could hear them playing upstairs. Soon they'd come down for lunch. She would jabber at the baby in her fast Spanish. He'd balk at the mention of a nap. I didn't want them to see me, but I needed to hear their voices drifting in and out of other rooms. Sandy had been unrecognizable, a strange voice across wide seas. What had happened to him? What was the worst Claude could have done? Asked a favor from him? That wasn't so unusual. Or had he somehow conned him as he had conned so many others?

Sandy could have never taken a bribe. He used to joke about his maître d's job in Detroit, how he'd made more money running a restaurant for the mob than he'd been paid as a federal agent. Each week he'd turn in his restaurant salary to his IRS contact. "I never wanted anybody else's money," he'd say. Any problems that he'd had in his career had come up because he was too straight, too dedicated. He sometimes bent official guidelines to satisfy a case. He might agree to an unwise favor or make a stupid judgment. But take a bribe? For what? For drugs—never. He was his father's son.

When we'd moved my things from Eighteenth Street, he had flushed my three-year-old joints of marijuana down the toilet. I had shocked him many times. It was easy to shock him. What had Claude done? Something had changed between Sandy and Claude. But what?

I sat in the living room doing nothing for fifteen minutes, for half an hour, until the telephone rang. It was the administrative officer from the DEA, the same man who had come to dinner at our house with Jacques Kiere. I listened to him speaking with a spanking brand-new sense of his authority.

"You should know, Joanne, that Sandy's been suspended. He'll be notified tomorrow. It's still unclear what that means for you. If you want advice from a friend, I think you should consider packing out immediately. I'm not sure that DEA will pay to move you. Do you know when your diplomatic visa expires?"

"No," I said. "My passport's here somewhere. Upstairs. Do you want to hold on while I check?"

"Not necessary. I'll find out from the consular office. This is—how shall I say?—confusing. The guidelines don't cover this kind of situation. We don't know what to do with you or your boy. It would cost you a hell of a lot to ship out yourself. You might consider selling everything."

He hung up. We must have said good-bye; I don't remember. That conversation was a door clicking shut. I tried not to panic, not to think about it. In the breakfast room Concha was singing to David: *"En el bosque, la chinita, la chinita se perdio* [In the woods the little Chinese girl was lost]."

I called Polly, who agreed to fly to San Antonio with me early the next morning. We planned to return by Tuesday so she would be ready to leave Mexico permanently with her family on Thursday. I called the airline to make two round-trip reservations. I called our Canadian friends, Sara and Paul, to ask if they would keep Concha and the baby at their house. Then finally, I called Concha to the living room.

She stood awkwardly in the doorway. Her gray sweater sleeves were pushed above her elbows. One knee sock sagged; a line of yellow lace hung below the hem of her uniform. For the first time all day, I was sad. It was a relief to know what I was feeling.

"Tomorrow morning you and David are going to stay at Señora Sara's for a few days, Concha. I'm afraid you won't be able to go home this weekend to see your girls. Maybe you should call and leave a message for your mother. I'm sorry, but it's an emergency. It's my husband. I have to go to San Antonio to help him."

"He's all right, the señor? He's not sick?"

"No. There are other problems."

"We could stay home, señora, David and I. We've stayed alone before."

"Not this time, Concha. This time is different."

She didn't argue. Whatever she might be imagining, she knew it was bad. She searched my face; I weighed every word. But it wasn't humiliating the way it had been with Polly or the lawyer. Without knowing, she understood. She was closer than Sara, than Polly, than anyone.

She excused herself and came back with her knee socks hiked up, her slip out of sight, and tea for me in our best china cup, laid out on the lace tray scarf that she hated to iron.

"Concha, come and sit with me," I said. But no, she couldn't, she had to put the laundry in.

I sat alone drinking the hot tea, staring at the paintings, the books neat on their shelves. I believed that administrative officer, accepted his authority. I would prepare myself to be thrown out of Mexico by the DEA, bereft of table linens and hand-me-down chairs. When the phone rang again, I didn't want to answer it. No more bad news or sympathy, no more information. Concha got it on the seventh ring.

"*Quien es?*"

"*La Señora Himmelfarb.*"

Did Helen know already, in her jewelry store on the Zócalo? No, it couldn't have gone that far already. I was about to ask Concha to say that I was out, but Helen was Sandy's friend; it didn't seem right to leave her hanging. I pictured her in one of her enormous caftans, leaning on the counter in her family's store, cabinets overstocked with ornate bracelets, stuffed alligators, carved leather bags, malachite key rings.

"Hello, Helen?"

"Where have you two been? We missed you at my son's bar

mitzvah. We've missed Sandy at the store. Just the other day my mother asked about him."

"I'm sorry we missed the party," I said, "but Sandy's been so busy. Are you calling from the store? Is everything all right?"

She would be on her chair behind the counter, shrouded in fabric. I could bury myself in her billowing skirts, lose myself in her wide lap.

"Everything's fine. Business is slow, but Christmas will be coming soon. Really, we're okay now. Tell Sandy to stop by when he can, and both of you must come for supper soon."

She had that practiced English, only its lilting cadence gave her away. I hated to let go of her soothing voice.

"We will, I promise. And Helen?"

"Yes."

"Be careful."

"What do you mean?"

"Nothing, just take care of yourself. Give our best wishes to your son."

She clicked off; I had spared her. If I could keep Helen safe from knowing, there was hope for the others—for my parents, for Marisa, Sandy's sister in Ohio, for Franco and Marco and Sandy's father in Vieste. They didn't have to know. If it were just a terrible mistake, we could let them in on the joke when it was over. I'd write letters to them, rooted in their safe places, in their houses where the roofs would never collapse. Sorry we haven't written, haven't called, but there is only our usual routine, Sandy's work keeping him busy and David changing by the day.

Or perhaps I was wrong, and Helen had a right to know. She'd enjoyed a long friendship with Sandy that had involved her mother and brother, her entire family. He had bailed her brother out of trouble once in the States. There were many people in Mexico who had tugged on Sandy. I would have to let them know sooner or later, after their yearly Christmas cards arrived recounting their gratitude one more time. The agent's wife in Guadalajara who had called Sandy day and night when her husband had abandoned her. Sandy had cajoled and reprimanded the agent though it had done no good. He answered all the wife's sad questions: What shall I do? Shall I wait for him? Should I take the children and leave Mexico?

He was a soft touch, Sandy. He had conned the consular office out of visas for the brothers and sisters of maids. He traveled with the families of his informants to the Houston clinic when they got sick. He worried through a long letter from his brother-in-law in Italy about moving to the States. Even Sara, our competent Canadian nurse and neighbor, had counted on him when her baby arrived two months early, while her husband was on business in Peru. Paul was unavailable in Machu Picchu, so Sandy kept the car ready, came home early every night, slept near the phone where her doctor's number was scratched in red on the bedside table.

Playing at God, weren't you, Sandy? Playing your lucky streak for all it was worth. You showed us that you knew the meaning of action when it counted. You played at being that white knight, collecting people on the edge like you collected rare and delicate seashells. Or maybe you weren't being noble after all. You simply needed to take risks, to toy with boundaries, to change the rules of everybody's games, like jumping from the side of that boat in France when the shooting started, into the deep, blue Mediterranean Sea.

21

Polly and I took a nine o'clock flight on Sunday, a clear cloudless morning. I sat beside the window thinking how often Sandy and I had flown the same flight out. Tourists heading home from Acapulco or Puerto Vallarta with sunburned cheeks dragged their straw shopping bags up and down the aisle. I knew the contents of their bags by heart, tennis rackets, manta shirts, clay ashtrays copped from poolside tables. The Mexicans would reclaim empty suitcases from the baggage belt in San Antonio, to be filled on daylong shopping sprees, the latest clothes, chocolates for the children, chemically flavored puddings in six-pack tins to be smuggled through customs with a *mordida* and a wink. I could've recited the breakfast menu before we even left the runway: cheese omelette, soggy Moctezuma pie, refried beans, and hot sauce on the side. I sat by the window, comforted by every boring, familiar thing.

The stewardess passed out the morning Spanish paper and the English weekly row by row. Polly and I guarded our empty middle seat and did not speak. When we left the ground, I watched the city out the window. The lake bed was puddled and tinged with green from months of rain. We banked to turn, the landmarks beneath us clear and clean: the Hotel de Mexico, the Viaducto, the old Olympics site. The mountains rose and fell like ocean swells, the solitary roads that cut across them looping slowly back and forth. It was an empty, willing landscape, to be infused with anything you liked.

I closed my eyes. Sandy's bond had been set at five hundred thousand dollars. The intelligence agent who had lived next door to us in our second house had told me the amount outright. He was going against the advice of other agents in the office, he said, because he and Sandy had once been friends. They were both the same grade, both supervisors. When we accepted a dinner invitation at a junior agent's house or were expected to attend an embassy reception, we often went with Ron Garibotto and his wife. I thought I understood him. We were the same age. He had fast-tracked through the ranks of the DEA in Detroit, in Ankara, Turkey. He carried his ego around on his shoulders, overbuilt from lifting weights. He was the new breed, educated, with understated suits and European shoes, a collection of oriental rugs rolled up in his basement. He never talked guns. Language was his tool. He had a way with words, a belief in memos, outclassing the competition with fancy footwork.

His had been the last of many calls on Saturday. He wanted to know if I was going soon to Sandy, exactly when I was supposed to leave. I was in bed for our conversation, in knee socks, a flannel granny gown. "I've booked an early morning flight," I said.

"Listen, I want to come over. Alone. There are some things you should know before you see Sandy. You shouldn't make any decisions until I talk to you."

I couldn't imagine going to the closet for my thick bathrobe. I was so tired. I wanted only the quilt over my head, the rains to come back, hailstones the size of quarters.

"Joanne, are you still there?"

"I don't think I can talk anymore now, Ron. I'm not sure I want to know what you want to say."

He was good at playing hurt. When the telephone was sitting on the nightstand again, I turned off the lamp and buried my shoulders in the quilt. The drapes were drawn across the window, but Sandy had insisted on leaving the glass door to the terrace bare. Even for the privacy of sex, for mornings when we might have slept late, he wouldn't sacrifice the view. The persimmon room absorbed the light. The rubber trees climbed the terrace wall.

There were shadows crisscrossing the drapes and lamplight coming through the glass door. I couldn't sleep. I sat up, reached for the phone, and dialed the embassy.

"Could you please connect me with the legal attaché's residence?"

Terry Gaither, the legal attaché and Polly's friend, was groggy. He spoke guardedly, as though he knew his telephone was tapped. Place a call through the embassy switchboard, and the tape kept rolling, so everybody said. "Joanne? I'll call you back direct."

"I'm sorry to keep bothering you, Terry. I know you were asleep."

"It's been a long day, but we're still awake, reading in bed. What's wrong?"

"An agent from the DEA just called. He wants to come over, to tell me something about this case. Should I see him or not?"

Terry's slow, quiet voice took over. "If it's not too much for you, I think you'd better. You need to know everything you can."

But I don't want to know.

I switched on the lights, upstairs and down. I found my bathrobe, called Ron at ten past ten, had a pot of coffee ready by the time he arrived.

We sat at the dining-room table, our admission that the conversation would be formal. He tried so hard to look at ease, just a friend. I watched him push the high-backed chair away from the table, his arm resting on the tabletop, his collar starched, his blue jeans pressed and creased.

"I know this is hell," he said, "that you've absorbed as much as anyone could in a single day. But we want you to know how we see this at the office. We don't believe this crime, if I can call it that, is within the range of Sandy's normal behavior. In one sense or another, it's a tragic mistake. But the charges are real, Joanne, they won't go away."

"What do you mean?" I asked, not trusting him, wondering whether I was an informant he was trying to debrief.

"You know there's been a lot of tension at the office. I'm sure you also know Sandy and I haven't been getting along. But you may not know why. He's been bizarre, unpredictable for months. His agents never knew what to expect when they stepped inside his office. He screamed, jumped on them, made unreasonable demands. He fought me tooth and nail at every management meeting, he and his precious general, his informants. He was obsessed, we all agree. In the past year, he went over the edge. Maybe you haven't noticed. He probably tried to protect you, but he's been very strange. Then his hair falling out, overnight almost. It must have been very hard on you. . . ."

I couldn't speak. I wanted to believe in Ron's concern. I wanted to tell him what the year had been. Maybe he was our friend; maybe he really wanted to help.

"I tried to tell Jacques," I finally said. "At his New Year's party. You remember, last year, his son's band was playing? We were sitting on the stairs. It was hard to concentrate—the music, everybody dancing. I asked him to talk to Sandy, to make him ease off. His ulcer was bad, Claude was on his back. I told Jacques that Sandy wasn't well. But then the music, the general was out there, Jacques had to go. He promised to help, but I don't think he really heard me."

I looked up at Ron, expecting—what was I expecting? I would have told him everything, the fights, the nights in separate beds, the times I'd told Sandy to see a psychiatrist. But then I looked up, and there was Ron, lost in his technique. Eyes painted with sincerity, neat, square hands on his coffee cup. He was distant, professional, as close and intimate as he had to be. He was part of them. For all I knew, he might be the enemy. No more teasing me about my advanced degrees or women's rights; no more trips to Xochimilco.

"I can see," he said encouragingly, "that Kiere might not understand. Maybe he thought you were talking marriage problems. We saw the changes, yet we didn't. The issue is where to go from here."

"It won't be pretty. No one will believe that Sandy's wrecked. You're the one who has to make the tough decisions, how much to risk riding this thing out. Kathy and I are concerned about you. We hate to think of you destroyed by this.

"Don't let Sandy lean on you too hard," Ron had warned me. "Don't let him suck you under. The government's case is tight. There's no way he can win. Don't sacrifice yourself, your son, to him. To fight will be suicide for all of you."

The captain's disembodied voice came on and filled the cabin, telling of clear skies, a good tail wind, and perfect visibility. We were due in San Antonio at eleven-thirty local time.

The stewardess cleared the trays, handed out landing cards. Polly finished her coffee and smiled at me. "Did you sleep? It seemed a shame to wake you for gruesome in-flight food." I left her to her magazine and turned back to the window.

We were beginning our descent over Monterrey. The city flattened out below—smokestacks, underpasses—until the empty spaces opened up again, roads narrowed down, disappearing. The uncluttered, bare, despairing space between Monterrey and the border was like a long farewell. Over the river, Texas was another country. The neighborhoods outside the border towns were definite, neat little squares on drafting paper. They scared me for some reason. The belly of the plane left its shadow on the valley as we floated north. We seemed to hang in the sky, but were moving, over treetops, the wide white interstate, taco stands, billboards. Texas didn't feel like home.

We stood in the immigration line for U.S. Citizens Only. We waited in the lobby for our bags to come through.

"I guess I should rent a car. We'll need a map."

Polly nodded, nervous and trying not to show it. She grabbed our bags when they came around. "Where shall we stay?"

"I don't know. I'll make some calls. We'll get the car first and go to a motel, then call the Kerr County Courthouse."

I took out the blue spiral notebook where I had written down the laywers' names, three of them given to me by Terry late the night before. I had his warnings in my head: "You don't have much money, don't make a commitment over your head." On the second page of the notebook I'd scribbled, "Motel, Ramada Inn," trying to remember which Ramada Inn I'd been to with Sandy. Near a shopping mall, on the Loop near the airport. It seemed important to go to the same motel—good luck when we would need it. I found it in the phone book, called and booked a room.

The rental car was red and white inside and flashy. It was hot in San Antonio. We used the air conditioner for the three-block drive.

The motel lobby was ugly and oversized. I had to stand on

tiptoe to fill out the registration form at the high counter. Polly saw the newspaper headline first, stretching across the front page, clamped by the metal rim in the vending machine. She pointed to it without speaking. It was at least a three-inch head, "Federal Agent Arrested on Bribery."

The clerk checked my credit card and signature. The quarter sounded hollow when it dropped in the slot. Polly opened the case. The clerk turned his back, reaching for our key. I read the lead over Polly's shoulder while we both stared at the photograph of Sandy. She covered it quickly with her palm, then folded the newspaper just before the clerk turned to tell us where to park the car. She didn't want anybody looking.

The first-floor room smelled mildewed. The double beds were covered with blue, green, and ocher spreads, overblown chrysanthemums. The blackout drapes were drawn. Polly opened the curtains, the windows, unpacked our bags, arranged bottles, jars, deodorant cans like Hummel figures on the vanity. She didn't look at me. The newspaper lay face down on the dresser.

I pulled the limp spread off the bed by the telephone, propped the pillows, and put the map out on the bed. It was fifty miles on open four-lane roads to Kerrville. In the clean notebook, on the first page under the lawyers' names, I found the number for the jail.

Someone answered in a long, lazy twang, "Kerrville sheriff's office."

"Could I please speak to the sheriff?"

"He's not here."

"Well, a deputy then."

"Nope, deputy's upstairs."

"With whom am I speaking?"

"The dispatcher, ma'am."

"There must be someone in charge?"

"On Sundays just the deputy and me. Who's calling?"

"My name is Mrs. Bario. I'm trying to find out about my husband, Sante Bario. I want to make arrangements to see him if I can."

The line seemed to have gone dead. "Hold on, ma'am," the dispatcher said. "I'll go get the deputy."

But it wasn't the deputy who answered after five minutes of holding on. It was Sandy. "Joanne? Where are you?"

"I'm here, Sandy. I'm at a motel in San Antonio."

"I'm so glad. I want so much to see you."

I played it light. I changed my voice and tried sounding like his sidekick. "I'm coming. Like old Mick Jagger says, wild horses couldn't keep me away."

"What?" he asked.

"Nothing. It was stupid. I'm sorry," I answered, feeling clumsy because I understood so little. "I have a car. I'll drive out right now if they'll let me see you."

I could feel him slowly moving back to safer ground. I'd never heard him sound so timid. "I'm sure it's okay. I'll ask the deputy. They've been nice. Can you hold on a minute?"

His voice, muffled by his hand, as if that could protect me: "It's all right. You can come."

"I've got a map. I'll leave right now. I guess it should take about an hour."

He didn't want to let me go. "Is Polly there? Did she come with you?"

"Yes, she's here."

"Ask her to come, too."

I was impatient with him already. "Okay, but I can do it alone. I'm fine, you know." I was fifteen and annoyed, wanting to drive solo. I was a high school senior, capable of everything. Out to take control, set Sandy free.

While I talked, Polly lay on the other bed, her long back to me and paper resting on her knee. When I got off, she folded it, sat up.

"What does it say?" I asked.

"Not much. Just about the arrest at the Hilton, his job in Mexico."

"I want to see the picture."

"Why? You know it's awful. It doesn't even look like him."

I slipped the map into my purse with the notebook. "If we're going there, I think I'd better."

She handed it over slowly, the photo still folded on the inside flap. It was like unwrapping a dead bird swaddled in newsprint. It wasn't Sandy, yet it was. He looked up from heavy brows, as if he were surprised. The photographer must have called his name; he looked directly at the camera. He was like a survivor off a ship, from a war, his eyes accusing and terrified. He wore his gray suit; I could tell from the lapel. The skin seemed to hang between his collar and chin. He looked sixty at least. It isn't fair, his eyes were saying, it isn't what it seems. There was a black slash running from the side of his nose across his cheek. I thought it was printer's ink at first, but it belonged to him, the shadow from a deeply folded ridge of skin—as if his face were caving in.

I rolled up the newspaper and left it on the bed. "We'd better go. If you don't mind driving with me."

San Antonio was all interstates. Loops and underpasses, ramps and exits everywhere, built in the sixties by Lyndon Johnson. San Antonio and adjacent Kerr County were Johnson territory. The Johnson ranch wasn't far from the Kerrville jail. The interstate we drove was wide, expansive, like the countryside. Beyond the farthest suburbs, there were rolling, barren hills, cactus, few trees. I could have blinked and believed we were in Mexico again. We drove through dynamited passes in limestone cliffs, tinted by the sunlight. We didn't talk, didn't listen to the radio. We became that drive. There was no one on the road on Sunday afternoon. It was so flat, so straight and empty, I was doing ninety and couldn't feel it. We were safe; no one could touch us. We'd been touched already. Those cliffs, the hills, the emptiness of sky to trick us.

We left the interstate, followed the signs to Kerrville on a flat, common two-lane road, passing gas stations, a Pizza Hut, a Holiday Inn that seemed deserted.

The courthouse stood on Main Street. The parking spaces were all empty on the curb. The shops were closed. A man and his son crossed at the traffic signal. Ours was the only car. I stared at the building with its cream-colored paint and Greek columns as if it could give clues to what we'd find inside. It looked deserted, too, though the lights were on.

I was wearing a dress, high-heeled shoes, like a grown-up. My skirt stuck to my stockings as we crossed the street. I batted at it impatiently. They'd have to be nice to me, I thought. I was so middle-class, so ordinary. Excellent grades, good marks in conduct my whole life through. I refused to seem rattled next to tall, poised Polly and rode my head high, pulled my shoulders back, just the way my mother taught me.

A modern brick extension had been built on the back of the courthouse like a bad joke—tinted glass, aluminum window frames. I thought that must be the jail, rising three stories above the domed courthouse roof, its narrow windows lined up like prison bars. That's where I headed as we crossed the street. "Shall I wait outside?" Polly asked. I shook my head, voice bouncing as my heels tapped the ground. "No, come in and wait. They may not let me see him." The side door was locked. We walked to the front, climbed the marble stairs. The oak doors were tacky with varnish, the brass knobs polished to a shine.

It was dark inside, with the smell of disinfectant. At the end of the long hall, two fluorescent lights cast an eerie wave on the polished floor. We listened to the echo of footsteps, but no one appeared. Finally, a woman came through, pushing her cleaning cart out the door with her heel. She was stringy, blond, and tense as she gave directions to the sheriff's office.

There was coffee heating on a hot plate and metal folding chairs lining one wall outside the sheriff's office. Polly hung back while I went in.

The long, narrow room was empty, the front desk cluttered with papers, Styrofoam cups. A file cabinet was piled high with folders and telephone books. But what I saw most clearly was a small, flat blackboard hanging on the wall, ruled in white paint, with small lettering down the left-hand margin: name, date, time, place, charges. There were only three names written down: the last was Bario.

I just kept staring until an enormous man in tan cowboy boots and new dark jeans came up behind me. He sat down at the desk, his cheek bulging with what looked like chewing gum. "Help you?"

"Yes. I'm looking for my husband." I pointed to the chalked name on the blackboard.

He held his finger up and turned away—to sneeze, I thought—while reaching across the desktop for an empty coffee can. He spat, pulled a cloth hanky from his back pocket, wiped his lips.

"You'll have to wait, ma'am. The deputy will be back in a minute."

I had gone out in the hall to sit with Polly when the door opened and there was Sandy in his wide-striped shirt open at the collar, in the slacks we'd bought in the Zona Rosa. He was standing the way he always did, knees locked, his back thrown out a little. I couldn't see his face in the bad light, but he looked so normal. He could have been working as he often worked on Sundays in half-dark, empty rooms.

I moved toward him, called his name—Sandy—in the long gray corridor. We came together, hugged. His palms were wet. When I looked up at him, his eyes seemed bruised, his eyelids trembled. He looked past me into the room he had just left, then down the corridor at Polly. "Hello, Polly," he said in a sad, deep voice that carried. She answered in the same tone and didn't move.

"Come with me," he said, holding my hand for a moment. I followed him into the corner room. The venetian blinds were up. I'd almost forgotten that it was daylight out. The two men inside half turned to me, half turned away, as if they didn't know exactly what to do. One of them was tall, dark-haired, in his forties. He wore a three-piece suit, a ruffled shirt, high-heeled boots. The other looked fresh out of school. His blue eyes smiled deferentially, eager to give us center stage. This young lawyer had been recommended to Sandy by the sheriff and must have known right away that he was onto something big. He'd called his more experienced brother-in-law in the ruffled shirt who flew straight up from McAllen, in a private chartered plane.

I didn't like the ruffled shirt even before he started talking. I rejected his walk, the sound of his high heels clomping. I didn't like his craggy face or the five o'clock shadow on his chin. He wore his confidence like a diamond pin. I handle federal agents every day, the tapping of his boot seemed to be saying.

I had my notebook in my purse with three good names, a San Antonio public defender, an expensive defense attorney in Houston, and the third name, underlined in felt-tip marker, a local San

Antonio defense attorney recommended by the legal attaché in Mexico as our best choice.

Terry Gaither had called all his contacts in Texas and had spoken at length with the San Antonio public defender to find the right man, a sharp young lawyer in his thirties. In San Antonio we'd need a native son who knew the judges and the drug-world scene, who could begin to sort out the complicated facts. Gerry Goldstein, the underscored name in my notebook, had a strong regional reputation, knew his way around the federal courtroom, and was known as a troubleshooter who liked to take on causes. He was interested in civil liberties cases, and the legal attaché was afraid Sandy's civil rights might be at stake.

I sat down. The older lawyer from McAllen stood behind the desk, with Sandy looking up at him from under those deep brows. Our first course of action, the lawyer said, was to get me out of Mexico. He advised me to go home, get packed, and return to San Antonio as soon as possible. That is, if I intended to come back to San Antonio. Sandy looked at me. I rolled my eyes and winked. Sandy smiled formally like his father in Vieste. "Good," the lawyer said. When I returned, he would expect his fee. He cleared his throat. He and his brother-in-law had already discussed the fee with Sandy: thirty thousand dollars plus expenses. Once we had agreed and I'd brought back the money, they would begin the real work, getting the bond reduced, getting Sandy released from the Kerrville jail. The five-hundred-thousand-dollar bond was ludicrous and would be changed.

They looked at me, three men waiting to hear what I'd say. After all, who was on the street, who could walk out the door, down the marble stairs, grab a plane? They had to count on me to get the money. I could call my parents, Sandy's family, our friends, friends of friends, to beg for money. I wanted to leave the lawyers hanging there, ten minutes, half an hour. I could have. Nobody was stopping me. But then I looked at Sandy.

"I'd like to talk to my husband alone," I said, "before making a commitment."

They left, handshakes all around, closed the door behind them.

"It isn't like it seems," Sandy said, not looking at me. He held his paper coffee cup, addressed the burnt black coffee when he spoke. "I didn't do what they're saying, Joanne. I didn't take a bribe, I never meant to keep Claude's money. He asked me to hold it for him, to keep it away from the girl, the same old story. It was a favor, a stupid, fucking, crazy favor."

It was too painful to watch him or to listen. When I closed my eyes, I heard his voice as if it were coming from a mine shaft after a fatal accident. I got up from the chair as though to get away in that small, square room belonging to no one. The desk was bare, not even a loose sheet of paper around. The room was filled with smoke, the first time it had been filled with anything.

"It doesn't matter," I said, looking out the window at the empty street.

"What do you mean?"

"You can tell me some other time, when you're out of here and we're sitting in a different kind of room."

He didn't answer. I turned slowly from the window. He was wearing his wig from Mexico, real human hair dyed Sandy's color. He had paid four hundred dollars for the most expensive model, human hair fitted on a plastic scalp. It looked real and absolutely artificial. I hated it, although I had been the one who'd talked him into trying a toupee, anything to replace that hat he wore day and night, in the house and on the street. He had bought his latest hat last summer at the beach, a white sailor's hat, its colored band bleached out by the sun. Anything to make him get out more. He had turned down every invitation, and who could blame him? He looked like a dog with mange, like an old bewildered lion at the zoo. He was indignant at first when I suggested a toupee, but when he began to realize that he would lose all his hair in tufts and patches, he had asked Marta to research the best salon and had taken off from work for fittings. The day he came home wearing the wig, he had looked painfully at me, waiting to see if I would tease him. Later, he'd put his head on my shoulder and cried. But he wore it, every day. It took him half an hour to get the adhesive right. He had to set it on his palm to comb it. Looking up at me from under his wig, under those half-collapsing eyes, he had changed. He was and was not Sandy.

I crouched on the floor beside his chair, put my head on his lap.

His hands were wet and clammy, stroking my hair, my temple, my cheek.

"I want to tell you about it," he started again, "everything that's happened in the past six months. For myself, to understand it better. I tried to tell the other agents during the arrest that it wasn't what it seemed, not like that at all. They believe I took the money. They could never understand how I wanted that case, how Claude could get his hooks in me."

I put a finger gently to his lips. "Not now, Sandy. There isn't time. We have to make our moves, the right decisions. We need a lawyer. We have to fight this the right way." I muffled my voice in his wide-striped shirt, "We don't have time to talk."

He held my face, lifted my chin. "You don't have to stay. Have everything shipped to your mother's, and wait for me there with David."

"Fat chance," I said with an exaggerated frown before I pushed away and stood up. "You'll be out in no time. DEA will have to reconsider, will begin to understand. In the meantime, we have to find a lawyer. Terry gave me a name, but I haven't called him yet. I wanted to talk it over first with you. But I think he's the man we should try to get. I'll get in touch with him this afternoon and meet with him tomorrow. I have till Tuesday, then back to Mexico to work out the transfer. DEA doesn't want to pay to ship us. We may have to sell our stuff. I don't think they can do that to us. I'm sure Terry will help."

He sat staring at the floor. "This isn't a mistake, Joanne. They're out to get me. DEA doesn't want an explanation, they want blood. They set it up here, in San Antonio, because the judges here, they're known, they have hard reputations. They set it up. God knows what Claude said, why they decided to believe him, but DEA is after me."

"We'll figure it out. Don't worry."

He looked at me the way he'd looked at the lawyer in the high-heeled boots, wanting to believe.

"Just so you're all right, so you can hold yourself together here."

He smiled sadly. "It isn't so bad. The sheriff has been nice to me. They don't make me stay upstairs much. I sit in the office with them. They're sorry for me."

"Do you need anything before I leave?"

"I could use a mirror," he said, touching his chin. "I'd like to shave. And maybe some crackers for my stomach."

"Does it hurt?"

He shrugged.

There was a knock at the door—the deputy in his plaid shirt, blue jeans with a turquoise buckle. He was young, with pale blue eyes withdrawing from the smoke and from our conversation as if he'd caught us in the act of love. Sandy introduced us; he shook my hand almost without touching.

"Would it be all right to buy some things and leave them for my husband?" I tried to smile.

"What kind of things, ma'am?" he asked, pushing in the chairs at the desk, throwing Styrofoam cups in the trash. I could picture him with Lysol and a cloth, wiping down every surface.

"Just some crackers, a tin of Jell-O. He has an ulcer and can't eat much. A razor, a mirror so he can shave."

He lowered the venetian blinds, closed the slats. "We don't cook here," he said, "just TV dinners. Don't allow no glass, no mirrors. You'll have to clear it with the sheriff first."

"But the sheriff's not around."

"Nope, Sundays he ain't here."

"May I leave them, then? I could call the sheriff for his permission."

Sandy interrupted, "Forget it, Joanne. It doesn't matter."

"I could leave a bag of stuff on the dispatcher's desk."

The deputy was at the door; he flipped off the light, turning the room a brackish green. I could sense Sandy moving to the doorway from behind me. I turned and he looked back once. "I almost forgot. The sheriff let me keep this for you." He reached in his pocket. "It's the key to my room at the Ramada Inn, near the airport. I paid three days ahead. Try to cash in my airline ticket. My bag's still there with all my things."

"Leave the groceries if you want"—the deputy gave in—"but I can't promise anything."

I waited till their footsteps faded before digging through the trash. The deputy had carefully placed Sandy's cup of untouched, cold black coffee upright so it wouldn't spill. I set it on the empty desk, proof that we had been there. I wanted that room to seem changed by us.

Half an hour later, Polly and I found a 7-Eleven, where I was tempted to buy a hundred things. We settled on the smallest jar of peanut butter, a box of saltines, deodorant, a toothbrush and paste, two large bottles of Mylanta, and a disposable razor. I almost cried when the clerk said they didn't sell any shaving mirrors.

Polly stayed in the car with the motor running while I ran back inside the courthouse, high heels clicking on the polished floor. The fat dispatcher was sitting at his desk when I rushed in, out of breath and grinning. I pretended it had been arranged already, but the dispatcher was suspicious. He reached for his tobacco, tore off a strip, and stuffed it in his cheek. He removed each item from the bag and made two piles. "Don't allow no glass," he said, setting the peanut butter to one side. He dismissed the razor, the can of deodorant which might explode. He opened the Mylanta and took a sniff. "Just leave it all here," he said. "The sheriff will decide."

I didn't run out, but walked slowly through the domed entranceway. That was hopeful, I told myself, looking down the stairs at Polly, who waved and smiled from the car.

22

It was after five and we were hungry when we got back to the motel. The coffee shop had dark red carpeting, booths divided by plastic partitions designed like fake stained glass. I left Polly to order and went to look for Sandy's room.

It was upstairs, on the opposite side of the building from ours. I expected to find it sealed off by the police, but everything looked absolutely normal. The suitcase Sandy had bought for me before our aborted move to Rio lay open on the bed; his suit hung in the closet. The vanity held his bottle of Mylanta, a box of adhesives for his toupee. I felt like a thief collecting his belongings. Sandy's airline ticket lay in the drawer with his address book. I flipped through the book, calling cards dropping on the bed, Licenciado Campos, colonels, captains from the MFJP, four numbers for General Mendioleya on the back of a reporter's card from ABC. The last page of the book listed his informants through the years, with black lines crossed through several of them, "dec'd" written in Sandy's parochial script. Claude's name came last, numbers in Mexico City, Guadalajara, Cuernavaca, Acapulco, hotel rooms with extensions written down.

I'd never understood the risks. I had made up Sandy on midnight walks along the Sparkill creek, on all-night train trips through the south of Italy, when his real life was written out in the small black address book in his coat pocket. I'd never understood the risks. Too late now, I closed the book and stuck it in my purse like a souvenir.

The same headlines called out from the vending machine at the front desk. I put Sandy's key on the counter, explaining politely to the clerk that my husband had left on an emergency and had overpaid one day. The clerk checked his register, didn't blink or ask my name, we were that unimportant. He set twenty-four dollars and change on the counter without seeing me.

I should have looked irreparably different, change on my face, in my body, my walk, but there was nothing. It was the same when I was eighteen, the first time I'd had sex, afterward going shopping in the mall at Seven Corners with my mother. No change; she never even noticed. So this is it; after the warnings, the waiting, the lectures and advice, my own mother couldn't even tell. I'd been relieved then, too, yet sadly disappointed. Sandy and I were so small and unimportant. He could be sent away for years; no one would mind.

The gold plastic domes in the restaurant turned everything yellow. Polly had ordered steaks, two glasses of red wine. She was smiling and tried to cheer me up. "You won't believe the waitress. I asked for burgundy. She says, 'We don't have any burgundy, ma'am, just red or white.'" My Connecticut Polly, trying to sound like a dumb Texas broad, jangling her head.

"Listen, Polly," I said, "I'm going back to the room to try the lawyer. Maybe he could meet with me tonight."

I only had Gerry Goldstein's office number, which I tried on the off-chance he was working on a Sunday. I had a friend, a criminal lawyer in New York, who always worked weekends and nights. But when I rang Goldstein, there was no answer.

There were two Goldsteins listed in the phone book with the same work number. I wrote down both home numbers, tried them; no answer either place. I finally called Terry's public defender at home. Yes, he'd talked to Terry, he said. Yes, he'd read the morning and the evening papers. He'd help, any way he could. The case would be big in San Antonio, maybe even nationally—an alleged crooked cop was always news. He was convinced Gerry Goldstein was our best shot.

I tried the other numbers again with no results. I thought of calling the expensive lawyer in Houston, to see what he'd say. There was nothing to do but lie on the bed, staring at the nubby plaster on the ceiling. Sooner or later, I'd have to call my family. I was going to need their help. I'd probably have to borrow money. I would have to ask my mother to fly to Mexico and pick up David. Who could say how long it would take to arrange our shipment or to get Sandy out of jail? I thought of David and Concha, that song she had been singing, *"La chinita en el bosque, la chinita se perdio."*

Polly thought I was sleeping when she came back—my head on the pillow, my eyes closed. I wanted her there, but didn't want to talk. I wished she'd take a bath. It would have been nice to hear the water running. I almost said with my eyes closed, Please, Polly, go and take a bath, but she would have thought that I was crazy.

I opened my eyes, sat up, shook my head to say I hadn't reached the lawyer. "I think I'll take a bath," she said.

When she was in the bathroom with the door shut, I tried both Goldstein numbers again. Gerry wasn't home, but an older man answered at the other number.

I cleared my throat though my voice still trembled. "Mr. Goldstein?"

"Yes?"

"I'm trying to reach Gerald Goldstein and saw that you have the same business number. Perhaps you're related to him?"

"He's my son. May I help you?"

He sounded so confident and relaxed that I wished he were in the room with me. "I hope so. I have a terrible problem. I must reach your son."

"He's been in Austin for a trial but should be back by now, I think. Are you able to wait until tomorrow?"

He had a wonderful grandfatherly voice, stirring up images of white hair, of leather-bound books in a paneled study. I didn't want to say my husband was in jail. "It isn't me," I managed, "but my husband."

"Try to stay calm, miss," Mr. Goldstein said. "I wish I myself could help you, but I handle corporate problems. Your husband is in trouble?"

"Yes."

"And needs a criminal lawyer?"

I nodded as though he could see me.

"I know it's frightening, but you mustn't worry. I'm sure my son can help. He's very good."

I was crying. He tried to get off gently as if he knew. "Don't worry. There are usually solutions to these things. Just keep dialing my son. He should be home soon."

After Mr. Goldstein hung up, I didn't consider the call to my parents but simply gave their number to the operator. My mother answered, excited to hear from us, ready to let go with her best local gossip, which of her bridge cronies had the flu, how many seedlings my father had planted in the depths of their backyard. I cut her off before she could get started. "Is Dad there?"—businesslike and calm. "Yes," she said and went to find him.

It was a signal we both knew. I was seventeen again, the narrow road coated with oil, with the mist of summer rain. I pulled around the corner in their green Pontiac, saw the school bus, lights flashing at the bottom of the hill. I braked and jerked the wheel. It was like coasting on our old Flexible Flyer. I stared at the belly of the school bus, at the neighbors who came running from behind a barricade of trees. Knees were examined on the bus, shoulder blades, scraped cheeks. I was lucky, the policeman said when he arrived. He'd take me home, arrange to have the car towed. But no, I wanted my father, dark hair combed sleekly back, cigar tucked in his teeth. He parked at the top of the hill behind the traffic and came down slowly, hands stuffed resolutely in his pockets. No cause for alarm, nothing to get hysterical about. He smiled crookedly at the big cop. He might have slapped him on the back and got away with it or could have brought him home to supper. He circled the car imbedded in the bottom of the bus, pausing to rub the soles of his shoes on the oily blacktop. "Pretty damn slippery," he smiled at the cop. They toured the site, my father's face impassive, concentrating. He shook his head, kicked the oversized bus tires, as if his exaggerated gestures could excuse me. Once he'd answered the policeman's questions, he started slow and easy up the hill. I followed five or ten feet behind him, anticipating an awful lecture. On the front seat beside him, I banked my body against the door and pulled my knees up to my chin, trying to make myself small enough to disappear completely. We drove in silence farther and farther from the accident site. My father didn't look at me. Please, get it over with, I thought. I'd admit it was my fault. He pulled into our drive, shut off the engine, dropped his dead cigar in the clean ashtray. "No one was hurt," he muttered. That was all he said.

But it wouldn't be as painless this time, not after seeing Sandy at Kerr County Jail.

My father always said hello like he wasn't expecting much. He didn't like the telephone. I aimed my voice above his thick, white forelock.

"Dad, I have awful news," I said.

He listened. It must have been worse than his image of the school bus crashing, than the drive to the accident not knowing how bad it would be. He didn't ask why Sandy had been arrested. He didn't assume it was some clerical mistake. He believed me. I pictured him in the kitchen, the receiver in his right hand, his left hand balled up in his pocket, and his eyes on the pattern of their linoleum floor until finally I'd got it out.

"You call when you need us to get David. Give us enough advance notice to get the money." That was all he'd said. He didn't even ask if I wanted to speak to my mother again—as though he could protect her.

Smelling of sandalwood soap, Polly edged into the room like an intruder and slipped beneath the sheet.

I spent the night on the telephone. Poor Polly couldn't sleep. I called Marisa, who thought we were playing our annual joke. I called the waspy Houston lawyer, who said I should drive through the night to meet with him at 8 A.M., who'd charge two hundred dollars for the initial interview, thirty thousand dollars if he took the case, who said Sandy could end up in jail for fifteen years. I reached Gerry Goldstein at home at seven the following morning and arranged to meet him at his office in an hour.

Goldstein's office was on the twenty-ninth floor of the Tower Life Building, the tallest building in the city, according to his secretary. She greeted me like we were chums from college days. Diane with her blond hair, her toothy smile, sat behind a high-paneled counter decorated with cardboard pumpkins even though it was only October 8. Two days earlier I'd been as innocent as she.

The waiting room was comforting, like a soap opera set of a law office, exactly as it should have been. I wrapped the room around me, hid in one of the deep leather chairs, and ventured a thin smile at Polly. We'd be all right now.

There were voices coming from the corridor, one I was sure was Gerry Goldstein's. I wanted very much to like him. I was sure we'd understand each other, that he'd be nothing like that waspy Houston lawyer. Then there he was, walking his clients to the door, laughing fitfully with his suit coat open, his shirt dissheveled, slipping his hand inside the waistband of his blue wide-bottomed pants to tuck his shirttail in. The couple with him were tall, sleek, black. The woman looked like a model for an expensive glamour magazine. Goldstein was a full head shorter than the woman but held his ground. He opened the quiet oak doors for them. He said, "Hot damn." I wouldn't have been surprised to see him shove them gently with his heel.

His arms loose, eyes nervous, he looked at me and nodded. I watched him leaning on the counter where his secretary sat, head down on his arms while she read his messages and told him I was waiting.

He offered his hand a little disdainfully, I thought. "Come on in," he said, leading the way to his back office. I looked over my shoulder at Polly.

The room looked like him—books and papers in stacks on the floor and on the chairs. Before he even asked my name, the telephone was ringing. He rolled his eyes, dropped heavily into his swivel chair. Leaning back, with his feet on the desk, he was in deep conversation. I watched him draw black arrows on the top border of his legal pad, then run his fingers through his thinning, curly hair. He loosened his tie a little more.

I could see immediately how he saw me. He got off the phone, hands flat on the desk, shrugging his shoulders to apologize. He tried to focus on me while I told him about the arrest, the charges, Sandy's job, the lawyer in the ruffled shirt, everything I thought might matter. I watched him write me off—a drug agent's wife. He'd never approve. Ten minutes into my long saga, I wished I could run it backward, that I'd brought my curriculum vitae, a snapshot of my Virginia neighborhood. I thought of blurting out that I'd smoked dope and marched on Washington, that I carried in my head those *Life* magazine photos of napalmed babies, anything to make him believe in me.

He was thirty-five and full of swagger. He'd taken the Piedras Negras case *pro bono publico*, those American kids beaten down by macho Mexican feds while DEA agents stood idly by, filing their blunt white fingernails. His house was written up in *Texas Homes Magazine*, the brick exposed throughout, a wood-burning stove, barroom fans. If he seemed arrogant, he was right to be. He'd made his choices, adopted the good fight. His Bentley was downstairs in its private parking space. He didn't like me, didn't like even the idea of Sandy, but I couldn't stop hoping that on some fluke, he'd decide to take our case.

He asked if I'd made a commitment with the lawyers in Kerrville; I shook my head.

"The guy from McAllen is pretty good. I've worked with him before and wouldn't want to squeeze him out. In fact, he called about your husband's case. He wanted me to do the trial and split the fee."

I drew my shoulders back and looked Gerry Goldstein squarely in the eye. "It's Sandy's decision, not some deal between you and your friend."

That didn't please him. "I live here and work with these people. My relationship with them matters to me. It's a question of professional ethics." He doodled with his desk pen. He could have been a stand-up comic in a West Side bar on his way to the big time in Vegas, with that studied, casual sense of marking time. He stood, fiddled with the papers on his desk, looked down at his expensive watch.

I was furious and afraid I'd start to cry.

"Look, I'll be frank. I'd like to take the case. I'd like nothing better than to take a stab at the DEA, but it's not gonna be easy. You say the facts are unclear, complex. This Claude, this informant, what's in it for him to fuck your husband over? I'm not promising instant relief. You think the bond is a real fuck-up. It's common in this district, the judges think they've got a big drug case. Cocaine, a crooked cop—they ain't gonna give your husband away."

He shrugged. That's the way it is, sweetheart.

"So, if you want me, you handle the business with the other lawyers. Be discreet, a friendly call, a polite letter. We'll talk about a fee. I can be reasonable if you can. There's gonna be a lot of work involved."

I nodded; there wasn't much to say.

"It would help if you could stick around. With your husband out in Kerrville, they'll be a lot of legwork. You know some of the facts, the people involved, colleagues at your husband's office. You ain't gonna do anybody any good in Mexico. Don't get me wrong, I'm not advising you on personal matters, but it'd be easier on everyone involved if you were here."

He gathered up his papers, came out from behind his carved oak desk. His boots were laced with dust, scuffed at the toe to show he wore them everyday at home with old blue jeans. He expected me to follow him to the door as he tossed his closing comments over his shoulder. "I'm due in state court now, but I'll send my associate out to Kerrville with you if you're free. We'll interview Sandy, try to get down some facts. But like you said, it's Sandy's choice."

He was eager to get rid of me and stopped in the doorway of a small outside office. "Bobby, can you come here a minute?" he asked, shifting his weight from one leg to the other, chatting with Diane about his afternoon commitments, not bothering with me.

Bobby Ozer came out, looking rattled in his shirt sleeves, his wingtip shoes. He threw his head back to clear long, fine hairs from his eyes, dark nervous pools. He held his pen and his legal pad, which made it hard to shake his hands. I could have been his baby-sitter when he first learned to ride his new two-wheeler.

"Do you have a car?" he asked.

I nodded.

"Just let me clear some stuff off my desk." He was so distracted, I wanted to take care of him.

I made plans with Polly while waiting for Bobby to come back out. We'd drop her off at the shopping mall across from our motel; she'd take a cab home. She promised to look for a shaving mirror to give Sandy.

Bobby didn't even try to make small talk in the elevator. He stood in the corner, squaring the edges of his three legal pads. He'd brought four felt-tipped pens and an empty plastic folder. I couldn't quite imagine him interviewing Sandy. But I liked him, which was more than I could say for Gerry G.

It was easier in the car after Polly left. I turned on the radio, drove as if I'd been to Kerrville twenty times. We had a forced, friendly conversation with wide spaces in between. Bobby Ozer said he'd graduated from law school the year before, worked unhappily for a year as a prosecutor for the DA, and had come into his own with Gerry Goldstein. His heart fluttered writing briefs for Goldstein's civil liberties cases. Goldstein was his hero.

The drive was completely changed from the day before. I could pretend I was anyone with Bobby—his brother's girlfriend, an older sister. I liked everything he said and wasn't anxious to arrive. I wished we were headed for a laid-back country bar where we would swap college stories and sip beer. I was a safe bet for Bobby Ozer—sexless, ageless, spoken for. Until he met Sandy, he was safe for me.

23

Kerrville was alive that Monday morning, the parking spaces taken on the curb. We walked two blocks, past a hock shop, a western-gear store, a beauty shop called Betty's.

Bobby Ozer was so nervous that I tried to reassure him, it would be all right, Sandy would be nice. We waited in the corridor while the deputy went upstairs for Sandy. Sitting on the folding chair, I could feel myself coming down from the drive into that dark, gray hall with Bobby next to me, a good kid but still a stranger. I couldn't lean over in my metal chair to whisper in his ear, "Help me, Bobby." We were at some point of no return. I was about to give Bobby Ozer an irrevocable gift, hand him Sandy like a hot potato, like a broken wind-up toy. It was awful, waiting for the parade to start in those fold-up metal chairs. It couldn't work, couldn't come out right.

Ray Holliman, an older, gray-haired deputy, led Sandy down the corridor. Sandy didn't even notice us till I stood up. Ray Holliman gestured toward his office; Sandy shuffled in. "I think I'd better go in first," I said to Bobby.

Holliman closed the door and left us. We embraced. I hid my face in Sandy's shoulder. I couldn't look at him at all.

"They gave me the bag you left," he said.

"I'm glad."

"Who's out there?"

It was my entrance line, and I came on strong. "He works for Gerry Goldstein, the lawyer I told you about. If you want him, Goldstein's agreed to take the case. I think he's our best choice, Sandy. Those other two had already called him behind your back and offered the trial for half the fee. Anyway, the kid outside works for Goldstein. He's here to meet you, to start taking down the facts of the case. He's pretty nervous and young. I don't know if he's ever interviewed a client. He told me he's been working on briefs for Goldstein's CLU cases. His name is Bobby Ozer. I think you'll like him."

I finally pulled away and looked up. He was smiling a regular Sandy smile, which set me back. I'd believed that picture on the front page of the paper. I was as unfaithful as they come.

"What's so funny?"

"Nothing. You." He took my hands, then dropped them. "Worrying about that kid out there when we're in this mess. You don't understand it, do you? You still don't know what it means."

"I know some of it, that it was Claude. I know you didn't take a bribe, and that I never trusted DEA."

He broke away, pacing, ending by the window. I watched the slope of his back, his long waist. His body was so real. He stared out the window, at the mowed courthouse lawn in the sun.

"What will you do?" he asked. "If the worst happens, if the bond continues. Five hundred thousand dollars. I'll be stuck in here until the trial starts, which could be months away. That's not so bad, I guess. I suppose I'm guilty of some crime in DEA's eyes, a mistake in judgment, trusting Claude. Who'd believe I could feel sorry for him or understand his life? And it was worse than that, Joanne. I covered for him. I didn't turn him in when I realized what he'd done, because I felt sorry, but not just that, because it would undo all my work, ruin the case, humiliate me in the region. I bought his bait, he conned me after everything I knew about him. I wanted that Añez-Vaca case so bad that I could taste it. What have I done to you and David?"

He turned, looked at me. I couldn't take it.

"The bond will be reduced," I said, "you'll get out, there'll be a hearing—"

He covered his face with one hand, put the other up to stop me. "You'd better call that lawyer in," he said.

I wanted to leave after introducing Bobby, but Sandy looked so anxious that I stayed. I couldn't tolerate watching him behind the deputy's desk in that stuffy little room, looking like the oldest absentminded professor on sabbatical while Bobby sat across the desk furiously taking notes. So I took out my blue spiral notebook and started writing, too. Later, I found my notes matched perfectly with Bobby Ozer's. I couldn't have left out anything important, not this champion note taker from graduate school. My notes were always in demand—neat, well organized, underscored in red. Comprehensive as they were, they didn't help.

Claude had met Vierzon in Guadalajara before he was fitted with a listening device by the DEA's internal security section. There was no way to verify anything he had said, but supposedly he'd convinced Vierzon to purchase the cocaine in Mexico. The first big meeting was set up in Mexico City, with Añez-Vaca at the Fiesta Palace Hotel. Salvatore Bonanno appeared as Claude's boss. Campos was supposed to bring Añez-Vaca and make the introductions, then slip away. But this meeting was already the beginning of the end. Añez-Vaca was nervous about remaining at the table without his contact, Alfredo Campos, so both Claude and Campos remained. This was the first time that Claude and Campos laid eyes on each other. When they met again in Santa Cruz, Campos would become suspicious that Claude, too, worked for the DEA, but what could Sandy do about it? He thought it would be okay. Later, he would reassure Campos that Claude was a legitimate middleman, and neither informant would be any wiser. Besides, Claude worked hard at that hotel meeting with Vierzon. If Añez-Vaca actually dug in his heels and refused to transport the cocaine from Bolivia to Mexico, Claude would convince Vierzon to move it. As usual, Claude produced best out of need, and he was needy then. He was dead broke, in debt to his French Embassy friends. He had even bounced a check to Sandy's shopkeeping friend Helen Himmelfarb after selling her some jewelry months before to raise more cash. Sandy had been pissed off about the bounced check. He had trusted Claude to play it straight with his friends. Claude knew he was in hot water with Sandy, knew he couldn't go much longer without earning another big reward, so at the Fiesta Palace that afternoon he really danced. He finally convinced Vierzon to accompany him on a dry run of the Mexico–Bolivia–Mexico route.

There were too many names, I thought, too many spilling out too fast. I checked my spelling against Bobby's notes while Sandy went on to explain that everybody except himself ended in Santa Cruz together. Añez-Vaca insisted on Campos' presence, so he followed on a later flight. Claude and Vierzon traveled together, stopping over in Panama to meet Art Sedillo, the undercover DEA agent who pretended to be a crooked customs "guide" who would get them through Panamanian customs with their sample coming back. Añez-Vaca had agreed to advance a small sample to Vierzon and Claude, to prove the purity of his cocaine while they tested the route.

It felt like we had been writing for hours when a knock on the deputy's door interrupted us. "Shall we stop for now?" Bobby asked, and Sandy nodded. The sheriff came in. "Could you leave for a moment, ma'am?" he said to me.

I gathered up my notebook and looked back at Sandy, trying to say with my eyes that it would be all right, that I'd come back as soon as the sheriff would let me. I headed down the corridor and ended up alone in the main lobby. I sat on an empty wooden bench on the far side of the room, opened my notebook, and began reading my confusing notes. It sounded innocent enough to me, but what did I know about any of these cases? I was just a dumb girl who had spent her brief working career writing two-inch blurbs, but this wasn't anybody's fiction, this had happened. I tried to imagine what Claude had said to DEA security. Was the meeting in the Fiesta Palace part of the case he was making up? I was relieved to be let out of it, to be free for a while from the fear in Sandy's eyes. I had wanted out of Bolivia, out of that stuffy little room. Let them tell their boyish secrets, let Sandy and Bobby continue their Bolivian adventure, let them reconstruct the alleged crime, whatever it turned out to be. I didn't want to know it.

I closed the notebook and my eyes, listening to muted voices coming from upstairs. The jail was overhead. Strangers walked through the lobby on ordinary business, to register their cars or take their driving tests. Someone was probably getting married on another floor. Then suddenly, there were footsteps and voices at my side, coming at me: "Hello, Joanne."

Two DEA men from Mexico stood over me, the one whose wife had called to tell me the big news and the administrative officer who had said to get out of Mexico fast. They pulled up folding chairs and sat down, wearing their best funereal expressions. They could have been insurance agents, briefcases full of choice policies at their feet. I closed up, tucked myself in, as if they might attack, as if I'd committed some kind of crime. Guilt by association, guilty by my very presence. I didn't want them contaminating me.

The administrative officer just stared while the other agent did the talking. "We're here to give Sandy his suspension letter. It says he has thirty days to resign. If he doesn't, he'll be fired. When you see him, tell him it looks better if he resigns. It's much less damning if it comes from him."

I didn't answer. I just hugged my arms and waited. The three of us hung out until, finally, the sheriff came. He looked down at me while he talked to them: "You can try to see him, if you like."

I watched them at the opposite end of the hall: Bobby, Sandy, the men from the DEA, the deputy sheriffs. I could hear Bobby get hysterical. "As counsel," he was shouting, "I request protection for my client from these men." He shielded Sandy from them; he waved his arms. "He doesn't have to talk to them or see them." The taller agent tried reaching over Bobby, holding the suspension letter like a gun, trying to drop it on Sandy's person. They were like the Keystone Kops, like Saturday cartoons, that bunch of men.

"Don't touch anything, Sandy. Don't accept it," Bobby said. Sandy raised his arms, backed away.

I stood up, started taking little steps across the cavernous lobby, wider than RKO Keith's when I was ten. The agent trailed Sandy in and out of office doors, trying to grab him. He stopped dead in the hall and threw his hands up, looking to the sheriff for support.

I was next to the sheriff by then, so close we could have touched. "I guess nobody's got to talk to nobody," the sheriff said, "nobody's got to see who he don't want to see."

The sheriff took my arm lightly at the elbow, led me down the hall into Ray Holliman's office at the far corner of the building.

We let him place us, one by one. Sandy came into the room. The sheriff closed the connecting door to the dispatcher's office. He closed the door to the main hall. Sandy and I listened to the key in the locks.

We heard the agent saying, "I need to use your phone."

We heard Bobby pacing and the sheriff arguing with the administrative officer in the dispatcher's room. "This is absurd, this is bullshit," the man from the DEA was saying.

I took Sandy's hand, led him to a desk chair in the center of the room, sat down on his lap. I didn't look into his face but played with his chin with my fingernail. He'd nicked himself shaving with the throwaway razor. He had no mirror, after all. We were safe, locked in. We could have been in any kind of waiting place—a bus depot, Grand Central Station. I considered writing graffiti on the walls or laying myself out on the bare scratched desk to make love to Sandy. Or not to Sandy, but to that nicked chin, that wide-striped shirt that smelled like Sandy.

His voice came over me through smoke, through stale, burnt coffee, until I looked up from his chin to his lips, to those sad eyes. He wasn't looking at me but at the window.

"We were in San Antonio a year ago October," he said. "You'd come to get your leg checked after that infection. You were medically evacuated, remember? We stayed in the same Ramada Inn where you're staying now with Polly. An agent dropped us off in his service car, one of the agents who arrested me. You were at Fort Sam Houston two days, sure you had lupus, TB, or some other rare fatal disease. I think it was really the death of your love you were feeling.

"We'd left the baby home with Concha. Not even Claude could reach us. We were completely on our own, alone. It should have been so close, a new beginning. The first night, before your first appointment in the morning, we ate in a restaurant on River Walk. It was warm, we sat outside. The trees had small white lights wound in all their branches. I was thinking hard about that dinner last night in my room. I could almost smell the river. I should've reached across the table for your hand and told you everything that I was feeling. But I couldn't. You were wrapped up in your fear of dying. I was afraid of losing you. The next day it was too late. I walked you to the doctor's office, across those wide, grassy lawns on the base, thinking my job had ruined us. We didn't speak."

I put my hand on his lips. "Don't say it, don't." I got up and stood beside the window, smiling over my shoulder at him as if nothing were wrong. The windows were so ordinary; there were no bars on them. I reached for the sash, unlocked the bottom pane, raised it above my head. "Come and see," I said.

We looked out on the window well, on the courthouse lawn, waist-high. We could have reached out, picked clover from the grass. The sidewalk was beyond our view, below a neat stone wall. The street was quiet. No one would have even noticed a woman in a two-piece summer suit, a man in a toupee and shirt sleeves. We could have climbed circumspectly from the window well.

Outside the locked door the agent's voice was loud, insistent. "Dammit, Sheriff. The man's our employee. We have a right to talk to him."

"That's hardly an accurate appraisal," Bobby Ozer spat out. "You're his accusers. You'll see him in court."

I was offering a gift, I thought. One more step out of the ordinary; Sandy couldn't balk at that. It didn't matter anymore. I was offering the day—open, endless sky. It was just crossing one more invisible border. We could have one long October day to replace the one we'd wasted the year before, walk down to the river, back to the restaurant with its delicate white lights, retracing every mistaken step we'd ever made. We'd get another chance to reach across that outdoor table and do it right, at last.

I must have been joking; I couldn't have meant it. Except it made so much more sense than Claude and Campos, Vierzon and Añez, in Santa Cruz.

Sandy closed his eyes, shook his head. "No, no," he said, so serious and somber.

24

It was dark when we left the courthouse. Hours had passed since the DEA agents had slipped Sandy's suspension letter underneath the door and disappeared. Bobby and Sandy had talked, but I'd refused to listen. Sandy outlined the history of Claude Picault, as much as anybody knew. I was sick to death of Claude.

I drove the flashy rental car, but my eyes were barely open. Bobby was riding an adrenalin high and wanted to talk. "Let's stop," he said, "and get something to eat." Since he was in charge of Sandy's life, I tried to be obliging.

He gave directions to a place he knew, three rooms that looked like they were glued together. The bar was lit with neon advertising. The dining room was dark and smelled of grease. Bobby borrowed a match, lit the candle on the table. His eyes bobbed around the room by candlelight.

He ordered a beer, so I did, too. It didn't matter that I'd always hated beer. Bobby Ozer had become my leader. The dark room, the Texas drawls and laughter seemed unreal. I wanted to go home —to Mexico. At least in Mexico I'd begun to understand what was expected. I wanted to push back time, to be hanging in that empty sky with Polly on the seat beside me. Anything was better than landing in the dark, in a roadside joint in Texas.

Bobby jiggled his foot against the table leg and smiled. He'd just come down from his best pep rally, was anxious for the game to start. His button-down shirt was stained from perspiration. He'd caught a drop of saliva at the corner of his mouth.

The beer was heavy, sweet on Bobby's breath across the table when he began to speak excitedly. "It was a stall tactic, that's all. That's what Goldstein called it when I got him on the phone. But those DEA agents misjudged the situation. They thought they could push the sheriff around. It was great to watch him. He wasn't taking any shit."

"What did you think of Sandy?" I took another sip of beer and swirled it in my mouth, watching Bobby's face.

"It's going to be a tough case. Just the facts are confusing, and we don't have them all yet. I told Sandy I'd come back tomorrow. He wants you to be there, too."

"But how did he seem to you?"

"Scared."

"That's what worries me. It hasn't even started yet. How's he going to make it? Unless Goldstein can get him out of jail."

Bobby was arrogant and cocky. "He'll make it. He'll get used to it."

"What do you mean?"

"People adjust to situations. It's new to him now. He feels betrayed. He's still in shock. But he doesn't have it so bad. The sheriff is a decent guy, a redneck maybe, but rednecks have a lot of heart. They don't make him stay in his cell, they haven't stripped him of his stuff. They're impressed, feel sorry for him. They'll treat him right. It could be a hell of a lot worse, you know. He could be in Bexar County, where the jail really stinks. They do time in there for good. You have to harden up. Be realistic. You're soft and middle-class about this."

He ordered steak and salad. We agreed to split the bill. I waited for the mean-looking waitress to move off again with the smell of grease and Texas chili in her hair. The jukebox played country and western, sentimental stuff. Bobby was right. I was being soft and middle-class. I *was* soft and middle-class, and what was happening to Sandy shouldn't have been happening to me. I wanted my old self back in New York, in blue jeans and a scruffy shirt. Before I was anybody's wife. Before I was an embassy dependent. I wanted to be like Bobby Ozer, who was sure he knew the score.

I considered spilling my beer in pools on the plastic tablecloth or knocking over the basket of stale rolls. It wasn't fair. If I couldn't go back to New York and start over, I could at least be in Mexico again, playing at safe middle-class games that Bobby Ozer would disparage. I belonged in Mexico—*huera, gringa,* dumb. I wanted to be at dinner with General Mendioleya and his wife in my own house. The waiter we've rented wears a snow-white coat. The candles turn everything to amber. The general's small dark eyes are smiling at me. He has seen it all, *mi general,* more deception than Bobby Ozer could conceive. He saw the revolution, when they strung up the clergy by their heels, when the haciendas were razed and the lands divided. He might have been in the crowd at the railroad station when that famous photograph was shot: the young girl suspended between the cars of the train, her long black hair drawn away from her face by the wind. She's framed by soldiers in the windows of the railroad car, though she doesn't see them. She tries to keep her dress from clinging, holding on while the train lunges forward, searching the faces in the crowd for someone that she's left behind.

I wanted to explain the general to Bobby before his steak and salad arrived. General Mendioleya would understand. He looked on Sandy as a son. I would call him myself when I returned to Mexico. But then the actuality began sinking in. What could the general do for us now? He had no files on Claude, Campos, Añez, or Vierzon. The DEA kept its files under lock and key and did not share the information in them with the Mexican authorities. The DEA must have planned the case on Sandy to outfox the general with his Mexican connections. They had known all along that Sandy was diplomatically immune in Mexico, and so had set up the case to end in San Antonio where the judges were rock hard. Claude had intentionally drawn Sandy to San Antonio. It had all been worked out carefully.

Much later we would learn that the DEA had counted on Claude to know Sandy's every move—when he was leaving for an arraignment in Chicago, when he was going to San Antonio to see the specialist who shot him up with cortisone in a last-ditch effort to save his hair. At the Kerr County Courthouse Sandy had made much of Claude's last trip to Canada to see another prospective buyer for Añez-Vaca's load, a man named Alain Chaillou, whom Sandy hadn't met yet. Alain was documented in the official case report, according to Sandy. It had all gone through DEA channels. But how were we supposed to get hold of the DEA's reports? Not through General Mendioleya or through Jacques Kiere. "There's something suspicious about the meeting in Canada," Sandy kept repeating, as if he expected us to find out.

We were limited by Sandy's understanding of the facts. In the last week of September 1978, he was about to leave for Chicago. It was peculiar, he must have thought, Claude's sudden, urgent call. But then again, it wasn't so unusual. Claude stopped over in Chicago en route to Mexico after meeting Chaillou in Montreal. It was a scheduled stop on the flight to Mexico from Canada. "Sandí," Claude says by telephone, boldly calling the Chicago courthouse where Sandy is appearing before the grand jury in another case. "Can you come to the airport to meet with me? I need your help. I want to report on my meeting with Alain." That much Sandy clearly understood. It was annoying. It pissed him off, more demands to hold Claude's hand. But of course, he went. "I'll be there," he said, "when we break for lunch."

Claude was in the terminal, tense and breathless. "I need a favor from you. I have some money here. I can't take it to Mexico—the girl will find it. She searches my clothes, the car, the apartment. What's worse, I'll give it to her if she asks. I always do. You understand? I can't afford to give away my money. Will you keep it for me?"

Claude handed Sandy an airline envelope with four thousand dollars cash enclosed, and Sandy took it. Later we would learn that DEA agents on surveillance saw this exchange from their hiding places, out of earshot, out of sight. They had carefully wired Claude for this crucial conversation, though later when they went to play the tape recording, they would discover that the cable attached to Claude's waist had "mysteriously" come unplugged.

But as Bobby and I sat together in the restaurant, we didn't know any of the facts about Sandy and Claude's Chicago meeting. I knew only that the general couldn't help. Bobby's steak arrived. We set our notes on empty chairs beside us. We were ignorant about that meeting in Chicago, ignorant of the DEA's case within a case. There wasn't even an indictment yet. The charges against Sandy weren't yet formal.

I watched Bobby cut his meat as I drank my beer to the foam in the bottom of the glass.

"I didn't mean to be so hard on you," said Bobby.

"I asked for it, I guess."

"This won't be any picnic, but don't get discouraged. Goldstein is amazing in the courtroom. He comes on with both guns, it's like a barroom brawl—the hottest game in town."

"I just can't believe this is happening to Sandy."

Bobby wiped his mouth and shrugged. "He believed in his job. He thought he was doing the right thing, making the kind of cases they wanted. Everybody secretly wants to be a star. Sandy was out to be the star of the DEA in Mexico. You shouldn't blame him. He just picked the wrong agency, the wrong informant. Everybody makes some wrong moves. He broke away from the team, and now they want to bench him."

"What will happen, Bobby?"

"I don't know. You never know. Goldstein says going to trial is like shooting craps. It depends on the docket, which judge gets the case, who's on the jury. We haven't seen an indictment yet. It depends on the government and how they decide to play it. The prosecutors might fuck up. They might put Campos on the stand. The judge would split his spleen at the idea of Campos, an attorney stooling on his clients, buying every case in court." Bobby's eyes lit up. "Even I could tackle Campos on the stand. Or Claude. Wouldn't Goldstein do a job on Claude. . . ."

The empty beer glass sat on the table with the tinny flatware and the paper napkin at my place. There was laughter coming from the bar in the other room. Going to trial was like shooting craps. A roll of the dice. A matter of luck.

"But until the trial, what happens? Sandy stays in jail?"

"Maybe, maybe not. We have a shot to have the bond reduced."

"But nobody's proven anything against him. He isn't supposed to be treated like he's guilty."

Bobby jabbed the piece of steak left on his plate and looked at me. "That's what they want you to believe. But that's not the way this game is played."

25

Sandy continued his story at the courthouse the next day in that same smoky room. It was horrible to watch him in his crooked toupee and dirty shirt. It didn't make sense that I couldn't bring clean clothes for him.

"Everything went the way we planned. I got a call from Claude at home late at night during carnival. The next day at noon the agent called from Panama. They got through customs without a hitch. The agent played a crooked customs agent who spent the night in their hotel with them to 'protect' the stuff. The agent said they were on their way. I notified General Mendioleya that the sample was coming, asked if he wanted his men at the airport when it arrived. We'd have our own men on surveillance, too.

"It was a mess at the airport. They'd changed the international arrival gate because of some construction. Campos was supposed to show his face, to show Vierzon that we were thick with Añez-Vaca's Mexican contact. He was late and came in just as Claude and Vierzon appeared. Vierzon was grinning, couldn't believe how easy it was. He came through the gate arm in arm with Claude, full of plans to leave for Guadalajara right away and call his French associate to make sure they'd be ready with the money when the big load traveled. Claude, Campos, and I walked him to the gate to catch the next flight to Guadalajara. I was nervous that Campos came along, but I didn't want to make much of it when Vierzon was there. Besides, it was looking good. Vierzon couldn't get over Santa Cruz, the great time he'd had with Claude, the ease of doing business."

"In other words," said Bobby, "he bought the bait?"

"Completely. Campos left as soon as Vierzon had boarded to call Añez and report the safe arrival of the goods. Claude and I walked back to the parking lot. We had two men waiting. We didn't need a big backup team, since there wasn't going to be an arrest. He opened his suitcase and took out the plastic bag with the sample. One of the agents checked the purity and took charge of the bag. Claude was staying overnight in Mexico City before returning to Guadalajara in the morning. I gave him a ride into town, and that was when he told me."

"So the agents went back to the embassy with the dope, and you and Claude were alone?" Bobby was stronger now, carefully sorting out the facts.

Sandy nodded, looking from Bobby back to me. I could tell he didn't want to go on late that Tuesday afternoon, but if he wanted me to be there, he didn't have much choice. Polly and I had reservations at eight o'clock the next morning. We were already behind schedule. Dan had panicked when Polly called to ask him for one more day, one more meeting between Sandy and me. Really, there was no reason why I had to be there. I couldn't help. I didn't need to know all this.

Sandy played with the corners of a sheet of legal paper, creasing them over and over until they fell apart. "His tote bag lay between us on the front seat," he finally went on. "He hadn't checked it with his other luggage. There was nothing suspicious in that. He always carried the shoulder bag when he traveled. We went by way of the Viaducto from the airport. The traffic was heavy, backed up before the entrance to one of the tunnels. I had the windows closed because of the pollution. Claude said he had to advise Añez that he'd arrived. I said it wasn't necessary, that Campos would tell Añez everything was fine. Claude said no, because Campos didn't understand the real situation. I looked at him, slumped down on the seat so he could stretch his bad leg out. He didn't face me. He said he had brought back more than just a sample. Añez had advanced him two kilos. He touched the satchel between us on the seat."

"He hadn't paid Añez for the two kilos?" Bobby asked.

"No," Sandy said flatly. "Claude said he hadn't asked for it. He wasn't prepared. He didn't have any money, but they had been out drinking one night. There was music. The bar was loud and crowded. Añez had been bragging that he kept a cache of cocaine like a kitchen maid kept soap powder. He could get his hands on as many kilos as he wanted, any time of day. A few grams, a few kilos, it didn't matter. Let Vierzon see what real powder was like. Let him show his men in France that the Bolivians could deliver. Let Claude really test the security of the route. Anybody could make it through with twenty-five grams, he wouldn't trust any route with that. The real trick was to carry out more than a kilo."

Sandy looked at me so intensely, I felt my left eye begin to quiver. He was pretending to be Claude. " 'You see,' Claude said, 'Añez wasn't drunk. He wasn't bragging. He was testing me.' "

I hated hearing Sandy repeat Claude's words and look at me that way, as if he were Claude, as if he could ever be like Claude. He must have seen the revulsion in my face, or noticed the way my eyelid trembled, because he looked down and continued ripping his sheet of paper until he'd made a pile of confetti on the table. Finally, he turned to Bobby. "I didn't know what to do. I didn't have any way to seize the cocaine in the car, with nobody around to verify my actions. Claude could have said anything he wanted if I turned him in. I couldn't believe he had gotten in so tight with Añez-Vaca. Campos had said that Añez was losing interest, that he hadn't approved of Claude and Vierzon throwing themselves around Santa Cruz. But if Claude *had* somehow conned him into fronting the dope, then Añez was ours. He'd make the runs now, once he knew the two kilos had safely arrived. And I would have him. Don't you see, I needed that case? Then in comes Claude with his private stash, and when I looked at him, all I could see was the whole case crashing."

Sandy turned to me again. "You were in Washington, Joanne. You were going to leave me. Oh, maybe not yet. I knew you'd come back from that particular trip. I'd worked so hard fixing up the house, but it was over. We both knew. It was crazy, but I thought making this case could change something. After a case like that, I could afford to coast awhile. I'd take some medical leave—I had eight hundred hours or more I'd never used. I'd spend all the time I could with you and David, take care of myself, for once. With a case like that for ammunition, Jacques would have to let me go."

His voice dropped lower. "I should have busted Claude right on the spot. I could have driven him to the embassy and dumped his tote on Jacques Kiere's desk. But if I seized the two kilos, it wouldn't have been just the end of Claude. I'd have lost Vierzon, Añez, everything. Claude would go to jail, and all the work I'd wrecked myself for would have been for nothing. It had been a terrible year. I could see myself becoming a ruined old man—my hair had started falling out, I'd lost weight, my stomach kept me awake all night. All of it for nothing. How would it look when the MFJP found out? Or the ambassador?"

He looked back and forth between me and Bobby as though we really could have answered him. He shook his head. "The State Department would have gotten exactly what they wanted if I turned Claude in—a scandal. They'd say DEA couldn't even control its own informants. I wanted to grab Claude and take him apart piece by piece, right there in the car, but he had it all worked out. We didn't have to lose the case, he said. Añez was coming to Mexico City in two days for his money. He wanted twenty thousand dollars for the two kilos, then he would organize the big load. Claude said 'twenty thousand dollars,' and my stomach dropped. 'No, no, Sandí, listen,' Claude said. He could have it all sewn up tight with Añez by then. Claude planned to place the coke with Asaf y Bala, just as Añez wanted. He'd take the chance, make the first contact. Then Añez himself would go to the prison, see his father, give Asaf y Bala the high sign. Añez would get his money, Claude could pay his debts, DEA would get its case. He said he'd worked other cases like this in France and Montreal with DEA, that we could sidestep all the bullshit channels—it was done all the time—that he was just paving the way before the big load came down. Añez could provide enough for Vierzon in France and Alain Chaillou in Montreal. The bigger the case the better.

"I told him to shut the fuck up, that I didn't want to hear it. I needed to think how to make it all right, how to get it through DEA after all. I went on driving, wouldn't talk. At his friend Dédé's house where he was staying, I told him he'd be lucky if I didn't haul him in this time, that this better be the only time he'd made his own plans. He had his tote bag on his shoulder like a hundred times before. I never even saw the coke."

I watched Bobby lean across the table, his felt-tip marker in his hand. I wanted to excuse myself before he spoke, to be where their mouths moved, but there was no sound. I stood up. "Let's stop now, okay?"

"No, we're not stopping," Bobby said. "We have to get through it all once today. I still don't understand how Campos fits. He didn't know about the two kilos? He still thought Claude had just brought in the sample?"

But Sandy wasn't listening to Bobby.

"You see it now, don't you?" he asked, as if Bobby weren't there. "He sold the dope for Añez, and I didn't stop him. I let him walk."

"Go ahead, tell Bobby. I can sit in the hall until you're done."

"No. I want you to stay. You can't make a decision without hearing this."

"I have no decisions to make," I said, but I sat and heard how Campos called Añez, found out about the two kilos. Campos wanted in. After all, Añez was *his* find, Asaf y Bala and his brother were his sources. He found out Claude's number in Guadalajara through Añez. It was easy. He called Claude direct. He threatened him, unless Campos were cut in on the coke, he'd blow Claude wide open and stool to Añez.

It was ugly, how the daylight faded in the sheriff's office, the stale smell of smoke, our bodies closed in. Bobby flicked his hair out of his eyes over and over as he wrote. Sandy folded an empty matchbook cover to shovel up his pile of confetti and dump it in the trash. It was five o'clock. It was a quarter to seven. I watched the cars one by one as they left the parking lot. The overhead light was harsh and yellow. Sandy kept going: "I figured Campos knew about the two kilos, but I wasn't sure. He never mentioned it. I never actually saw him with Claude, but they bitched to me about each other. They blamed any stalls in the case on the other fucking

up. Añez came to Mexico. I didn't see him. Claude swore he gave one kilo back. I assume he got his money from the other kilo. He never told me, just kept saying not to worry. The big load would move as planned in April. By April, it would all be over. . . ."
I couldn't stay. It was dark out, my stomach ached. Polly would be waiting, packed, impatient. There was so much to do before our early morning flight. I tuned out the tremor in Sandy's voice, opened the door to the outside corridor. They didn't stop; Sandy kept on talking. But I'd have to wait for Bobby. I paced the halls, shoes clicking. That was when I met Deputy Ray Holliman under the dome, when he gave me his wrinkled handkerchief, his calling card with the sheriff's star printed in blue, and put his arms around my shoulder like I was anybody's pathetic lost kid.

26

It was nine o'clock when I dropped Bobby off at the office. He drew me a map of the shortest route back to the motel, said he was tired and wanted a shower, but he was pleased to begin understanding the vague outlines of the case.

I watched the Tower Life Building recede through the rearview mirror, past the dome from the old world's fair, the Hilton where Sandy had been arrested, then the city was behind me, lost in trees. The expressway was empty. I could recognize some of the street names on the exit signs.

Polly's dinner tray was outside the door of our room. She was in her nightgown, reading on the bed. She'd taken my messages like an efficient secretary. Terry had called, Sandy's sister, my father. Goldstein left his message at eight forty-five. I took off my shoes, lay down on the flowered spread, stared at our packed bags parked neatly by the door. I listened to Polly on the phone to the front desk. "We'll be checking out tomorrow," she was saying. "We have an early flight and need a wake-up call at six." She set the phone down, clicked off the lamp between the beds. I listened to her pull down the covers and fit herself between the sheets.

"I spoke to Dan again," she said. "The packers are finished. They'll be loading the truck tomorrow."

I stared at the ugly floral spread beneath me. "Good. You'll leave on schedule then."

"He sounded so upset that we didn't make our flight. He's checking into a hotel with the kids tonight. They're nervous I won't get back in time."

"It's understandable, the move and all."

"Yes, I suppose." She paused, her voice already thick with sleep. "I bet you'd feel better if you took a hot bath."

I didn't answer, but I rolled over, got up. Polly's face was buried in the pillow. I turned off the light in the dressing room, shut the bathroom door behind me. The heat lamp turned everything red: the hollows underneath my eyes, the washcloths hanging on the rack by the sink, the unused roll of toilet paper. I ran the water. Polly had left my nightgown folded on the toilet seat.

It had been easy avoiding a messy farewell, at opposite ends of that long dark hall. Bobby came out first, his legal pad hanging from one hand. Sandy waited by the door for me. I was the one who was supposed to make a move, out of love and understanding.

The bath was hot. The fan went on. The heat lamp was at my back with the water rising.

It had been easy not to move. I couldn't see his eyes, just the deep shadows cutting his face like scars. I was supposed to have held back like a new, shy lover, no endearments, no embrace, trusting Ray and Bobby to play their parts. Bobby stopped midway between us, flattened himself against the wall. Ray Holliman stepped back. It was supposed to be a dramatic, classy moment, the sound of our heels in a quickening pace. He'd lift me up. We would be lost in shadows.

The water found its level on my breasts. My kneecaps turned red from the heat of the water, from the filter on the lamp.

But I hadn't moved. The three of them waited, counting on me not to let them down. Three minutes, maybe five, then it was over. Ray Holliman's discomfort was written on his face. He shuffled down the hall to Sandy, drew Bobby along with a hand on his back.

"Been a long day, hasn't it?" he said. "You men need another cup of coffee." Sandy stared at me. I cocked my head, waved, shoved the blue spiral notebook in my bag. I'll call, I might have said and let it echo.

I was underwater when the phone rang. It would be my father

or Gerry Goldstein calling back. I rose, water dripping, and grabbed a towel. Three rings, a fourth, a sleepy moan from Polly. I felt my way by the light of the heat lamp, turning the room to spoiled wine. I was old and flabby, slippery and comic, netting the phone on the fifth ring. "Hello?" "Joanne?" It was Sandy.

"Will you drive out? I've asked the deputy, he says it's okay. He'll let you in."

"It's almost eleven o'clock," I said. "The drive will take an hour—"

"I know. It's important. I need to see you."

I turned on the bedside lamp. Polly rolled over, blue eyes open. I hid beneath the sheets. "All right," I said, tucking the bedclothes underneath my arms. "All right," and then we hung up.

I didn't want to get up with Polly watching. Maybe she realized, because she turned over, covered her head. From my suitcase by the door I pulled out the first things I could find: a sweater, a pair of summer slacks whose hem was coming down. I put them on quickly, not bothering with underwear.

"What are you doing?" Polly asked, sitting up.

"I'm going back to Kerrville. That was Sandy."

"Do you realize what time it is?"

I nodded.

"Then I'm going with you."

We were getting good at that drive without any words. It was like the last tired shuttle to New York, like carpooling to the farthest suburb. Polly laid her head back, closed her eyes. There were a thousand stars, no traffic. I could feel myself working up to a real confrontation, the anger easier than pain. Traitor, I'd call him, fool. I made my moves through those limestone cliffs, reviewing the case from a domestic standpoint. Forget Añez and Vierzon. It was Claude coming courting. Claude in a tightly woven sweater, in expensive leather clogs, his stiff leg out for pity. We might have been part of a small French film with our twisted *ménage à trois*. Luncheons on the terrace, the backs of the chairs holding the sun. Pâté de foie gras and caviar over whispered conversations. I had only walk-on parts in the shadows of deep green lawns. The real focus, all the movement, lay in the balance of those two men, perfect foils, completely different, yet somehow the same. In one rich lawn or another, during one or another smuggled-in French meal, I'd lost my Sandy from the third-floor landing on Eighteenth Street. This one in a soiled striped shirt, with his toupee and tremor, had been conjured up by Claude.

Claude must be played exactly right for the scene to work. He can't be seen as all bad. In another language, from a distance, he looks sad. He's generous with parties, with spectacles, with gifts. They win him sympathy because they never do him any good. He's every woman's patsy. He fails buying friendships, buying love. He gave me a narrow, hammered gold collar when I delivered my first son. I couldn't give it back. "It's worthless," he said. "I had it melted down from an old bracelet I never wore. You can't insult me by saying no." He is the type who hangs on the insult of each rejection.

He must be seen in search of bodyguards and heroes. He lives on the edge, takes great risks for money which he throws away on anyone.

He plays Sandy as his find, his father or big brother. This is where the story turns, where the scene gets murky.

My hands tightened on the wheel: What did he really want from us? Sandy was just another target, another case, another fat reward. If he was more, he was the finest feather in Claude's cap, his last case in Mexico, his most decorated sucker.

We drove past a lit-up Holiday Inn off the interstate. The marquee said Happy Anniversary to Peg and Jim, but the parking lot was empty.

Ray Holliman was waiting at the courthouse door. "I made a fresh pot of coffee for you. Have some while I go bring your husband down."

Polly took a cup and waited on the bench beneath the dome. I sat outside the dispatcher's office. Sandy appeared. He'd taken off his toupee. I followed him into Holliman's office, where he locked the door by pushing in the button on the knob. It couldn't do us any good, such a tinny lock on a jailroom door. Sandy waited for Holliman's footsteps to fade. He leaned against the door frame, flicked off the light.

"I'm sorry to have called so late," he said without looking. "I had to see you. It was awful when you left."

"That was my fault. I should apologize."

"There was so much I wanted to say, but it was impossible with Bobby here. I thought we'd have time alone when I finished with him. Then you were gone."

"I couldn't listen any longer."

Still not facing me, he turned, ran his hand up and down the door frame. "You think this Goldstein is the right man?"

"I think so. You might not like him at first. I didn't, but they say he's the best, and it looks like you're going to need the best."

"You hated it today, didn't you?"

"What can I say? That it was fun? That I'm glad this happened? I hate seeing you here, how sad you look. I hate to think what it may be like before it's over."

He kept sanding the door with the heel of his palm. "You ought to hate me. I did this to us. I ruined everything for myself, for you and David."

I considered walking across the room, slapping him across the face for getting in so deep with Claude, and hated myself. He was like an old balloon when the air is seeping out. He hadn't meant it to be like this. He'd pictured the case coming down around him. He'd imagined everything changing once he'd saved his case as he'd imagined everything changing each time we moved. He was all I'd ever wanted, my romantic Sandy. I kept my hands flat on the desktop, my voice clear.

"We can't talk like this, not now. I'll walk out again. I won't listen."

He dropped his hand and turned. With his patchy baldness in the patchy shadows of the room, he was the oldest man I'd ever seen. If he started toward me, I'd back away. I wouldn't let him touch me, bare breasts on wool. I didn't love him, hadn't loved him since New York, I told myself. He'd tricked me into marriage with his promises. He had conned me. He was just like Claude, and I'd have told him so right then, except he kept coming closer with his eyes above me reflecting that row of streetlamps down that dark, empty street. I could see the ridges in his face deepening as he deflated. He was bearing down, holding tight. He kissed me:

stale smoke, burnt coffee, the echo of footsteps down a marble hall.

It was wrong, reaching out, pressing back, but I recognized his hands on me, could close my eyes and see him naked as I had a thousand times before. I knew the slope of his back, the line of his legs, his hard buttocks. I saw his walk in David's. That was worth something, a caress, an embrace, half felt, half made in anger. I leaned into him, my forehead against his chest. He touched my back all over. His damp, cold hands reached for my bra that wasn't there. His fingers were like spiders up my neck, across my belly, on my breasts.

He pressed his mouth against my hair, kissed my ear, whispered, "Don't leave me, please."

"I won't," I said.

He slipped his hands from underneath my sweater and placed them on my shoulders. I had to strain to understand him. "I'm not bad. I'm not a criminal. I wasn't moving dope. I was only trying to save a case that mattered, to make things right again in my job, with us. I was terrified that you would leave. I don't understand this thing, Joanne. I don't know what's happening to me."

"Please don't, Sandy."

"You'll leave tomorrow. You have to go back, I know that. This is my last chance to explain. After that first trip, Claude had me. I wanted to tell you, but I was afraid. I was sure then you'd really go. You warned me, you knew he was all over me. When you were in the States, it was much worse. He called all the time, was in touch with Añez behind my back. I lost control of him completely. He knew he had me, that I couldn't do a thing once I'd let the sample pass. He would have turned me in. He could have told them anything he wanted. He kept me dangling with the case. He kept saying nothing had changed, that it would go down as I'd planned it from the start. . . .

"At night I sit up there listening to the drunk in the next cell. I hear a car drive by on the street and wonder if it's you. Music on the guard's radio reminds me, everything reminds me. I know it's crazy, it's the middle of the night, but I can't stop myself. I think maybe you've found out something, that DEA has changed its mind. They've decided to call the whole thing off, they've reviewed my record, the case file, the informant's file when they check on Claude. Or maybe Claude has changed his mind and can't go through with it. After all I've done for him, he repents and tells them how it really happened. They'd believe him, funny isn't it? They'd believe him, a crook, a stool, when they wouldn't believe the same from me. And they know me. Jesus, Jacques Kiere knows me, Garibotto knows me. What about Marta, my own secretary? Why doesn't she tell them what it was like, locked in that office like a prison cell? When the others would disappear in the Jorongo Bar for a few shots, but not me. I had what I wanted, had it there, right in my hands. I was out to make up for all the time I'd wasted, all those years when I lived like Claude, from one city to another, changing hotels in the middle of the night, leaving clothes behind, paying bills for rented TVs and plastic couches.

"I couldn't stand Claude's rooms in Guadalajara or Cuernavaca. They were too familiar, those depressing photographs of his latest girl pasted on the walls to make it seem he had somebody, like he was home. That's why I couldn't throw him out. I knew what he was, what his life was. He used everybody, everybody used him. I remember Paris, when there was nothing to do except write another report, make another meet. I used to make things happen to escape my rooms. I used to really push, to push my luck just to make it clear what I was doing there. Still, weeks would pass when nothing happened. Carmen was out visiting her niece, Roger Lanz was in another city. I used to walk by the embassy sometimes, to pretend that I belonged. Once I walked by with Carmen, you know, as a joke. I'd planned it with Kiere. He had the secretaries behind the curtain at the window, watching."

His voice hurt my ear. My collarbone ached from his hands pressing down. I held him around the waist, gently tugged until we were sitting on the floor together, his head resting on my summer checkered pants.

"When we found each other in New York," he said, "I thought everything had changed. I'd been depressed. The case in Paris was winding down, ending like so much nothingness. My briefcase was filled with used-up airline tickets, Paris–New York, New York–Paris. Some nights I couldn't remember where I was. I'd wake myself up, talking so loudly in my sleep in English or French, terrified I'd said something wrong that somebody would hear. Claude knew exactly what that was like. Every place I found myself was wrong, the cabaret in Montmartre, the U.S. attorney's office in New York, my wife's house in Washington. I was so unhappy in that house. I'd sleep on a chair all night in front of the TV and hate myself, but my kids were there. They were all I had outside my work. Until you. With you I thought I'd changed all that."

I stroked his hair, or what was left of it. Whenever we touched, more of him fell out. He was Claude's straw man, coming undone beneath my fingertips in the dark, in Deputy Sheriff Holliman's office.

Sandy, I should have said, unzipping my pants, slipping the scratchy sweater over my head. No one would have seen us. No one would have known. We were flat and spare beneath the window ledges. A face at the window would never even have guessed. We were part of the furnishings, the desk, the file cabinets. The streetlamps cast shadows on us on the floor. We could have made love and distinguished ourselves from the shadows.

I should have, but I couldn't. I pushed myself back, a fraction, an inch. I held Sandy's head gently in my arms. We were not ourselves. I had no feelings for that altogether other woman, that altogether other man in the dark, in Deputy Sheriff Holliman's office.

The woman is rumpled, unkempt. Her heel catches in her hem and pulls it down. She's perspiring. She expects to pick that fellow up in pieces and put him back together. But see him through the shadows: The lamplight glints off patches of white scalp. He holds her down. The muscles in his neck are working. His voice is relentless, absolutely clear. It's the strain of making out his image in the dark that makes his European accent sound so grating.

"No, don't get up," he says. "Not yet. We were so happy in New York. I was—completely happy. You must remember, now that it's over and nothing can be done. It doesn't matter what the charges are, no one will believe me. But you must admit how much it meant. We were on top of something. We could have started over as we said. What went wrong? I need to understand. You must explain. I lost myself in Mexico. How? I've tried so hard to understand what went wrong."

He grabs her wrist in one hand, her brittle bones. She can't explain, she doesn't understand. She wants to pull away but cannot risk it, snapping like a twig on the courthouse lawn. If she shuts her eyes, she can almost hear her own bones breaking in the dark.

27

"That's impossible," Polly kept saying to the ticket agent as she leaned her elbows on the high counter, glaring at him. Our flight had left an hour early because of an air controller's strike in Mexico. The remaining flights were booked solid two days running, every available seat preempted by travel agents en route to an international convention in Acapulco.

"I want to speak to the manager," Polly said, hauling out her big guns. The vice president of American Airlines in Mexico City was another one of Polly's friends.

We were treated like VIPs when we touched down in Mexico City. Polly's friend sent his limousine to meet us.

When we drove up outside my house, nothing seemed to have changed. Polly got out to hug me at the gate. "I'll call with the number at our hotel. Try not to worry. Dan and I may have to leave, but we won't abandon you." Then she disappeared in the back of that big black car and the driver carried her away.

The front hall smelled of wax. The living-room doors were closed. I dropped my suitcase in the kitchen, put the kettle on the stove. I didn't call to check on David or the embassy or my parents in D.C.

I grabbed a pen and paper, sat at the dining-room table, drew four columns on the top sheet of the pad: to sell, to ship by air, to ship by truck, to take to San Antonio. But I didn't catalog a single object. I had no idea what I might need, what to dump. Where would I send the shipments? To my mother's?

I decided to look for Sandy's box of clippings from old cases. Those I would take to Gerry Goldstein to prove who Sandy was. Somewhere there were diaries from his cases in Detroit, Miami, Paris, New York. The carton was in the storage closet with the vacuum cleaner. I dragged it to the kitchen, made some tea before the water boiled down.

There were three diaries dated 1972, 1973, 1974. I laid them on the tea tray and went upstairs to look for Sandy's photo albums. The leaves of the rubber trees tapped on the casement windows in our room. It had begun to rain.

There were loose papers folded in the pages of the diaries, a creased black-and-white photo of Sandy and Carmen at the bar of Le Gavroche, the walls behind them hung with drawings of real *gavroches,* street kids who'd run underground messages in Paris during the war, boys like Jo Attia had been, *niños perdidos,* alone and tough. Jo Attia smiled up at me when he was twenty, dressed in satin boxing shorts, a towel flung over his shoulder. There was a glossy article about him from an old French magazine, neatly stapled together by Sandy: *"Jo Attia, dit Jojo-le-Moko, est le truand le plus célèbre de France."* I worked my way through the pages slowly: Jo Attia the most famous crook in France, romantic antihero of the French press, of the people, born Joseph Victor Brahmin Attia near Rennes in 1916. The article was a pop psychology treatment of Jo's life in crime—in an orphanage when he was six, in jail at seventeen. He'd learned to box in prison, was the star attraction, a war hero at nineteen, a fighter, Jojo-le-Moko, Jojo-le-boxeur, Jojo-le-Tunisien. Attia didn't give up when they threw him in prison; Attia came out fighting.

I set the papers on the couch and flipped through the diary entries. "August 23, Paris, France. 8–10 A.M., at my residence, no activity. 1:30—lunch with Nicole Attia at Chez Bichette, 7:00—Le Gavroche, meet with Carmen re shipment through Madrid. Details of activities, expenditures, filed separately with the Paris Regional Office."

Where did he keep his diaries when he lived on Rue Joseph de Maistre? I flipped back a few pages: "July 18, New York City. 7:00

A.M.—on duty, awaiting call from CI—# in file. 7:35 A.M.—observed dark blue Cadillac Eldorado custom convertible, D.C. lic. 892-270, on 1st Ave. & 63rd St. 10:15 A.M.—in conf. w/ Asst. U.S. Atty. Rudolph Giuliani re Peraffo & D'Ambrosio." He sounded worried about that Cadillac convertible. Why hadn't he ever sounded worried with me? I closed the diary, set it on the coffee table.

I didn't have much time. I had to collect David, call the embassy to make arrangements to get out. I had no time for Sandy's cops and robbers, for photos of him when he looked like Sandy. I had to take him as he was, take him or leave him, my only choice.

He was innocent or guilty. Either he took Claude's money or he didn't. The diaries weren't talking, the photos held no clues. He looked untouchable in the photographs he saved, so innocent. He was innocent. Or he was guilty. In either instance, he was mine.

I called Sara: "Could you bring Concha and David home?"

I called my mother: "Do you think you could get a flight tomorrow to pick up David?"

I talked to the DEA's administrative officer: "I want to leave as soon as I can. I need to know whether DEA will ship. I'll warn you now, I'll fight every inch of the way to make you pay."

Then I closed myself back in the living room and waited.

Sara and Paul arrived together with my son, theirs, and Concha. Sara took the children upstairs to get them settled. Paul sat on the pink chintz chair, trying to make sense of what had happened.

"I'm getting out as soon as I can," I told him. "I'll sell everything if I have to. I've got to return to Texas within the week."

"Slow down a little," Paul said. "You're rushing this, you're being premature. DEA can't throw you out. You haven't committed any crime, and for all they know, neither has Sandy. You say he hasn't even been charged yet. This is obviously some blunder. You've got to give them time to work it out. Sandy could be back within the week and this whole thing forgotten. Why not send David home with your mother, close the house up as it is, and go to San Antonio to wait?"

"Our visas expire the end of October. They've already said they won't be renewed. I have to get out now."

He rattled the ice in his gin and tonic, looked down at the floor. "This is insane," he said.

"I'll need your help. They've suspended Sandy already, which means his salary will stop. I'll have to sell as much as I can, fast. We have about twelve thousand dollars in the bank from selling our car and Sandy's apartment in New York. I'll have to pay the lawyer, it won't go far. I'm going to need the money from the household sale before I leave. I'll want the new tenants to buy the carpets, the curtains, the appliances. I just can't do it by myself."

Sara came in and closed the doors. "We'll help. I know someone at the English paper who'll get a late ad in for us so we can have the sale this weekend. We'll advertise the house as well. You don't have to be here. I think you should come and stay with us. I'll start calling friends this afternoon to see if we can raise some money for the bond."

I looked across the coffee table at her, could picture her starched white uniform, her opaque stockings and silent shoes. I'd want her in the operating room, her firm hands on the instruments to save me, but I could have laughed: "Some money for the bond?" For the five-hundred-thousand-dollar bond?

By the time they left, it was decided. I'd leave Mexico for good within the week, sale or no sale, shipped out or not. If we could manage it by Saturday, I'd sell what I could, rent the house, gather the clippings, files, personal documents from Sandy's office that Goldstein might need. I'd find a home and job for Concha, pack David's clothes, his crib, his toys, to send with Polly's air freight to D.C. I'd make arrangements for our car, ship it to Texas if I could. I'd walk through the house that night marking every object, every piece of clothing, to sell, to ship by air or truck, to take to San Antonio, so friends could pack me up and move me out after I was gone.

Paul and Sara left; the phone started ringing. The administrative officer had cabled Washington. If I moved quickly, the DEA would ship, but I had to be out of Mexico before Sandy's suspension took effect. My mother called, panicked. Because of the strike, she could only get a flight as far as Texas. I didn't waste any time calling Polly's VIP. He got my mother onto Braniff the next afternoon and booked two reservations back to D.C., one adult, one child aged two. Polly called to say she and Dan would come by at 6 A.M. to load David's things for their air shipment. It was dark when the telephone stopped, and still raining.

I gave David his supper, read him a story in his room. His toys were on their shelves. The rocking chair was quiet on the rug. He asked me to sing the song that Concha always sang about the Chinese girl in the woods getting lost.

I asked Concha to have coffee with me. She wouldn't sit at the table but stood in the doorway, her coffee mug in both hands, her narrow shoulders resting on the frame. "Please, come and sit."

She shrugged, giggled, shook her head.

"We're leaving Mexico, the boy and I. We're going in less than a week. We have to talk."

Her pockmarked face was tired. Wisps of hair hung from the ponytail she'd tied with yarn. She sat across the table from me, eyes wet and unbelieving.

"It's my husband, he's been arrested. My mother arrives tomorrow to take David home with her. There will be a household sale this weekend. I'm calling the landlord tonight to see if I can place the house. By next Friday I'll be gone. Could you stay this weekend? You could bring your girls here and let them stay with you until I leave. I have some things I'd like to give you. I'll call some friends to find a place for you—"

"No," she said, crying.

"You won't stay the weekend?"

"No, I don't want a new position. I don't want to work in a house with children or with embassy families anymore. If you really go, I'll look for a job in the factory near my village."

I reached across the table, touched her hand. "You can get the girls this afternoon. If you'll only stay another week."

"You know I will. But I won't bring my girls."

"Why not? They can sleep in the guest room upstairs."

"No. I'm afraid. It's not safe."

I looked at her, not understanding.

"None of us are safe," she repeated, "from the work your husband did."

She got up, put my empty cup on the tray. I stood, hugged her, brushed the loose wisps of hair from her face. The telephone rang.

It was Jacques Kiere, calling through the embassy operator to make sure our conversation was recorded.

"As you know, Sandy's been suspended, but your transfer has been arranged. We opened his safe today by court order. We've confiscated his badge, his service revolver. There are certain semi-official documents which still belong to him. Shall I have them delivered to your house?"

"Please, as soon as possible. I need to know how much there is before the packers arrive."

That was all. Before he hung up, I'd marked the table, the planter, the throw rug in the hall "to sell" in red.

Sandy called at ten that night, crying. I could barely make him out. "I'm leaving Kerrville tomorrow morning. Goldstein says it's too far to travel, fifty miles each way from San Antonio, says he can't see me often enough here. They're sending me by truck to the Bexar County Jail. When will you be back? I won't be able to call again. It will all be changed. I'm frightened. When are you coming back, Joanne?"

"Don't worry, Sandy. Don't cry. I'm coming."

In a week, less than a week, as soon as I can be there.

28

There was a crowd outside the gate at 8 A.M.: maids in search of used bras, and shoes for their children; women in Pucci scarves and leather boots; professional buyers who wanted only electrical gadgets, U.S.-made. The ad said the sale would start at nine. By eight-fifteen they were piling in. The bad rains came at ten.

Two men wanted to see the TV. They stayed in the den for an hour, fiddling with the color tuning, watching American football on the cable channel.

A woman in her early thirties was interested in the house, though she wouldn't commit herself to the carpets and curtains. She didn't need the refrigerator. She had a double-door GE already.

Concha and I stayed upstairs, packing clothes for Sandy—dark, subdued suits for the trial, jeans and sweaters in case it was cold in Texas when the bond was reduced.

My mother stayed in David's room, playing with his train that had too much track to fit in Polly's air-freight shipment.

Sara was downstairs showing the stove. At three Paul ran up to say he'd sold the washing machine for three hundred dollars. Later a stranger knocked at the bedroom door saying someone from the embassy wanted to park his station wagon under the portico where the racks of clothes and tables of linens had been set up.

The administrative officer had a yellow pad of notes for me and a carful of cartons of papers for Sandy—documents, framed awards from the DEA and Treasury, an autographed picture of the U.S. Attorney Whitney North Seymour, Jr., from New York; "To Sandy Bario, with thanks for his invaluable contributions to the fight against narcotics."

He carried the cartons through the rain and dumped them in the front hall, where a woman in mink asked if their contents were for sale.

I gave him my carnet and the embassy phone book. He asked where I wanted to ship the car. Texas, I'd thought at first, but soon the bond would be reduced, soon Sandy would be out of jail and we'd return to Washington to stay with David and my parents until the trial started—if there was a trial, if the charges became real. Yes, Washington, I decided.

He got up, slipped my carnet in his pocket. The movers would come to pack me out on Friday. Someone would have to sign if I wasn't there. I was entitled to thirty days free storage of my furniture, a termination physical for me and David. He said good-bye. I didn't shake hands or walk him to the gate, though I did watch him drive away in the rain.

At five the embassy lawyer called. I'd have to come by with my mother before she could leave the country with David. I'd have to give her power of attorney to travel with him through Mexican immigration. It was illegal to take a child out of Mexico without both parents' written permission.

At six the sale was over for the day. At seven the woman who had wanted the house came back with her husband. They took the carpets, the curtains, a built-in bookcase in the den, reluctantly.

By nine o'clock, Concha and David were both in bed. The front gate was locked, the racks of clothes set under the portico covered with old sheets. I'd made a fire in the fireplace, feeling like a thief burning logs from the stack of wood I'd sold earlier that day for thirty dollars. My mother was cold, sitting on the floor near the fire, wrapped in a rebozo. The rain was falling hard.

I dragged the cartons from the DEA into the living room. There were thirteen in all, marked Personal Effects of Sante Bario. Investigative files bulged with travel vouchers, housing records, notes from cases finished years ago. There were slips of paper pocketed by Sandy during surveillance on the streets. My mother and I went through every folder, every box, without understanding much of what we saw. I set aside every slip of paper that might refresh a recollection. We made two piles—to ship, to take to San Antonio—making wild stabs in the dark.

The telephone rang at ten, collect from San Antonio. I accepted Gerry Goldstein's charges while watching my mother open yet another carton, lift another set of folders out.

"Frankly, I'm pissed," Goldstein was saying. "Sandy's acting like a child. Christ, nobody said the county jail was a garden party. So they took his clothes away. So they wouldn't let him keep your wedding picture. He's a federal agent. He's been in plenty of jails before. He's locked enough guys in the slammer himself."

My mother opened one of the folders, set the papers on the floor, began to read them one by one. Her blue eyes went blank and sad.

"The arraignment is Friday next week. He's got to get himself in line. We have work to do, we need his help."

The coals in the fire hissed. Another folder, another set of papers. Something fell from the folder to the floor. It looked like a ticket envelope bound with a rubber band. My mother removed the elastic, slipped it on her wrist. She opened the envelope—a pile of money fluttered to the floor.

"You'd better get here quick," Goldstein was saying. "Someone's got to put your husband back together."

29

Goldstein was our lifeline. He'd save us, he'd know what to do about the money. Everyone in Mexico agreed, take the money to Goldstein; let him tell you what it means. My mother had uncovered four thousand dollars in cash in that file from Sandy's official safe.

I was hanging an awful lot on Goldstein. He'd explain arraignments, pretrial hearings, indictments, how magistrates differed from federal judges, and the four thousand dollars returned to me by the DEA. It was true he'd lowered his fee for us. He normally expected a fifteen-thousand-dollar retainer in such a complicated federal case, but was only charging us six thousand dollars, a rock-bottom rate. I'd agreed to help, to do some legwork, to copy documents and hand-deliver letters. Maybe his cut-rate fee meant he wouldn't answer any questions, but no, that couldn't be.

Paul, my mother, the embassy lawyer, all agreed—take the money to San Antonio, give it to Gerry Goldstein.

Sara flew up with me, waited in the customs line nibbling her lip. I didn't lie to the customs' agent. I had forty-six hundred dollars in my purse, but I didn't have to report the money. I was legitimate enough, a citizen coming home from a diplomatic tour of duty overseas.

At nine o'clock sharp on Thursday morning I was waiting in Goldstein's office with my blue spiral notebook and the four thousand dollars. Like the new girl her first day on the job, I was eager to learn from Gerry G., prepared to work as hard as I knew how to help get Sandy out of jail. But first Goldstein had to tell me what the money meant.

Sara was waiting in the motel coffee shop across from Gerry's office. I thought I saw her from the waiting-room window on the twenty-ninth floor. I could see our room, not such a bad place, Sara kept saying. The motel had a pool and four dusty deck chairs in the parking lot. The Mexican room clerk spoke to me in Spanish, said I had a nice, clean *latina* face. "He likes you," Sara said as we unpacked. "He'll keep an eye on you after Paul and I fly home." In the meantime, they'd get me settled, help me find a cheaper place near Goldstein and the jail. Paul would arrive on Friday night; they'd both go with me on Saturday to visit Sandy.

Diane led me into Goldstein's private office. He was on the phone, eating sunflower seeds from a cellophane bag. He nodded, pointed to a chair, but I wouldn't sit. When he finally hung up, I dropped the envelope of money on his desk.

"Do you know what that is?"

"Four thousand dollars in cash, marked American bills," he said.

"How did you know?"

He shrugged, offering the bag of sunflower seeds. "DEA called about the money yesterday. They fucked up. They gave you their evidence of Claude's first strike. It's what they were looking for when they opened Sandy's safe."

"Then it's true, he took the money just like they said?"

"I don't know. I haven't even talked to Sandy. This was the first setup in Chicago, the week before Sandy's arrest. Claude went to DEA, offered them Sandy, a crooked cop. They want proof Claude's on the level, so he goes to Chicago where Sandy's testifying for the grand jury on another deal. All Bobby's gotten out of Sandy is that Claude met him, asked him to hold this money for him, and Sandy said yes. He took the money to Mexico, put it in his safe for Claude. Now you see what we're up against? Somebody's got to make Sandy stop crying so we can talk."

But I didn't see at all. If he was only keeping the money for Claude, where was the crime? It was my first day. I didn't want

Goldstein to think I was stupid. "What do we do with the money?" I asked.

"We keep it here while I get some legal advice. Maybe we're not bound to turn it over. It's their mistake, their loss. Maybe we'd be better off to turn it in at trial, to show that even DEA hasn't figured out this case. But now, first thing, we go see Sandy."

We drove the eight blocks to the jail in Goldstein's antique silver Bentley, each of us hugging a stained upholstered door. It was as if the money lay between us on the seat, the money Golstein had wrapped in brown paper towels and laid on his secretary's desk to be locked in the office safe. I'd heard him tell her, "I don't know what this is, I haven't seen it. Just put it in the safe." He was treating the money like a hot potato. It had to be important, so why couldn't he open up and tell me what it meant?

"It's hard to swallow Sandy's manner," Goldstein said, stopping at the traffic light. "He cries enough. He pisses and moans about the food, that everything is made with chiles. He lived in Mexico. He should be used to chiles. It's hard to believe he's so naive."

"He has a bad stomach."

"So I've heard. I don't mean to be unsympathetic. It's a lousy place, we know that. We have a civil suit pending over the facilities. It's a contract jail for the feds, they get federal money, so where are all the services? No doctor on staff, no special diets. What can I do? Why bitch at me? I had to have him moved. I couldn't drive fifty miles to confer with him, not at the fee I'm charging you. Not unless you'd care to buy my time for the next six months."

Six months, that's all I heard. After paying Goldstein, I'd have six thousand dollars left to pay court costs, witnesses who had to travel, to pay for a room, food, the telephone. Sandy's salary had stopped. I had to find a job and a cheap place for at least six months.

"Will it take that long—six months?"

He shrugged. I stared at his undone tie, his curly hair, the way he leaned against the window. I watched him from the corner of my eye.

"I know you can't estimate the time exactly," I continued, still not looking. "But you could give me some idea so I can make a reasonable decision about staying, about my son. I can't leave him in Washington too long. He's only two and needs me."

He turned the Bentley into the lot of a white-brick building and rolled his window up. He got out, locked his door. I watched him over the sleek curved roof, frowning, wrinkling his thin nose.

"Look, those are your decisions. Don't ask me. I've told you what I can, that I could use your help, that Sandy wants you here. I admit you're a notch above the wives of my other clients. But your kid—" He grabbed his briefcase, tucked it under his arm, and started walking. "I've got a wife. I can't take on another. And as for kids, I've been very careful all these years. I never wanted worries over kids."

The single pleat of his suit coat flapped in front of me. I had to run to reach the curb behind him. "I'm not asking you to worry."

"What?"

"I'm just asking how much time, that's all."

He stopped, cocked his head, smiled. "Two months, six, it depends on the judge, on the prosecutors, on Sandy. Everybody's got a right to a fair and speedy trial."

"Then I'll wait," I announced. "I'll take care of myself and my kid. I was only asking for the time."

"Good," he said and started walking. "I'm glad we understand each other."

I stomped after him. Fat chance we understood each other, Mr. G. No wonder he seemed so cool about the money. Sandy was just a name on an indictment, a docket number. Goldstein didn't care. Or maybe he was like the doctor whose patient is terminally ill. Why bother understanding now, when the dude will kick off soon? My knees were shaking—could it be that bad?

Goldstein held the door for me, politely, Texas fashion. I followed him down the first-floor hall, where the courtroom doors were paneled, the seats inside plush red. There was a sign hanging by the elevator door: "Children allowed on visitors' floor weekdays only. Keep children away from automatic doors."

Goldstein buttoned his collar, tightened his tie. Not my kid, Mr. G., not weekdays or weekends in a hundred years.

He prepped me in the elevator. "We'll go straight to the attorneys' visiting rooms. I'm not sure I can get you in, but it's worth a shot. Sandy may try harder if you're there. I'll play it up big to the chief, that you're not just a wife, you're a witness."

I sat by the guard's cage on the third floor while Goldstein was conferring with the chief of the jail, Mr. Ray Olivarri, his name in gold on tinted glass. The glass door opened silently. The chief was short and fat. He'd crooked his arm casually near Goldstein's back to lead the way, careful not to touch him. The guard's face came to life; I heard my name in whispers; the guard nodded. The chief headed back to his office, shoes shining, chest out.

Goldstein sat beside me. "It's all set. I'm not sure how long we'll get away with it, but I said we needed your help with dates. You'd better straighten Sandy out. He can't afford to feel sorry for himself like some kid whose Boy Scout troop has let him down. It's bullshit, you tell him. DEA's no fucking Boy Scout troop. This is real and happening to him."

I nodded, tried to pay attention, but there was some distraction at my back, a kind of motor running. I turned to look. The reinforced steel door was cranking open, the bolt thudding when it broke free. The door was painted yellow like the cinder-block walls, soft yellow. I watched the guard in his cage playing with the lever. I could see him through the convex mirror reflecting down an interior hall. The shift was changing; the door swung open; a group of men came out in street clothes with sports bags on their shoulders. They joked with the guard, whose eyes relaxed. He stared blankly after them, one hand on the lever, as they reached the elevator and the buttons lit up. He waited to see who came out the elevator doors. He was deadpan, legs splayed, butt out, and ready.

Sandy was somewhere inside those yellow walls.

Goldstein waited, leaning an elbow on the back of my chair, his foot tapping. I wanted to take his arm away, but it wasn't touching. How could Goldstein understand? He'd argue his case the best he could. He'd keep the money in his safe and ask the right tactical questions. He'd see his name in print in the local papers, maybe even put his reputation on the line. But he wouldn't go to jail. No pale yellow walls for Gerry G., no plates piled high with chiles.

I didn't say it. I was perfectly behaved, a good girl, a young lady.

When our names were called, I followed Goldstein to the cage and left my purse with the guard as instructed. The cinder block was paneled in the attorneys' rooms, the booths made of simulated wood with a window between lawyer and client so papers could be passed, signatures given. Each cubicle had its own door for privacy, though the doors were glassed. The guard could peer down the rows of bodies, marking anyone he chose. Sandy sat in the last cubicle, farthest from the cage.

He was wearing a light gray uniform, one piece, monogrammed on the pocket, Bexar County Jail. They'd taken away his toupee and wedding ring. He laid his paper, pen, a pack of Marlboros on the counter, resting his hands on top of them.

Goldstein raised the window, cleared his throat. "I'd leave you two alone for a minute so you could talk, but I think it's better not to chance it. They're already nervous about this arrangement. Let's not rock the boat."

"That's all right," I said and didn't look at Sandy.

"We have a lot to do. First, the indictment came down. I brought you each a copy. After tomorrow's arraignment we'll start preparing for the bond hearing. We'll move to reduce, they'll move to continue the full bond in effect. It's the usual bullshit. They'll argue you have no family in the district, that given any opportunity, Sandy would split. He's Italian, he'll go to Italy. He could go to Mexico or France. They'll say it's his business to get lost. He's used phony names before and has the documents to back them."

I was busy reading:

United States District Court
Western District of Texas
San Antonio Division

United States of America,	X	*Criminal No. SA 78 CR 225*	
Plaintiff	X		
	X	*INDICTMENT*	
	X		
	X		
VS.	X		
	X		
Sante Bario,	X	(18 U.S.C. 201 (c) (3):	
Defendant	X	Bribery of a Public	
	X	Official)	
	X		

THE GRAND JURY CHARGES:

That on or about the 7th day of October, 1978, in the Western District of Texas,

SANTE BARIO,

being an officer and employee of the United States Department of Justice, that is a Special Agent of the Drug Enforcement Administration, corruptly did, directly and indirectly, ask, demand, exact, solicit, seek, accept, receive and agree to receive from Claude Picault, a thing of value, to wit, approximately $5,000 in United States Currency, in return for the said SANTE BARIO being influenced in his performance of an official act in respect to the enforcement of the controlled substance law, in violation of Title 18, United States Code, Section 201 (c) (3).

COUNT TWO

That on or about the 24th day of April, 1978, in Mexico, D.F., Mexico, being out of the jurisdiction of any particular State or Judicial District, Defendant,

SANTE BARIO,

being an officer and employee of the United States Department of Justice, that is, a Special Agent of the Drug Enforcement Administration, corruptly did, directly and indirectly, ask, demand, exact, solicit, seek, accept, receive and agree to receive from Claude Picault, a thing of value, to wit: a sum of money consisting of a portion of the profits to be derived from the sale of certain cocaine, in return for the said SANTE BARIO being influenced in his performance of his official act in respect to the enforcement of the controlled substance law, in violation of Title 18, United States Code, Section 201 (c) (3), the said SANTE BARIO, having been first arrested in the Western District of Texas.

A TRUE BILL

Jamie C. Boyd
United States Attorney

By Jim Bock
Assistant U.S. Attorney

I looked up from the paper in my hand—*corruptly did, directly and indirectly, ask, demand, exact, solicit, seek, accept, receive and agree to receive from Claude Picault, a thing of value, to wit:*—I looked up, through the open window. Sandy was reading slowly, couldn't seem to focus. When he turned the page, it trembled in his hand. *A thing of value.* To wit: the money, the meaning of the four thousand dollars in Sandy's safe.

Okay, the money was the first count. But Sandy had explained the money. He'd held it for Claude as a favor because Claude asked him to. There wasn't any crime in that. He'd never meant to keep the money. Where had the money come from, though? From the crime, Claude's crime, for suddenly I knew there was a crime. I believed in the crime, the crime was real. It was carnival in Santa Cruz when Añez fronted Claude the coke that wasn't just a sample. Claude made his first independent move; the crime began when he brought back two kilos from Santa Cruz. Sandy's crime was not arresting Claude in that pink-lit tunnel of the Viaducto when he found out. But that wasn't what the indictment said, count two. The indictment said it was bribery, more money, money from the sale of coke that Claude brought in.

A thing of value, to wit: the money. The four thousand dollars was in place. The government had its money; that is, until they gave it back to me. *Corruptly did, directly and indirectly, receive and agree to receive from Claude Picault, a thing of value.* The amount in April wasn't named. I looked at Sandy, reading still. He'd been ambitious, desperate, had needed his silly Añez case to prove himself to me and to the region. But to take Claude's money for the sale of coke? No, I knew it wasn't so.

But then the thing of value had never been the money. There were silver buttons on the denim jumpsuit Sandy wore. Buttoned up from crotch to neck, he slowly raised his eyes. His pupils were contracted points of light drawn in, disappearing. His hands were white. He was Claude's thing of value, wrapped and ribboned, Claude's final gift.

30

I didn't laugh, but I knew the afternoon should have been funny, comic relief after our Saturday morning at the jail. Eight of us sat in the converted garage of a San Antonio ranch-style house in the suburbs: the host and hostess, big Texans in their fifties; a young Colorado couple who were weekend guests; a slow-talking hunter who'd just returned from his tenth African safari; and the three of us—Paul, Sara, me—fresh from our joint session with Sandy.

Paul hadn't known there'd be other guests when he encouraged me to come. "We've been invited to lunch. You can't say no. These people are our only San Antonio connections. He's a decent guy, owns a club in Mexico, has a homey wife. They're just the kind of folks you'll need. They'll be a port in the storm when I explain your situation."

But explaining wasn't easy. Sara and I sat against the bar making idle conversation while Paul helped the host load a large roll of film on his projector. His wife had already turned off most of the overhead lights. She was waiting on an old couch against the wall for her husband's order to kill the lights completely.

"I've got it," he said. The remaining lights went off.

I was relieved when the room went dark. The carcasses on every wall turned to silhouettes: a spread-eagled polar bear, a grizzly, several antelope. Two giant elephant tusks, luminescent in the dark, appeared to be suspended in thin air. The projector lit the screen; the motor ticked. I focused on the light until I couldn't see the mounted lion any longer, licking fake blood from his fatal wound. He'd been shot, the host painstakingly explained, many years ago, before there were even the vaguest rumors of vanishing species on the central plains. Not that the hunters were to blame. The blame belonged to native poachers, living off the profits from the animals they killed.

The film had sound. The narrator's careful voice introduced the hunters as they set off on their first photographic African safari. The camera panned the group of men and settled on our host.

It was comical, really. Paul kept waiting for the right moment to take his Texan aside and tell him what we were doing in San Antonio. Sara and I had avoided each other's eyes at my introduction. "Meet our closest friend," Sara had said. "What's such a pretty girl doing alone in Texas?" the hunter asked. "Her husband's here on business," Paul too quickly answered.

The camera cut from one rare animal to another.

"That elephant, that very one," the host exclaimed, freezing the frame. "We call her Lady. Look at her tusks! We've followed her on four trips now."

Someone behind me dropped ice in a glass, poured liquor from a bottle. Paul pretended total absorption in the film, his high forehead reflecting light from the screen. We knew he'd never tell them who I was. It would have been too funny. "And where exactly does your husband work?" the wife might have asked in a slow moment. "He doesn't," I would answer. "He's in jail in San Antonio. If convicted, he'll be imprisoned for fifteen years."

Paul couldn't have managed the shame. At thirty-four he was fast-tracking in the hotel business, director of the Central American region for a chain of Canadian hotels. At forty he intended to be president of his entire company. He and Sandy used to fantasize opening a small, well-appointed hotel by the sea.

Fifteen years—that's what Goldstein had said driving back from the jail the day before. I watched the elephant called Lady nudge her calf from the brush, plod with him behind the rest of the herd down to the murky water's edge. She looked around, nudged the calf again, lowered her wide, enormous head and took a drink.

As we walked from the motel to the jail that morning, Paul

repeated a rumor he'd heard midweek at an embassy party. "Don't give it any credence," he said. He was only telling me because he'd been so outraged, hearing Sandy's name bantered all night long. Some woman had announced at table that if convicted, Sandy would be moved from prison to prison every six months to protect his life. He had a reputation, she'd heard, was a genuine secret agent, and everybody knew that an agent's life wasn't worth a cent in jail. What could that stupid woman know? The Canadian ambassador himself said Sandy deserved nothing but respect, that more than once he'd helped out the Canadians.

I tried to imagine fifteen years of following Sandy from one airless cubicle to the next. Sara and I had stayed close together watching for him through three walls of glass, over the heads waiting their turns by the automatic doors. We waited an hour and a half before they brought him up. Sara and Paul leaned against a steel beam in the center of the room while I stood in the long line to turn in the slip of paper with our names. The guard addressed me in halting Spanish, as he did all the other visitors, until he read my name, looked up, whispered something to the guard beside him. They both stared while I walked back to Paul and Sara.

We couldn't believe how long it took. The guards didn't bother getting up to carry their packet of names to the cage until they'd saved a pile big enough to make the twenty-foot walk worthwhile: "Mrs. Gonzalez to see Fred Gonzalez, Jaime Cortez for Jorge Cortez, Hernandez for Hernandez," on and on. Like the slips of names, the visitors piled up, filled the benches along the walls, eyes hidden behind newspapers, mothers busy changing baby diapers. The room was heavy with cigarette smoke. The infants grew restless and started crying. Women lined up outside the dirty restroom doors. Finally, the adults grew restless, too. They crowded in front of the steel doors on either side of the cage, though they hadn't yet been called, to watch the inmates lined up in the holding tanks inside.

"There he is," said Sara, and there was Sandy, sitting alone on a bench apart from the others. The young men locked in the room with him bunched up close to the glass partition and stood on their toes to flirt with wives and girlfriends in the waiting room with us. They sported colored scarves around their necks and pretended not to mind the Bexar County Jail. A young girl beside me recognized her husband, called his name, and lifted her baby up, waving him back and forth above her head. The father laughed, called out something in return. But Sandy wasn't laughing.

Sara began to cry. The three of us were stuffed into one cubicle, passing the phone between us to say hello to Sandy through a wall of glass. We had fifteen minutes before the line went dead. I started first, "We love you, Sandy. Paul will come back alone tonight. The sergeant said it was okay since he'd traveled so far. I'll come back next Saturday, maybe sooner with Bobby Ozer."

Sandy nodded, eyes tearing. There wasn't any way to comfort him. Paul poked Sara in the ribs, whispered sharply, "Stop your bawling." I quickly passed the phone, knowing Paul wouldn't let himself feel sorry.

He played it crisp and businesslike. "You've got to keep busy," he advised. "They must have books. Do you read the daily papers? You can do exercises in your room. They must let you out, in a courtyard or something?"

Sandy tried to answer. He took a sheet of paper, drew the dimensions of his room, pressed it up against the glass. There wasn't space between the cot, the wall, the toilet to stretch his body. Yes, he read. No, he never went outside. The others went in groups. He stayed inside alone. He was afraid to be around them.

The reel of film was running down. The camera cut from the campsite to the setting sun, a huge orange disc against the hills. A herd of zebras grazed in the flatlands, then for no apparent reason broke, dust flying from their hooves, changing colors as it rose— orange to taupe, then fading to black. The wife, still reclining on her couch, had it timed exactly, her finger on the switch until the screen went blank. The fluorescent lights came on. I wondered how often she had practiced.

"Beautiful," the Colorado woman said. Sara smiled, blinking. Paul murmured something which I didn't hear. The lion continued licking his wound. The elephant tusks were shining.

31

Sara and Paul helped carry my suitcase and Sandy's cartons into the Barron Apartments on Sunday afternoon. The building was vintage 1930s and across from the courthouse. We had a hard time getting in. The lobby door was locked. The manager's office in the basement was reached through an entrance on another street, through a labyrinth of halls. But Goldstein's secretary said the rooms were cheap, the building was walking distance from the jail.

The manager's name was Sue, a spare, drawn woman in her late forties with a face like a bird's, wide-mouthed, tense. The veins in her long, thin arms bulged out. She wore a hairnet and a cotton wrapper when she walked the halls at night.

She later said she had a real eye for people in distress, developed after years of running transient buildings in the Southwest. She'd learned to read prospective tenants, to pick out the good from the bad. She'd seen all kinds. "You got problems, you come see Sue"— that's what she said, but I never told her much. I never knew if she recognized my name from the stories in the local papers.

She promised a good room on the fourth floor, directly across from her own place. I could use her phone for emergencies till mine was installed. She told Paul that the building was safe, security tight. The front door was locked against riffraff in the streets. Meanwhile, she led us down the dimly lit hall.

It was an old-fashioned room with heavy molding, a single bed, dressing table, stove, sink, and small refrigerator. The two long windows were covered by one oversized venetian blind. The room looked out on an alley and a darkened office building fifteen feet away.

"It's clean," Sara said cheerfully. She opened the creaky oven door.

"The exterminators come once a month. I'll send them here this week," said Sue.

It was convenient, cheaper than the motel across from Goldstein's office. I paid two weeks in advance. The rent was seventy-five dollars a week.

That night Paul took us to dinner on River Walk. We sat outdoors, watching the flat touring boats on the water. The candle on the table flickered, went out. We drank two bottles of wine and didn't talk. Afterward I walked them back to the motel. They left the next morning on an early flight.

I didn't sleep that night, didn't even undress completely. I unpacked and hung up Sandy's suits. I shoved the cartons under the bed. Sue had left a note on the mattress for me: "These sheets are from the linen service. Will charge you later." I turned off the lights and lay on the unmade bed in my blouse and panty hose. The venetian blinds were down and sagging. I wished for a phone, though there was no one to call.

32

I couldn't wait to escape from the Barron Apartments the next morning. By 8 A.M. I was outside Goldstein's door. "You're sure early," Diane remarked when she arrived. "There must be something I can do," I said. "I could make a pot of coffee." I made coffee, copied a stack of documents. Bobby came in at nine sharp—"Good, you're here"—and I could've kissed him. "You want to help with the memo of facts? The bond hearing is set for November 3, that's about ten days away. We have a lot to do."

He made space for me at a table in his office, took off his jacket, found his notes. "Goldstein said to tell you to call or write your family, Sandy's, any friends who might help and ask them to send letters or telegrams to the court stating their relationship with Sandy and their belief that he'd conform to any terms set by the magistrate if the bond were lowered. We want to show his ties in this country, that he's not gonna run if he gets out.

"Also, you're gonna have to raise some money, about fifty thousand dollars is the best we can do in this district. They'll want a bond for the full amount with your name on it and any family members who'll sign, with ten percent up in the registry. Goldstein said he'll be in later to take you over to the jail and explain all this to Sandy.

"In the meantime, let's get out our notes. I'll catch you up. You left, remember, when Sandy was explaining the best parts." He smiled, to let me know that he was joking. "I'll take you through April, if that's all right. We'll have to go completely by Sandy's recollections. We won't get discovery until the bond hearing is over. But we do know there's a recording of the Chicago meet that we should get. Let's see, the Chicago meeting took place in September. Before then, Claude was on his own."

I was lost already, unprepared for this. I watched Bobby flipping through his legal pad, his notes triple spaced in his big hand. We'd move on to April, then. I couldn't avoid it any longer. April 1978, when the big load came in, count two in the indictment, the bribery charge. I'd rather think about the calls I had to make, the money I would borrow. How many calls would it take to collect fifty thousand dollars?

"We're clear about the February trip, Santa Cruz, Claude and Vierzon flying down to get the sample? Claude comes back with two kilos, doesn't report it, waits until DEA has taken away the sample, then tells Sandy when they're alone. This is the original setup. He figures Sandy will let it go in order not to blow the case, tells Sandy he'll place samples with prospective buyers who they'll come back to later, tries to lead Sandy on that they can make legitimate cases out of this, that he's worked this way before with DEA. The big question is, Was he planning all along to do Sandy in, to make a case on Sandy? If so, he's setting the scene, collecting his evidence. Maybe he figures DEA would pay him more for a crooked cop than for any other dealer. We don't know. We don't know if he collected from DEA for Sandy."

I stared at Bobby, his elbow on the table, forehead resting on his hand with his fine hair hanging. He was into it all right, concentrating, into his detective mode and sorting out the facts. What would it cost me in his eyes to slip out the door, down the elevator, back to my room at the Barron Apartments? I'd be made then, out from under cover. Bobby would know once and for all how unfaithful I was. All those years I'd been the big talker with the men I'd known, into truth and understanding—such a little girl, such a fool. Now I didn't want to know. I knew too much already, since I'd learned about carnival in Santa Cruz. If Sandy had a fatal disease and would soon die, I didn't want to know it. Give me pills to make me sleep and long afternoons in a hospital room with flowers on the windowsill. I preferred my ignorance to any truth.

But of course I didn't believe that Sandy took a bribe. Where was the money? Four thousand dollars—was that all it would be worth? How much did cocaine go for on the streets? I didn't know. It was incredible that I didn't know; married to a narc for three years now, and I didn't know the cost of his product on the street. Two kilos pure powder, that must have been worth something— even before the main load came in April.

"So we come to April," Bobby was saying. "They're gonna take Añez for this load, make his Bolivian associates at some later date. The deal is, Claude goes down for ten kilos. It's all arranged, cables back and forth from Washington, the general on alert, the surveillance team ready at the airport with the MFJP who'll make the actual arrest. Claude calls with the flight number, the date, with confirmation that Añez is cool and flying back to Mexico with him. The dope is in Claude's metal suitcase. Okay, so it goes as planned. Añez is arrested at the airport. DEA and MFJP agents seize the suitcase, take it to a prearranged hotel in the city where they've reserved a suite. Claude and Sandy are in one room, the agents in the other. The telephone is wired. The agents remove a sample from the coke for delivery to Asaf y Bala at the prison, they're gonna net him, too. Claude is supposed to place a call to him and to one Alain Chaillou in Montreal, another buyer. They're gonna keep this case going. Sandy's nervous because of Claude's secret stash when the sample came through, though he doesn't want to believe Claude would try for it again. He could, though. I mean, why not, when Claude already has Sandy in the bag? Sandy's already been compromised, right?"

Bobby looked up at me for confirmation. The bad news is coming soon, I know. Who cares about the hotel room, Claude's metal bag? Who's this Alain Chaillou, this Asaf y Bala? The April I remember six months past makes no reference to them. I remember April in our living room, saying to Sandy something's got to give. We should go to a shrink or a marriage counselor. We were fighting again. My worries were about divorce and David growing up without a father. How was I supposed to know that Sandy's problems led back to Claude? Sandy never said a thing, that creep, that gentleman from the old school, trying to protect me.

"Finally, after a couple of days, Claude lays his second bomb on Sandy. This time he brought in five extra kilos."

My stomach dropped and knotted. I'd have to buy my own Mylanta. Please God, I'll never ask another thing. I'll go to church, I'll have my son baptized, if only you'll say it isn't true.

33

Goldstein came in late, in his usual rush. I couldn't make myself stand up when he collected me from Bobby. Somehow we got into his private office. I had to make him like me, had to smile, but I couldn't. It was Claude's word against Sandy's, and Claude would win.

"Bobby told you about the letters and the cash?" Goldstein asked.

"Yes, he did."

"You'll have to bring in twenty grand. If the bond's reduced to fifty, they'll want a fair amount of cash up and plenty of reassuring names on paper. If we get it, we'll be lucky. We'll go for discovery as soon as the bond's decided."

"DEA will fight, won't they?"

"Damn straight they'll fight. If we lose here, we have an appeal in New Orleans. Bobby says Sandy's known in New Orleans, which will help. We'll go over to the jail and try to lay this out for Sandy. How is he? Have you seen him?"

"Saturday morning. He was down, badly down."

"Yeah, well, it's no picnic. You gotta try to raise his spirits. If he becomes any more a basket case, we've got real problems. We'll have to call somebody in. I know a good psychiatrist. We may be needing him later if Sandy's flipped. But I don't think it's tactically wise to call him in so soon. If the government got wind of it, they'd want to ship Sandy off to the Army hospital to be evaluated. If they found him incompetent to stand, they'd have him institutionalized. If not, they could start their own treatment and curtail our access. We don't want either."

When we got to the jail, Sandy looked awful. Goldstein explained the letters and telegrams I'd be asking for, the best we could hope for with the bond. Preoccupied, his eyebrows closing down, Sandy hung on Goldstein's every word. Gerry asked him to write the names and ages of his children, the names, addresses, relationships of his other family members in the States. Sandy tried to get it right, but the pen shook in his hand; he couldn't remember Franco's name or anybody's birth date. He even forgot when and where we'd married. I watched him bend over his legal pad, scratching out wrong numbers. First the pen wouldn't work, then his hand wouldn't function. He stared at the pen point. He put his left hand on his right wrist to steady it. He finally gave up, put the pen down, wiped his face with his uniform sleeve, and looked pleadingly at me.

"Help me," he whispered, "you've got to help me."

Driving back in Goldstein's car, I saw revulsion in his face. "That's it," he said. "We can't wait. I'll call the shrink today and set up a time for him to see Sandy."

It was unmanly and damned inconvenient, Goldstein must have thought.

The next morning Dr. Saul Rosenthal called and asked me to meet him at his office. He'd seen Sandy the night before.

There was another woman waiting when I arrived. She smiled, set her ashtray on the couch, flipped through the pages of a magazine. She was formless, unattractive, comfortable there. I assumed she was waiting for her weekly shot: Tell me, doctor, why I can't take hold of my life, why my work isn't thrilling, why I can't let go in anybody's arms. I envied her, wishing I'd come to Rosenthal for the usual reasons, anticipating years of fifty-minute hours, taking the time I needed to evade, act out. I could've suffered quantities of guilt with Rosenthal to guide me. "Tell me," he'd say, "the worst that would happen if your marriage fails, if you start another life. No one will die or fall apart."

The fat woman in the wrinkled shirt disappeared behind the

padded door. I opened my purse, took out Sandy's latest letter. I wrote long letters to him every night, delivered in the mornings by Bobby when he had his private sessions at the jail. So far, Sandy had written twice. "I'll shave tonight," his letter said, "in case Bobby brings you here tomorrow. We're allowed to shave or shower at 8:00 each night. I hope you come. I count on you to read the situation for me. I can't tell anything from here. I can't even tell you what it's like. I can't come to any strong conclusions. I trust you to make my decisions now."

The fat, formless woman plodded out.

"Come in," said Dr. Rosenthal.

We sat in wicker chairs around a low table.

"How are you holding up?" he asked, but before I could answer, his secretary buzzed. The far walls of the room were glass. The buildings of the University of Texas Medical Center jutted up across from us like unnatural growths. Rosenthal reassured his desperate patient on the line while I stared into a hundred treatment rooms, picturing bodies under paper gowns waiting for their particular diagnoses: cancer of the colon, irreparable holes in their children's hearts.

"Sorry for the interruption," said Rosenthal. Before Sandy was arrested, I would have smiled, relaxed, expected help and resolutions. Rosenthal wasn't from San Antonio; he was East Coast and kind-looking, but I didn't trust him. I'd been wrong too many times. I'd underestimated Claude, overestimated Goldstein. This time I wasn't taking any chances. I wouldn't look at Dr. Rosenthal. I kept staring into those tall buildings where the doctors went from room to room doling their prescribed measures of hope like sugar pills. The patients were a class beneath them, lumps of flesh. There was a clearly defined pecking order. Sandy turned to me, I turned to Goldstein, Goldstein had dumped us on Rosenthal now. Nobody had the answers.

"I've seen your husband twice already, late last night and first thing this morning. He's quite depressed. It's acute now, due to his circumstances, but the symptoms have been with him for some time. You know them, I'm sure: anxiety, crying jags, insomnia, ulcer pain, hair loss, tension headaches, impotence, loss of appetite. I've prescribed some medication. What I need from you is a sense of the changes you saw during the past few years."

I couldn't get beyond the list of symptoms. Yes, I'd seen them all, but they hadn't registered. I'd said he was crazy because he'd disappointed me, that's all. I thought, Dr. Rosenthal, that I'd been conned, that in Mexico my husband had revealed himself to me, that the man on those long walks by the Hudson, on the midnight train in Italy, the man who'd climbed to the top of the tallest pine in Boscotrecase, was putting on a show. I was too stupid, too naïve to see it happening. The prince changed into the ugly toad, that's all—it happened all the time in all the stories. He was too good to have been true.

> The *present illness* begins in April 1977. At that time Mr. Bario was officially confirmed in his supervisory role in Mexico City and a combination of circumstances and problems leading to his present illness began to intensify.
>
> In the first place, his previous work for the government had a strong impact on him and made his adjustment to a relatively normal life difficult. For approximately twelve or thirteen years he had been living among criminals on government assignment. During all that time he was in a situation where he couldn't make friends, he was under an assumed identity and dealing with hoodlums. He had hardly ever been home, he therefore had very little experience in dealing with coworkers and others on a cooperative and social basis.
>
> Also, due to the demands of his previous work, he had very little experience dealing with a wife and a family on a continuing basis. His brief visits home in his first marriage did not prepare him for the experience of living full time with a wife and new baby. This was complicated by the fact that his wife did not like his job and did not like living in Mexico and was placing pressure on him, both to leave Mexico and to find a different kind of employment.

Rosenthal's report must have been accurate, based on eight interviews with Sandy, several with me, corroborated by other psychiatric experts who saw us. He'd talked to Franco, to Sandy's former wife, to colleagues and supervisors at the office. Even

Jacques Kiere had guardedly agreed to speak to him, through monitored DEA channels.

Everything should have been fine in April. Truly, Dr. Rosenthal, I was learning to like Mexico. It was only that the office wasn't running smoothly yet, that Sandy was so seldom home. It was only that David wasn't gaining weight, wouldn't sleep, had stomach problems. The bacteria that got him seemed to breed in the dry, dusty air. I admit I hated Mexico for that, for the strangeness of the climate, the pollution, for the secret haughtiness I seemed to see in the eyes of everybody's maids. It sounds crazy, doesn't it? But even the nurse at the embassy said most diplomatic families went through it every year. It was only that Claude called every day, wanted meetings every weekend. Without those complications, I would have adjusted. Certainly, we had our days when the mountains closed in, when we couldn't talk or look each other in the eye, but every marriage has its moments. Please, Dr. Rosenthal, don't blame me.

> Mr. Bario's prior experience as an independent agent did not prepare him for the demands of a supervisory desk job. It was very difficult for him to relinquish control over his agents and allow them autonomy. He had great difficulty in delegating authority. He, therefore, ended up trying to manage all the cases of eight agents. He felt extreme work pressure, part of which came from above, as there were demands upon the office to make more and bigger cases. He worked long, long hours, didn't go to lunches like the other workers, stayed after everyone else went home and continued to receive urgent phone calls at home. This caused added friction between Mr. Bario and his wife. His ulcer continued to get worse and he was constantly drinking Maalox or other medication. This was observed by his supervisor, Ralph Saucedo, who also commented on the considerable tension between Sante and the people working under him.
>
> In addition to assuming the burden of his subordinates, Mr. Bario was pressed into the role of doing some of the work of his boss and negotiating with the officials of the host government. To quote from the report of July 11, 1978, by the regional director, "Additionally, group supervisor Bario found himself involved in a number of regional activities at a level not commen-

surate with his responsibilities, namely because the rating
supervisor did not discharge some of his own obligations or im-
properly delegated regional responsibilities to group supervisor
Bario . . . while I have the highest regard for group supervisor
Bario's professionalism, he did not receive the guidance he was
entitled to."

By the fall of 1977 Mr. Bario began to behave erratically. He
would stay in the office until late at night and then come home
to go right to bed. On the weekends he would just want to sit
around all day by himself or sleep. He and his wife began to
have frequent arguments and they moved into separate bedrooms. . . .

Autumn in Mexico was the best time; the rains tapered off, day lilies bloomed in the garden, the nights were cold. We moved to the top of our steep barranca in Tecamachalco in September. We had a clear view of the mountains before the smog rolled in. Sandy used to sit on the first-floor terrace every weekend sipping *té de manzanilla*. He didn't want to talk.

While Mr. Bario was well used to the strain of an undercover
solitary existence, he was unable to cope with the completely
different strain of administrative demands, supervisory responsibilities, and familial pressure combined.

I was his wife; I should have seen—I did see—that he couldn't cope. I should have done something about it, but I was too busy feeling sorry for myself.

Around Christmas of 1977 the marital situation became really
bad and Mr. Bario had severe outbursts of anger. As Mrs. Bario
remembers it, he was constantly angry, yelling and attacking,
and she was constantly crying. He was at this time under continuing tremendous pressure at work.

After Christmas of 1977, in early January, Mrs. Bario left for
the United States in a marital separation. She refused to return.
Mr. Bario became very depressed, unable to sleep, sitting up late
at night and thinking about his marriage breaking up, crying
almost every night and with continuing trouble from his ulcers.
He called her repeatedly and pleaded with her to return, and she
finally did in February. . . . Mr. Bario continued to be trou-
bled by insomnia every night, ulcer pains for which he drank

Mylanta, and crying at night. He also took Valium for anxiety. He had tension headaches and irritability with his wife and at work.

I came back, though, because I still wanted to believe. I came back for myself, and could not help Sandy. So blame me, Dr. Rosenthal, if you must.

> *Summary:* It is clear from the foregoing that Mr. Bario suffered a major depressive illness, beginning probably in the fall of 1977 and becoming severe in the early months of 1978. This illness continued and worsened throughout 1978 and certainly up to and including the months of October and November. This impression is concurred in by Dr. Bowden, whose consultation letters are also attached. Mr. Bario's judgment was certainly impaired, at least from January 1978. It is clear from many sources that his ability to appropriately perform his duties was severely impaired by his illness for many months prior to October 1978 and that Mr. Bario was disabled by his severe depression during these months.
>
> *Diagnostic Impression:* DSM-II, 298.0, psychotic depressive reaction. (In light of this strong, positive family history, an alternative possible diagnosis would be that Mr. Bario was suffering from an initial episode of manic-depressive illness, depressed type; DSM-II, 296.2)

34

There wasn't time to check out every lead or make intelligent decisions. A few days before the bond hearing Jimmy Breslin wrote a column about Sandy's arrest, claiming he was set up by a New York mobster in retaliation for the Norman Archer conviction in Queens. I asked Sandy at the jail if it could possibly be true. He shrugged. He shook his head. He had never heard of that particular mafioso, he said.

A reporter for *High Times* magazine was closer to target, Sandy seemed to think. A public relations officer at DEA had told the reporter that Sandy's arrest was a direct result of the DeFeo Report, a highly classified Senate committee report on corruption within the Drug Enforcement Administration. When I went to the jail again to tell Sandy the reporter's theory, he looked terrified.

"He wants an interview," I said to Sandy. "He thinks DEA is paying you back for your Senate testimony about Intertel's involvement in your Paradise Island case before your transfer to Mexico. He suspects CIA involvement in the Bahamas and in Mexico. According to Goldstein, DEA may act as a front for CIA in lots of places. Could it be true? Do you know much about any of this? The reporter is anxious to make a deal. If you agree to the interview, he'll give us those parts of the DeFeo Report that concern your testimony."

"Have you met him?" Sandy asked, squinting at me through the glass partition as though I might be keeping secrets.

"Not yet. This is all through Goldstein. But he wants to meet me. He suggested having lunch with Gerry and Bobby. I didn't know what to say until I'd talked to you."

"What exactly is he looking for? The CIA stuff?"

"Not according to Goldstein. *High Times* is some kind of druggie's magazine, I guess. I've never heard of it, but he says he's interested in the use of paraquat on marijuana in the eradication program."

"I don't know," Sandy slowly answered. "If DEA finds out I've talked to him, they could make it harder on me. What do you think? Still, maybe you'd better meet him. I think my Senate testimony is important. See what you think of him. I'm sorry, Joanne, but I'm afraid you'll have to decide."

"It's not my decision, Sandy."

He looked at me, fear in his dark eyes and deep black craters underneath them. He looked like he hadn't slept in months. I supposed in truth he hadn't. "Please do this for me, Joanne. If he seems all right to you, I'll have to chance it."

"Do you think he's right about the DeFeo Report?"

"I know DEA was unhappy with my testimony. Conein tried to change my report. There are people in DEA who wouldn't mind if I was out of reach for a while." He turned his eyes away. "No, I didn't mean that. I'm not sure. I don't even know what I'm saying anymore."

If Sandy didn't know how seriously to take the reporter, how was I supposed to? I met him for lunch with Goldstein and Bobby at a Mexican restaurant near Goldstein's office. Gerry ordered beers all around while I watched the reporter across the table eating guacamole. Goldstein was being charming and cracking jokes. The reporter laughed, looking perfectly agreeable. He seemed to be a regular guy and was nice to me, but I didn't know whether or not to believe his story. I couldn't anticipate DEA's reaction to an interview with Sandy in a drug-culture magazine. The agency would be outraged, I knew, but could they make it harder on Sandy with the prosecutor's office in Texas? Could they influence the judges in any way? I couldn't answer those questions. I decided to make whatever wild stab I could and leave. I searched Goldstein's face for clues: his thin lips, the way his narrow nose seemed to slide across his face. Go with it, his eyes were saying. So I did. Yes, I said, all right. I asked to borrow Bobby Ozer's car and left them to their beers. But before I could get out the door, the reporter caught up with me. He had his memo book in hand. "Shall we set a time up now?" he asked. "I'm sure your husband will want you to be with him for the interview."

Sandy and I met the reporter the following day in the attorneys' visiting rooms. The meeting could not have been more tense. Sandy's hands were shaking. He wouldn't take his eyes off mine. He kept asking the reporter to turn off his tape recorder while he clarified a question. Some things slipped through Sandy's guard, as if he himself didn't know how much he knew. Loads of drugs had gone through Mexico without knowledge of the Mexican Government, he said. Recently, sixteen tons of marijuana that had not been destroyed by the eradication program had been delivered to Canada under the DEA's control, and the Mexican Government was never advised. But when the reporter asked about the CIA, Sandy would say nothing.

I should have paid closer attention. I shouldn't have allowed Sandy's nervousness and fear to distract me so much. I can't remember what else was said. The truth is, I had my own agenda for Sandy that day. After the interview was finished, I managed to stay behind a moment, to sneak some time from the guard in his cage when he wasn't looking. I had to tell Sandy that I was going back to Washington for a few days, that when I left the jail that afternoon I was driving Bobby Ozer's rusted car on a search for a new apartment. I had already called and asked my parents if they would return to San Antonio with David and me until Sandy's bond was reduced and he was out of jail. That way, I'd be free to visit the jail, to work with Goldstein and Bobby, without leaving our son with another stranger in another strange place. David would have my parents, and Sandy would still have me.

I had started looking for a bigger place the day before, on Saul Rosenthal's advice. He'd suggested that a long separation would be damaging to David. Too much loss—the sudden disappearance of both parents within a week, and then to have been whisked away from Mexico by a grandmother he didn't really know. When I'd left Saul Rosenthal that morning in a rush to meet Goldstein and Bobby for lunch, the psychiatrist's words kept ringing. Who could think about *High Times* magazine or guacamole? The promise of a few pages of a report I'd never heard of meant nothing to me compared to my son. I had considered leaving San Antonio that same afternoon and flying to Washington to pick up David. I'd rent a crib and pack his umbrella stroller. But who would take care of him while I conspicuously parked myself at Goldstein's office? I didn't have the money to fly David and my parents back with me. I needed the time to drive back, to bring my car.

I had taken a cab from Goldstein's to the restaurant, making plans. My parents had generously agreed to come to San Antonio. My father had more or less retired. My mother's time was sort of free. My car was en route to Washington, where I had so ignorantly had it shipped. I wanted to laugh that it had once seemed so easy: Sandy would be released on his own recognizance, and we would stay at my parents' house until the silly business of his trial was over. But those plans had been made in a different life. Now I would fly to Washington to wait for my car to arrive, then we'd all drive back together.

I tried to explain it quickly to Sandy before the guard down the row of glass partitions happened to turn our way. I couldn't wait any longer. I was planning to fly to Washington on Saturday morning, the day after the bond hearing, which was only two days off.

"I have to find a bigger apartment," I was saying. "I'm going to look today. I'll testify at the bond hearing like Goldstein wants. But after that, I'm not waiting. I want my son."

Sandy listened hard—it had been a long, exhausting afternoon for him. He nodded as though he agreed with me completely, but he didn't understand. He thought I meant that I wanted to leave him, that I would stay in Washington until the trial started. I couldn't touch him through the glass to reassure him. I kept promising I'd never leave him for good, never. Even if the worst should happen and the bond wasn't reduced and he was convicted at the trial, even if he were sentenced to fifteen years and moved from prison to prison every six months like Paul had said, I wouldn't leave. But I wanted David and couldn't wait any longer. Yes,

Sandy agreed, I was absolutely right. I should go and get the car and drive back with my parents. But he didn't want to talk or think about it. He pressed his hand against the steel-lined window and said again, "Please don't go."

Bobby's old Dodge sputtered and burned oil. He had warned me to check it every half hour and not to panic if the car stalled. I had a road map of the city and a marked copy of the morning paper. I had made appointments to see three apartments that afternoon. They were furnished two bedrooms, all within twenty minutes of the jail.

Driving on the Loop, I made a list of everything I had to do before I left. Notify Sue when I'd rented a new place. Ask Bobby to help me move my stuff out. Call Goldstein to ask if he thought Sandy would be all right while I was gone. But I couldn't ask Goldstein. He would say those were personal judgments I had to make. I'd call Saul Rosenthal instead: Am I doing the right thing? Is Sandy strong enough for me to leave? Will you, please, go see him while I'm gone? But I was worried that I'd been calling Rosenthal too often. His time was adding up. He billed me for every fraction of a minute on the telephone, for his driving time to and from the jail, for telephone interviews with Sandy's supervisors, for meetings with other psychiatrists, for talks with Goldstein, and for consultations with Sandy at the jail. Eighty dollars for every forty minutes, that was his fee. His first bill had arrived that morning, itemizing every phone call, three minutes here, four there. The bill was five pages long; it totaled twenty-one hundred dollars. I couldn't afford reassurances from Rosenthal.

The first apartment was on the top floor. One mattress was torn—my mother wouldn't like it. The agent promised to fix a broken window in the kitchen. The bathroom tiles were caked with soap and had been painted a smoky shade of blue. I didn't take it. I finally chose a first-floor apartment in a new complex near the Loop. The apartment wasn't furnished, but it was clean, and the complex had a large playground with swings for David.

35

The woman is dressed in a plain beige suit and grim walking shoes. She has followed her attorney's instructions and worn no jewelry but her wedding band. Her fingernails are bitten down. Her face is pinched and somber. Although I've watched her countless times, timidly coming through the courtroom doors, she doesn't look familiar. She lacks substance, stature. It's easy to see why she's attached to the balding man sitting at the center table. They're alike. They're both losers.

The funny thing is that the woman doesn't know it. She honestly believes that her testimony will make a difference in that rehabilitated theater-in-the-round which is the federal courthouse building. Intimidated as she is by the reporters who turn to watch her entrance, by the court reporter winding tape on his machine, and the magistrate adjusting the wide sleeve on his long, black robe, she thinks they'll listen. Important issues will be raised, real questions of worth decided. She thinks she can just march up to the empty witness box when her name is called and start in talking. There will be questions, but in between, she'll say what she's come to say, and everyone will listen.

After all, she's the only person in the room who really knows the defendant sitting at the table with his head down, his shoulders sloping. She knows he won't run away. She knows it as surely as she knows her own name. She's lived with him. She's seen him at the jail, watched him come undone and read about it in his daily letters. He isn't what he seems. How ugly he looks, with his hair fallen out and his eyes gone dead. She's worried that the judge will think he's sinister, looking up from underneath his brows, concentrating so when anything is said. She wants to tell the magistrate: He looks like that because he's scared. His eyes hurt because he cries so much. He's concentrating just to understand. He needs help, your honor. I apologize for that, for how he looks, for his accent and his foreign ways and his peculiar occupation. He's an odd combination of qualities, sir. So sophisticated, so well traveled, yet naïve. He didn't mean to do anybody any harm. He was trying to help, your honor. That's how it started, believing he was charmed, believing he could make great cases. If you let me, I'll explain. It will only take a little of your time. It happened in the Viaducto, in Mexico City, last February. It happened after Claude returned from carnival in Santa Cruz.

Dizzy, dizzy dame. Dumb broad. Every time I see her, I want to make her over. She's the only woman in the room, and she's pathetic. I can even tell you what she thinks as she steps into the last row of wooden seats. They're like pews. The room is quiet as a church. Somebody coughs, and it echoes. This is serious, the room says, and she agrees. She sits with her back straight, liking the feel of the wooden benches. She presses her hand on solid oak, varnished to a shine, grateful that it holds her. That's what the godawful woman is thinking.

When she finally looks up, she's face-to-face with Jacques Kiere, sitting at the narrow table in the center of the room. They're lined up like football players for a pregame interview, Kiere and the prosecutor, Sandy and Goldstein, waiting for the skirmishes to start. Kiere nods hello. She could have really shook him up, forced him into one hell of a confrontation in that courtroom where he couldn't get away. She could have blamed him for everything she hadn't acted on herself: We tried to warn you, Jacques, didn't we? That Sandy was cracking up, that he was working too hard, that he was caving in beneath the pressure. The other agents, Marta, even I tried to tell you at your New Year's party. You knew the problems better than anybody. Why, you even admitted them to the inspectors when Sandy was arrested—how the region needed Añez to give the DEA a shot in the arm, to ease the tensions caused by bad morale. When the inspectors appeared, showed off their badges, said they were going to arrest Sandy, why didn't you tell them that he'd failed his State Department physical last summer, that he'd returned so soon because you needed him? Why show up now on the other side of that courtroom table, leaning into the prosecutor to give him your advice?

That woman could have made Jacques Kiere really squirm. But she simply turned her head away, no scenes, no misbehavior. She is the perfect lady, intact in her beige suit, last row center, waiting for the services to start.

> THE COURT Good morning, Ladies and Gentlemen. Please proceed on your motion, Mr. Goldstein, to amend the conditions of release.
>
> MR. GOLDSTEIN The defense, at this time, would call the Defendant's wife . . . and she has not been sworn, Your Honor.

She makes her way up the aisle to the witness box. She's duly sworn, takes her seat. Her knees are knocking. Before the questions even start, she's lost herself. She hears the court reporter's machine ticking, taking down the basic data of her life for the official record —your name, your age, your occupation, and that man, seated at the table, the defendant in this case, is he your husband? Goldstein leads her by the nose. Everybody's name is in the record: David's, her parents', her in-laws' and stepchildrens'. Where were you born? Where do you live? What do you own?

Goldstein moves carefully, asks permission of the magistrate: "May I approach this witness?" It's only part and parcel of the litany and doesn't help. Do you have a passport? Do your husband and your son? Do you currently have a visa to enter the Republic of Mexico? Will you relinquish all passports to this court? Not that we don't trust you, not that we think you'd run away. Do you own an automobile? Describe it for the court—what make, what year? Is it currently en route to the United States? Is it registered? Were you born in the United States? Were your parents? Was your son? Are you legitimate or fly-by-night and foreign?

He falls back, approaches her again. Do you recognize this piece of paper? Does it accurately reflect your financial situation? She wants to stop him. Nobody asked her permission to approach. Sure, he's trying to be kind, but he carries some stiff wind behind him blowing her back, taking her breath away. How much money do you have from loans, from savings, from telephone solicitations? Twenty thousand dollars? Are you willing to deposit that money in the registry of this court. How much do you offer to buy him out, to rent him for a month or two until the trial starts?

> Q. Mrs. Bario, you indicated to the Court your willingness to submit your passport and any other visas that you have and you have indicated that you will be able to raise, from family and friends, $20,000 to put in the Registry of the Court.
> A. I would like to make one more statement.
> Q. Sure.
> A. My parents are moving here, too. When I go to Washington to get my car, my parents—my father, who is retired, and my mother—
> Q. You will have to slow down. We have got a lot of time and just slow down and take your time.
> A. And my child is currently in Washington, he is staying with my parents; my parents are going to accompany me to San Antonio and will reside with me and with my child, and, hopefully, my husband, here in San Antonio until the charges against my husband are cleared.
> Q. All right. Is there any doubt in your mind that your husband, with that kind of security up, and the kind of people who have backed him and are willing to put their name to a letter and their money up, is there any doubt in your mind that he would show up at any time that he was required to by this court?
> A. No. His only desire is to stay with his family until he can go to Court and vindicate himself of these charges.
> Q. In the event that he were unsuccessful do you perceive your husband as the kind of individual to flee the jurisdiction—
> A. No.
> Q. —in order to escape punishment?
> A. No. My husband is an honorable person who would face whatever punishment was given to him.
> Q. Are you willing to sign the bond in the full amount as it is

right now, $500,000, and put $20,000 up in the Registry of the Court?
A. Yes.
Q. Can you give the Court your assurance that that would—
A. Yes, I can give the Court my complete assurance.
Q. All right.
MR. GOLDSTEIN Pass the witness.
THE COURT All right, sir.
You may inquire, Mr. Bock.

How formal, how proper and polite. We might have been waiting for the ball to start, the men in curled white wigs and morning coats. "Sir, you may inquire," "Your Honor, my husband is an honorable man. . . ."

She's an idiot, I tell you. She bought the whole show. She told the truth, believed every word she said. She swallowed the judge, Goldstein, the court reporter. A sucker for ritual and ceremony, she believes she's part of that high service, a witness to the sacred truth. She's on her knees, eyes closed, chin against her chest, *mea culpa, mea culpa, mea maxima culpa.* . . .

CROSS EXAMINATION

Questions by Mr. Bock:
Q. Mrs. Bario, I need to ask you a few questions and, if you will—You don't need to get upset—
THE COURT Let's take a five-minute recess.

It's like I said, she comes apart. Someone shoves a box of tissues in her hand. The marshall leads her to the ladies' room. She stands in front of the mirror and blubbers like a kid. She's humiliated. She wants somebody, but whom? She wouldn't let anyone see her now, laying herself out, gaped at by reporters. Not her parents—what could they do? She's a grown woman who's made her choices. Not her friends who have their lives on track, in order. She wipes her eyes, blows her nose. Suddenly, she recognizes—Concha; she wants Concha in her turquoise sweater, knee socks falling down. She'd be seated in the last seat of the last pew, back arched, her buttocks barely touching the bench, with wisps of hair framing her dark face. Even if the Court could understand, she wouldn't breathe a word. No judgments from Concha, no shock at anything that might be said. They would have hugged each other. Unless, unless even Concha would have said no. . . .

> (Whereupon, after a short recess, the following proceedings were had in open court.)

THE COURT Mr. Bock, you may proceed.
MR. BOCK Thank you, Your Honor.
Q. (By Mr. Bock): Mrs. Bario, how many foreign languages is your husband fluent in?
A. Italian and French.
Q. And Spanish?
A. And Spanish.
Q. And English?
A. And English.
Q. How long had you lived in Mexico before his arrest on October 7th?
A. Three years.
Q. And he had been working for the Drug Enforcement Administration for that full period of time?
A. Yes. . . .
Q. Now, your husband, during the time that you had been married to him, you say he worked under cover?
A. During the time that I have been married to him, yes.
Q. You are familiar with the term 'working under cover'?
A. Yes, I am familiar with that.
Q. And this is what you meant when you say he put his life on the line, so to speak?
A. Yes.
Q. As a matter of fact, he has penetrated several underground organizations as a government agent?
A. Yes.
Q. And he has worked for long periods of time under cover?
A. Yes.
Q. And he has come in contact, during those periods of time, with all manner of people in the underground world or criminal element?
A. I wouldn't know about that.
Q. Well, that was the purpose of his working under cover, wasn't it, ma'am?
A. Yes.

Q. All right. This undercover work not only was in Mexico, but in France?
A. Yes.
Q. And other foreign countries?
A. I don't know of any other foreign country.
Q. At least Mexico and France we know of?
A. Yes.
Q. Also because of his upbringing and relatives and everything, he has a connection in Italy?
A. He has family in Italy.
Q. He was raised in Italy, wasn't he?
A. Yes.
Q. Now as a matter of fact, in renouncing his Italian citizenship at the time he became an American citizen, he can merely return to Italy, and he can regain his Italian citizenship?
A. I don't believe that is true.
Q. Well, if the Italian Embassy says that it is true, would you—
MR. GOLDSTEIN Well, I object to this as being argumentative.
THE COURT Sustained.
MR. GOLDSTEIN Thank-you.

Yes, thank you, but the woman couldn't speak. Goldstein was her voice in addressing the Court, your honor. She was finally beginning to understand. She had no voice, no opinion, just yes or no, that's all. Goldstein knew this language, the magic words to speak. She'd have to hold her breath and wait. She couldn't excuse herself and run to Goldstein.

She wanted time out to talk to her attorney. Didn't he see where Bock was leading? It wasn't true. It was unfair for the government to use those undercover years against Sandy. They were turning him inside out. Those were dangerous, foolhardy years, perhaps. But what did Sandy know, the police chief's son who wanted to make good? He figured he was being brave, climbing on limbs, diving off boats. He believed he was acting the hero in his new land. He gave up his pearl of a town on the edge of the sea to see the world, to have adventures. Hold that against him if you must. I admit he's naïve, foreign, speaks four languages. He's dark and has an accent. But Goldstein, can't you hear? Bock is whispering in the magistrate's ear—this man is dangerous and foreign, he speaks other languages, he's worked with criminals before. His underworld connections will enable him to run away. Then you, your honor, Mr. Representative of the Court, will look the fool. It wasn't true, the woman was thinking, it wasn't true at all.

Q. Now, you said or answered a question of your lawyer a little while ago; you stated that your husband was being treated by psychiatrists?
A. Yes.
Q. But, as a matter of fact, that psychiatrist was hired by the lawyer in the representing of your husband in this case, wasn't he?
A. The psychiatrist was hired by the lawyer because I told the lawyer that I was extremely concerned about my husband's mental condition, and because I was new to San Antonio and I didn't know of any doctors that I could hire myself, so I asked the lawyer to advise me on whom I should hire.
Q. But the point is, ma'am, prior to October 7, the date of your husband's arrest, he was not being treated by any psychiatrist, was he?
A. My husband was working in Mexico, and the State Department has a very strong rule on the use of psychiatrists abroad.
Q. Ma'am, would you answer my question? Was he being treated by a psychiatrist?
A. No.
Q. Prior to October the 7th?
A. No, he was not.
Q. As a matter of fact, he was coming to San Antonio to be treated by a physician because his hair was falling out prior to October the 7th, 1978?
A. Yes, he was.
Q. Now, do you know the gentleman seated here to my left?
A. Yes, I do.
Q. Have you had an occasion to talk to him concerning the arrest of your husband, just after the arrest?
A. Yes, I did.
Q. I believe he called you to tell you about it?
A. Someone else told me about it. He came over to see me following my notification that my husband had been arrested.
Q. For the record, do you know Mr. Kiere's position?

A. He is the Regional Director of the Mexico City Region of the Drug Enforcement Administration.
Q. I then take it that your husband worked under him?
A. Yes.
Q. Or for him?
A. Yes.
Q. Has Mr. Kiere visited in your home or been to your home prior to October 7?
A. Yes, he has.
Q. Has he been out to dinner with you and your husband and gone on social occasions with you?
A. Yes.
Q. And you might consider him your friend up to October 7 of this year?
A. I would say that he was a colleague of my husband.
Q. All right. You did have social contact with him?
A. We had social contact.
Q. When he talked to you, did you not tell him in words to the effect that you and your husband had just patched up some marital difficulties?
A. Yes. My husband and I were having problems with our marriage. I think it related to the fact that my husband was having so many psychological problems.
Q. But on this trip to San Antonio to see this physician, he was seeing this physician for a hair problem, wasn't he, and not a psychiatrist?
A. I had discussed with my husband the possibility of seeing a psychiatrist and a marriage counselor and—
Q. Well, what does—
A. May I explain?
THE COURT: Go ahead.

It was no use. Even when she did break through, screwed up her courage and addressed the Court, she made a mess of it. She blurted out, ran on too fast. The words came pouring out with no control. It was the truth and nothing but the truth, but that didn't make it any more compelling. She was up on that stand, windblown and frazzled; she might as well have stripped and told them every moment as it happened: So many days we couldn't talk, your honor. So many nights we lay in bed, separate and tense. I'd turn and say to him let's try once more, go and see someone, a shrink, a counselor, anybody who can teach us how to talk again. But it did no good. And my job, he'd say, what happens to my job? If I admit that I can't make it, go to the nurse and ask for help? Send me to a doctor, find someone safe to straighten me out? It isn't done. They'll send us home. They'll stick me at a desk somewhere where nothing happens.

> A. I had discussed with my husband the question of seeing a psychiatrist or seeing a marriage counselor because we were having marital problems and my husband—I was very much in love with my husband and I knew that he was in love with me and I thought all the problems related to the amount of stress he was under in his job. I suggested that he go to see a psychiatrist in Mexico. He told me that he was concerned about that because any psychiatrist that he would see in Mexico would have to be cleared through the State Department, through the embassy, and he was afraid that it would jeopardize his job if he were to admit that he had psychological problems. The Drug Enforcement Administration has no civilian or complementary support systems for agents who have any kind of emotional or psychological problem. So my husband was concerned because of the agency's position, he was afraid it might affect his career, so, therefore, he told me that he wanted to wait until he was back in the United States and he felt that he could do that.
> Q. But the point is that he had not sought psychiatric help?
> A. No.
> Q. Until you sought it for him through your attorney?
> A. That is true.
> MR. BOCK: No further questions.

The magistrate leans forward, pulls his glasses down over the bridge of his nose, peers above them. He looks so big, as though he could reach his arms down in those wide black sleeves and envelop that woman. "May I inquire of this witness?" he asks flatly. "Certainly, your honor," Goldstein answers.

The questions start again, circling around her. As if with the right questions, they can take her apart like the engine of some infernal machine. What are they looking for? she wonders. Loose parts, missing parts she never even noticed. "Mrs. Bario, where did you marry?" "Where did you go to school?" "Do you have any brothers or sisters?" "Where are they; what do they do?" It's like being with Dr. Rosenthal again. She sees those buildings jutting, that flat emptiness of sky. She sees someone on the examination table. A woman. In a treatment room. The walls are yellow. There are steel bowls and rubber gloves in boxes. The woman sits nude on the table looking out the window with the buildings sticking up. The nurse appears. The woman lies down, scoots forward. Her feet fit neatly in the stirrups. She shuts her eyes. "THE COURT: Would your parents be willing to sign a bond if the Court—in any amount of bond the Court sets, would your parents sign and be fully obligated for that?" The lamp curves up from the floor, cold steel. She feels the lamplight on her. The door opens. The doctor takes his seat. "THE COURT: In regards to his brothers and sisters then and their respective spouses, would they sign a bond?" She is screwed down tight against the table. Sterile implements, cold steel. The nurse's cool, dry fingers run up and down her arm. "THE COURT: And in regards to his former wife . . . would she sign a bond?" How far, she wonders, will he go? She feels the clamp, the heat of the lamp on her. She feels his hands in rubber gloves and his authority, penetrating farther. "Yes, she would. Well, I don't know. I think she would. I haven't asked her. I'd have to talk to her—I have talked to so many people—I would have to ask her."

The nurse's voice is soothing, lie still, relax your breathing. "Are there questions? Do you have any further questions? Mr. Bock? Mr. Goldstein?" Yes, I do, that woman wants to say. I have questions, with her eyes so tightly shut. What's wrong with me? What parts are missing? What do you see with your light inside? Tubes and tissue in the dark and the tension of that man's hand reaching for her soul.

36

The first-floor hallway of the jail was filled with children's voices and the warnings of their mothers—*"No, gorda, déjalo"*—bouncing off the concrete walls. A metal table had been pushed against the wall that held the public telephone. The children climbed up and squirmed on it. I could smell the heat in their hair, the impatience, the boredom. There was no guard in sight though it was after nine. The elevators were locked. I dialed Goldstein's number and listened to the heels of sneakers thumping on the metal table.

My waiting was almost over. I'd flown to Washington the week before and raised more money, begged more signatures for Sandy's bond. Goldstein had called my mother's house with the good news. The magistrate's findings of fact and recommendations had come out in our favor. The magistrate had recommended Sandy's release on the condition that my parents, Sandy's family in Ohio, and his former wife would sign the bond, on the condition that I could raise a fifty-thousand-dollar deposit to place in the registry of the court. I was a good witness, Goldstein had said. I had convinced the magistrate that I was genuine. When would Sandy get out? Soon, Goldstein promised, by Thanksgiving, perhaps. As soon as the judge signed the order, which was pro forma now. According to precedents, the judge relied completely on the magistrate's recommendations. That's why the findings were required in the first place. The secretary answered. Bobby Ozer was on the line.

What? I couldn't hear him over the children's laughter. "Speak up, Bobby. I still can't hear."

"I said the judge denied the magistrate's recommendations. We just got word this morning. The bond has been continued in effect. Goldstein is livid. It's unheard of. The magistrate was the only one to see the demeanor of the witnesses, to hear their testimony. We're taking it to New Orleans on an emergency appeal. But Sandy needs to know. Where are you? Have you seen him yet?"

I watched a ten-year-old in a frilly yellow dress playing hopscotch on the squares of the linoleum floor. It was mid-November, yet her hair was matted on her face from the heat. Her net crinoline was sticking. When I'd arrived in Washington the trees had already turned colors, the leaves had begun to drop. The cool air seemed so clean. We had packed the trunks of my car and my father's tight with our expectations for Sandy's release. My parents kept saying they wouldn't stay long, they wouldn't need their winter coats. After Sandy got out on bond, they would drive back to Washington so we could be alone with David. We made space in their trunk for a roasting pan and candles for the table. Just in case the bureaucratic red tape of Sandy's release took longer than we thought, we packed Christmas ornaments and lights. We'd have something to be thankful for, my mother said. We'd have Sandy out of that degrading jail. We'd driven straight through Nashville, Memphis, Texarkana. When we stopped to sleep, the promise of Sandy got us on the road by dawn.

I watched that yellow dress hopping, those skinny brown legs like winter sticks.

Bobby said, "Don't worry. We'll appeal and win. I'm already working on the brief. Tell Sandy we'll have him out by Christmas." A long pause. "Are you there?"

"Yes, I'm here."

"Sure you're okay? I could meet you for lunch and try to get you in to Sandy."

"I'm at the jail right now. I'll try to get a special pass from the chief. I missed one visit while I was at my mother's. They might let me in."

I hung up. The guard appeared, herding women, children, a few old men onto the elevator with him. "No pushing," he yelled, repeating it in Spanish. Bermuda shorts, a striped rebozo. The sneakers had stopped drumming. The visitors bunched and shuffled in. Nobody dared punch the guard between his buttons, under his double chins. He held his hand on the keys in the lock and looked across the tops of heads to me. "You comin' up or not?" The eyes in the elevator waited. I wanted to speak for them, ears pricked, dark eyes watchful. "I'll walk up," I said. "Maybe they'd like to walk up with me. Unlock the doorway to the stairs." It was a weak, uncertain voice, but it was mine. There was disbelief from the guard and curiosity from the others: "What's happening?" "What's she saying?" You would rather walk up, wouldn't you? Without this pig? ¿Quieren, verdad?

They murmured to themselves. One old woman nodded timidly before the guard snapped back. "Nobody's walking. You ride with me or don't go up." The faces shrunk; the doors glided shut. Another visiting day had started.

I turned slowly from the elevator and walked down the hall, out into the heat. My car was parked in the first row of visitors parking, my own car. I had jealously inspected it in Washington when it arrived, outraged by a small nick on the door, by the empty Styrofoam cups tossed in back. I closed myself in, lit a cigarette, felt in my purse for the last letter Sandy had sent to my mother's. I didn't read it through again, but its opening sentences hung in the air—"I'm so afraid to believe the good news, that I'll soon be with you. You were so strong and brave at the hearing. Once I'm out of here, I'll be stronger, too. No more feeling sorry for myself, no more nightmares. I'll get a job, work hard to prepare for trial. I heard about a priest in San Antonio who might be able to help us. You remember, I mentioned him to you? Please try to find him when you get back. Tell him everything good you know about me. . . ."

I couldn't face Sandy in the jail that day, so I took out the map and went looking for his priest.

37

It didn't take long that afternoon to find Father Brosnan's reform school. Everyone I talked to in the Spanish-speaking part of town had heard of it and was eager to give directions.

The gatekeeper left me in a big bare room where I sat by the open door watching a basketball game on a distant blacktop. The players soon came filing in beside me. There were catcalls, the smell of body heat. I couldn't decide whether I was more afraid of an audience with the priest or outright rejection by the gatekeeper when he got back. I needed something from that priest before I returned to the jail to tell Sandy—there'd be no bond, no release. Scratch the Thanksgiving turkey; now we're putting down our borrowed funds on Christmas Eve.

I had come on a stall tactic, that was all. The judge's continuance had been sealed and delivered. There wasn't a thing Father Brosnan could do. No use dragging out Sandy's letter and trying to explain to Father B. that my husband prayed for a job at his school as his penance of good works for a year of bad judgments. Sandy's fantasy followed a tired Bing Crosby plot from the forties, the kind of Saturday matinee fare that Vieste's old theater manager, Don Luigi, had rented on the cheap. The kindly Irish priest with his heavy brogue and crooked cassock gathers streetwise kids around him and performs a miracle for Sandy—who is freed from jail and lands the ideal job working for the priest. By Christmas it's like

Charles Dickens in Texas. We're standing in the threadbare parlor of the training school, decorating an eight-foot tree—one happy, do-good family. Sandy reclaims himself for his false belief in Claude and hangs a gold star at the top of the tree.

"This way," the guard signals with a broad, flat hand.

I catch my breath. Maybe somehow it could be true, maybe our luck is finally turning.

I follow down a long hall, and there's the priest—just like Bing Crosby, graying, bald, compact. He flutters his robe and nods. "In here, my dear."

I sit across his cluttered desk. The sun is at his back, pouring in the barred, ground-floor window. His Hollywood eyes try to read why I've come. I'm racing inside. I take a breath and follow Sandy's script down to every scratched-through letter as though I believe this priest might actually help, as though I need his absolution. Forgive me, Father, for I have sinned. The tears start falling. His chair scrapes, his cassock rustles. He's got his arms around me. He really has a brogue. I can't believe it. I catch a whiff of his perfume as he reaches for the tissues, lilac on his starched white collar.

"Easy, my child. It can't be that bad, nothing is. Calm yourself. I can't understand you when you're crying."

Part of me is laughing at the thought of this drug rehabilitation center, at this man I've never seen in his long black coat calling me "my child"; and the other part of me leans into him, wanting his embrace, wanting it to turn out just like Sandy's fantasy. He puts his hand on my head, and I consider reaching for his fingers to kiss his holy ring. I should pull away. What can you do, you phony old priest, pushing your tired powers?

Puffy eyes and sniffles, a balled-up tissue in my hand. I wipe my eyes, try to smile. I'm so ashamed. "I'm sorry," I say as he draws back.

"Now, tell me. What can I do about your husband? Tell me from the beginning if you can."

Mexico, Sandy's job, Claude, the arrest, I stumble through it all again, laying the damp Kleenex on my knee, trying to include anything that might convince him we're worth saving. I pull out all the stops. A good Catholic girl, Father, duly confirmed. I did my time in parochial schools, memorized my catechism. And Sandy, an altar boy, a soloist in choir. Did I really say it? Looking up from underneath my brows as Sandy taught me, I realize it doesn't matter. It's no use. Knee-deep in the middle of my sordid little story, it's written in those priestly eyes. I've come to the wrong place with the wrong crime, the wrong kind of sinner. Father Brosnan's eyes are sharp on me. He's moved perhaps, but he's no wizard. He's strictly into street crime, blue-collar stuff, ripped-off liquor stores, an occasional armed robbery. No narcs, no former federal narcotics agents.

Stop sniffling; dry up and take it on the jaw. Father's bag of miracles doesn't cover international coke intrigue. He watches me with his smooth face. Even clerics have reputations to protect. He swivels in his leather chair, stares through the bars out the sunlit window. Another round of basketball is breaking up. A guard hands out clean towels to the sound of laughter. That blacktop court, six buildings, the grounds are Father's fiefdom. He enjoys an ear with certain judges on the bench. He does some good, he thinks. In the afternoon his classes, a group encounter. In the evening he'll say mass and still have time to prepare for tomorrow's court appearances where he might wangle a few deals for some tough kids. He's got to think of the school as well as his reputation. He swings thoughtfully back from the window, stands, spreads his hands on the desktop.

"You love your husband, Mrs. Bario, and believe in him?"

I nod, vigorous and humble.

"Then he has the help he needs most, your support, your commitment to your marriage vows." He steps out from behind his desk, knowing I'll stand, too, reaches for the rosary that dangles from his hip. "Now let's kneel and pray together—'Hail Mary, full of grace . . .'"

38

Our emergency appeal to reduce the bond is set for December 22 in New Orleans, according to Goldstein. How can I avoid seeing Sandy for so many days? Saturday will be here soon; Saturday arrives like clockwork every week. I'll pretend that I'm sick, that David has the sniffles. I'll send word to the jail by way of Bobby that I've been busy working on Goldstein behind the scenes. I go to Goldstein's office at eight o'clock each morning to pester him—what about filing for discovery, Gerry G.? Where are the facts of the government's case, where's their evidence, where is Claude and their hard proof? We'll have time to file for discovery after the bond appeal, Goldstein keeps saying. Be patient, Joanne. That's not so long a wait. It's December 1 already.

December 1. My God, I'm running out of money. The money I've borrowed for the bond has arrived, but I can't touch it. I'll get a job, go for interviews at private schools, at office-temporary agencies. There's an ad in the paper that looks promising. They want a sales rep for a New York publisher. I'll lie and say I'll stay in San Antonio forever.

I talk to myself in the car coming back from interviews. So what? Sandy won't be out for Christmas. Sandy won't be out at all. I've lost hope and dream of minimum and maximum security, picnics in a concrete box on Saturdays for fifteen years.

A friend from Mexico calls from the San Antonio airport—

come and have a drink, take the afternoon and we'll go shopping. A visit in the airport bar is tempting, an hour's pretense that nothing's wrong. My friend is bundled down with presents, takes out everything she's bought and shows it off. She sparkles like an ornament. We exchange stiff smiles, clink glasses with our stiff drinks. The hour drags in small talk about her maid, her daughter's ski trip to Colorado. She finally works around to the customary stateside favor: Would I buy that special bra she couldn't find and mail it through the diplomatic pouch? I sit staring at her, wonder what she means, why she's asking this peculiar thing. I have nothing to do with Christmas shopping, nothing to do with Warner's bras or embassies.

Wednesday, December 13. I'm in Chief Ray Olivarri's private office, in a room without windows, without pictures on the wall. I pinch myself to pay attention, tell myself this matters, this man has power. I've washed my hair for this interview, bought new stockings, smeared makeup on the circles underneath my eyes. If I'm believable and good, the chief will grant me special favors—no more Saturday visits in the jail. I'll avoid the telephone; I'll be able to speak to Sandy face-to-face. I can't pretend to be sick forever.

This interview has been arranged by a deputy from the extradition section of the sheriff's office, someone who knew Sandy when he looked like himself. His name is Bob Hernandez. He saw Sandy's picture in the paper, thought it couldn't be the same Bario who had been so kind in Mexico when Hernandez arrived on an extradition case. He'd hurried down to the jail to see what he could do to help. "Please bring my wife to see me," Sandy said.

Bob thinks the chief is a decent guy who'll try to work out something. It's tricky to hold a federal agent in jail; it's dangerous. The chief's responsible for his protection, no small deal in Bexar County. This jail is infamous. There are killings every year. They can't completely stop inmates from coming and going in the halls. Any of them might be proud to do in a former narcotics agent. They've got Sandy in the hospital section in the basement where he's isolated, though other inmates deliver medicines and food. It would be a relief to the chief to keep Sandy in his cell on Saturdays when half the jail is loose.

Hernandez talks as though the other inmates are the major

threat, but to me the real dangers are the DEA and Claude. Claude has the best motive to do away with Sandy. If Sandy goes to trial, Claude will have to take the stand, and who could count the targets of former investigations who'd gladly murder Claude?

"I want to help," Ray Olivarri says, but I refused to beg for dispensations. He doesn't even seem to notice my hard stance as he reaches for the phone. "Bring Bario up," he says, "from the hospital section."

My face goes white; my palms are wet. What does the chief think he's doing? Bob gently pats my wrist, the chief waits smugly at his desk, and I'm trapped on a black-and-chrome couch as the moments go by, sure that Sandy and I are about to be had. I won't feel gratitude; I won't, I swear.

A guard appears at the door with Sandy, his face the color of a winter sky. He's been two months without daylight, two months in his basement room. His eyes sweep the bunched-up furniture, Bob Hernandez, the chief. They touch on me and quickly look away as if I've caught him in some awful private act. Give him time to pull up his pants, to zip his fly. His white coveralls hang from his shoulders. His paper slippers flap against the floor. He clasps his hands low in front to protect himself.

"Come in," says the chief, already regretting this whim of his. If he'd known how pathetic Bario would be, he'd never have suggested it. He tries to reach for Sandy's arm across the desk and misses. Sandy pulls away, straightens up, shuffles forward in his paper shoes. "Hello, Bob," he says softly, passing him to sit on the other couch, near the chief's big desk.

"Go on," the chief says to me. "Go ahead and join him."

I grab my purse and quickly move, careful not to brush Sandy's bony knees. We're close enough to hear each other breathe. The chief fills in the silences: "Bob says you'd rather visit weekdays instead of the Saturday sessions. I don't usually hear special requests, but this is different. You're from out of town, there's security to think of. I'll send a memo to the cage permitting Mrs. Bario weekday privileges."

Sandy presses the tips of his fingers together, mutters, "Thank you, sir."

Relief is written on the chief, whose chair squeaks when he

throws his weight back. It'll be all right, no scenes from us. He's offered his charitable gift, and we've accepted. We might as well relax, let go. Share a few laughs, some easy remarks. But neither of us smiles. Sandy stares down at his cold gray hands. I am totally absorbed in Sandy. Bob Hernandez works hard not to look at anyone. The chief talks shop at him a little, asking if the sheriff is a sure bet in the next election, but Bob can't take up very much slack. There's no neat way to end this interview. The chief can't just excuse himself and leave.

He gets up, maneuvers around the furniture. "One more thing," he says politely. "If you'll follow me—" We stand, confused. "—as long as this is our little secret, you understand. Nobody has to say a thing. You don't even have to tell your lawyer."

He reaches for the door to a small, square room beside his office. The room is dark through the open door. We don't understand what he wants us to do. He flicks on the light to reassure us.

"Take as long as you like. Go on, it's all right."

Sandy and I touch, hold hands as the door closes behind us.

"This is what you wanted," the chief says through the paneled door. "To be alone so you can talk."

Alone with some file cabinets, two chairs, a desk, we're like former lovers meeting by chance years after our romance is over. We're shy without the glass between us, without the telephone. It isn't like Kerrville—no windows here, no pretending to escape. I wonder if they're watching us through peepholes or if a tape recorder is hidden in the room.

"Do you want to sit?" asks Sandy.

I choose the armless typing chair that swivels. "I'm sorry I missed our visit last week. There was nothing to report. Bobby says you know about the bond. I'm sorry."

He comes closer. "Did you find the priest?"

I push off with my toes; the chair spins away from him. "He won't help, Sandy. He works with kids who do drugs, not federal agents accused of bribery."

In the long pause between us, I'm sure I can hear the tape go around, though it doesn't matter. Let it all come out now. I'll confess, so will Sandy. At least we'll know what they have against us.

"I didn't take a bribe, Joanne. Did you tell the priest—"

I stop the chair and look at him. "He doesn't care. We can't make any deals with him. You're going to have to go to trial."

"Over what? Goldstein hasn't even filed for discovery. We don't even know what Claude said when he turned me in."

"Goldstein thinks DEA paid him."

"Sure, they paid him. Everything he ever did he did for money. He must have gone to them when I told him in April 'No more, never again.' I threatened to go to Jacques. I would have. I swear I would have, Joanne. I just had to figure out how to explain the sample, my letting him go the first time with the sample. I couldn't think. I couldn't get the words down—"

"But the sample isn't even in the indictment. They're saying you worked with Claude to smuggle cocaine, that you got paid for it."

"I swear I didn't. I kept the money in my safe for him, that was all. He gave me the four thousand dollars to keep it away from all the women in his life. I put the envelope in my safe, and that was it. Don't you believe me? If you don't, then everything is lost."

But couldn't he understand? We were lost already. During our weekly visits at the jail, I had watched him scribble down the important dates on his makeshift calendar, the cardboard backing of his legal pad. He must have realized that the DEA was closing in. On December 19, the government would take him to their Army shrink to have him checked for craziness. He would never pass their tests. But if by some chance he did and was found competent to go to trial, all we could hope for was more of this, months more of waiting, of trying to sort out unknown facts, months when Sandy wouldn't sleep, when he would be as rattled and as incoherent as he was being now. His hands trembled; his eyes drifted far away. The bond appeal was scheduled to be heard on December 22. Goldstein was convinced we'd win in New Orleans and that Sandy would be free for a meager fifty thousand dollars. Then I would get him, his bony knees and patchy head, in our first-floor two-bedroom apartment with its depressing rented furniture. What would we be like then? David would continue to sleep restlessly in his rented crib. Sandy would continue hearing voices in the night. He would cry through the mornings, his stomach would hurt. We'd be no competition for the DEA and Claude in court. Never mind Sandy's presidential commendations, his awards and trophies; forget his fifteen undercover names; Claude was too crafty for us, too well armed by his lack of feeling. Claude wouldn't fall apart. He wouldn't cry when he took the stand. Our only hope was that one of Claude's former targets, somebody else without any feelings, might come boldly in and kill him on the stand. I stopped the chair from moving and set my feet down on the floor. Had I really thought that? Could I mean it?

Sandy was pacing the small, square, windowless room. He reached for the other armless chair and wheeled it next to me, to sit with his palms flat on his knees.

"I got permission from the chief to go to the inmates' library to work. They take me at odd times each day so I won't be noticed. You see, I'm trying. I sleep a little now. Maybe Rosenthal's medicine has helped."

"I'm glad," I lied and then looked at him. If I squinted, I could remember Sandy. I could *see* him in spite of his uniform, in spite of his diseases. If he had saved that heart of him that was still Sandy, maybe he could fight. He would strain to remember the substance of the conversations Claude had managed to record. He would recognize the names from the cases that Claude distorted. He'd undo all Claude's innuendos. He would vividly recall the places where they'd talked, the circumstances—all the things that Goldstein couldn't know. Then there might be hope for us.

"The appeal looks good," he said.

"We can't count on it. We have to be prepared to keep working even if you're not released."

"But it looks good. Ozer said the court secretary in New Orleans went out of her way to be helpful. They know me there. It's different."

I played with the zipper on my purse and didn't answer. I pushed the chair again gently with my toe so we wouldn't be aligned.

"Do you want me to call the chief?" he asked, as if he'd read my mind. We weren't comfortable together any longer.

"It's been too much for you, hasn't it?" he said. "You've been so good these past two months, but you can't go on like this forever.

We should make other arrangements. You don't have to stay. It isn't fair to David or your parents. There are no Italian bakeries in San Antonio where your father can buy bread."

Stop, I wanted to shout, no more stupid, solicitous remarks. How could he go on as if it made sense to be closed up in this small, square room on the whim of the chief of the Bexar County Jail? How could he worry about my father finding bread? I didn't want his belated concern. If I could have taken everything I'd ever felt for him and dumped it at his feet, I would have. Don't need me. Don't count on me to save you.

"What about the arrest itself?" I asked. "Claude gave you money then, too, didn't he? How much was it—five thousand dollars? I've been afraid to ask about that. We never got around to it. What did he say to you that time?"

"It was the same thing," Sandy said, staring at me as if he couldn't believe I'd be so mean. "Don't you trust me, Joanne? I would have put it in my safe with the other envelope. If I'd ever meant to take his money, I could have really made a killing. How many kilos had he smuggled? At what value on the street? He had me, don't you understand? He had me as soon as I let the sample pass. Would I have risked my life or yours for five thousand dollars? Do you know how many cases I've worked all these years? I wanted the case badly, I admit. But I never wanted Claude's blood money."

I didn't think he'd meant to keep the money. I believe you, Sandy, I should have said. But my silence was the only way to prove my hopelessness to him. I didn't like his new control, his upbeat, got-my-shit-together mood induced by Elavil, Dr. Rosenthal's wonder drug. I wanted my real Sandy from New York, from Italy, before there was Claude or any hint of a crime. I wanted clear-cut, uncompromised outrage, the denial that there had ever been an unreported sample, or I wanted the complete collapse of will. Fight or give up, be absolutely innocent or absolutely guilty. If only it were true, if only he'd been truly guilty, I could tell him how I lie alone at night on my rented mattress, listening to David in his crib, his breathing regular as clockwork, while I count the years Sandy may soon spend in prison. How am I supposed to act? What will it be like if Claude can win with his bad record, with his customary lies? I see David at four, at nine, at seventeen—What am I supposed to say to David through fifteen years of weekly visits at some jail?

39

Two days after our private interview I went to see Sandy again at the jail, our first weekday visit, a Friday, December 15. "Get some sleep," my mother had said, "so you can cheer him up." But he didn't need my cheering. Perhaps it was Rosenthal's visits, his Elavil prescription, or just time ticking off the days until his appeal would be heard in New Orleans.

"Only a week more," he said through the telephone receiver. He even managed a brief smile. "Can you believe it? I'll get out of here, I know it. I'm fighting now. Once I get out of this place, they won't be able to stop us. Maybe I made a mistake to save a case, but I didn't take a bribe. I'm not the criminal here. Claude is. I just have this feeling now that we can prove it."

"I won't come tomorrow," I reminded him. "It will be our first Saturday off. Do you feel okay about it?"

"Yes, I do. It's better this way. Nobody around. Maybe they'll even give us a few more minutes. The Saturdays were so depressing —especially for you. Tomorrow you should do something special with your parents. Go for a ride, get out of town for a little while."

"Maybe. We could go to Austin. My father read in the paper about something going on in Austin. It's hard on him without anything useful to occupy him. You know why he won't come here to see you—"

He put his hand against the glass to stop me. "Don't say it. I couldn't tolerate your parents seeing me in here. I won't allow it. I'll see them when the bond's reduced."

"You know, Marisa calls almost every day. She's heard from Italy. They're sending money for the bond. They want to know if they should come—"

"Tell Marisa not to even consider it. No, I don't want anyone to see me here."

"If the bond's not reduced, I'm sure they'll come."

"But it will be lowered, Joanne. I feel it."

Time was up. The telephone line went dead. Sandy held up a finger to keep me in the cubicle a moment longer. He had paper with him, but no pen or pencil. He lit a match, extinguished it, and with the burnt end, scribbled on his legal pad. He held the note against the glass partition: "Come back Monday with Ozer. We have work to do."

That Saturday morning I drove to Austin with David and my parents. I didn't even mind the Christmas bazaar on Main Street or following my mother in and out of open booths. I bought an ice-cream cone for David, telling myself that Sandy was better. I could live through Christmas without him if he could begin to focus on the facts in his defense. We returned to San Antonio by 8 P.M. Our lights were out by ten. There were no calls.

How could we know what was happening that night, December 16, at the Bexar County Jail? As we slept, the inmates in the hospital ward were watching the ten o'clock news on the guard's TV. Sandy was in his cell making himself a sandwich. He had apparently saved a small cup of peanut butter from an evening snack, a slice of bread from his supper tray—though much later one of the guards would privately confide to a reporter that the jail had never listed peanut butter on its menu. He offered half the sandwich to a man in an adjacent cell who turned it down. Sandy took a bite, stood up. It looked as if he'd lost his balance. He wore a queer expression as he walked to the end of his cell, threw the sandwich in the toilet, and lay on his cot with his face to the wall. The inmate next door was sure he was sick. Then it happened—his back arched, his legs stiffened. The neighboring inmate heard gurgling from his throat. "Guard!" the inmate shouted. The guard telephoned the nurses' station. Sandy continued to choke and arch his back. When the nurse arrived, the ward was in a panic. She felt for a pulse but couldn't find one. She started artificial respiration. "Guard, an ambulance!" she ordered. The convulsions worsened as the emergency team began to work him over. The seizures were continuous and massive when they rushed him to the closest hospital, Santa Rosa Medical Center, eight blocks from the jail. It took two men to pry open his mouth and insert a breathing tube. They strapped him down to stop his body jerking. His mouth was set, his pupils fixed and dilated.

Sunday morning at our apartment complex stretched out before us, empty and cold. It felt strange to have missed my Saturday morning visit at the jail. I resisted the urge to call Bobby Ozer to see whether he had talked to Sandy.

I walked David to the playground, pushed him on the baby swing. A big kid in a baseball hat hung around the jungle gym playing bully. He led a pack of ten-year-olds down to the drainage ditch on the edge of the grounds and came back a few moments later dangling a snake from a stick. "It's a rattler," he called out. I didn't answer. "I swear it's really a rattler, lady." I picked David up and went to see, though I'd never recognize a rattlesnake. "You'd better put it where you found it," I advised before carrying David home.

It was a slow, boring day. My father said we ought to buy David a Christmas tree, but I ignored him. That night I wished someone, anyone, would call.

Bobby and I went over to the jail early Monday morning. I sat nervously outside the chief's office, chewing on a fingernail. He wouldn't let me in, I was sure, not after last week's private interview and my Friday morning visit by telephone. When Bobby came out jumpier than usual, I was convinced the answer had been no.

"You'd better come in," Bobby said.

"Must I?" Not that crowded, private room again, not the chief behind his desk.

"Yes," Bobby insisted.

The chief looked upset and worried. I tried to reassure him with my eyes that I had kept our bargain about the private session.

"It's Sandy," Bobby said. "He's been poisoned."

Some joke, Bobby. I even tried to smile.

"I'm terribly sorry," the chief was saying. "We have no idea how anybody could've got to him. They say it's strychnine, that's what they think."

"Where is he?" Bobby asked.

"Santa Rosa intensive care."

It was as if I wasn't there. I watched Bobby talk to Goldstein on the telephone. "What do we do?" There was silence while Goldstein gave instructions. Bobby turned to Olivarri. "When did this occur?"

"Saturday night, about ten o'clock."

But that wasn't possible; Saturday was two days ago. Someone would have called me sooner. Saturday night we were back from Austin at eight o'clock. At nine we were eating pizza from a cardboard box. By ten we were in bed. The phone never rang.

As though reading my mind, Olivarri said, "We would have called, but we didn't have your number."

I'd had the apartment more than a month; it was surely listed. Bobby hung up, turned to the chief. "We're official counsel. We should have been informed." Then gently, he asked me, "What do you want to do? We can go to the office first or right on to the hospital."

"To the hospital," I said.

"We'll walk. It'll be faster."

In my high-heeled boots and that unlucky beige suit, decked out for the attorneys on the off chance the chief would let me in, I kept pace with Bobby. He kept waiting for the tears that didn't come. I was more aware of Bobby's watchfulness than of the lights, the traffic, the Christmas shoppers. Just outside the hospital doors I touched him on the arm. "Maybe this is better," I tried saying. "He'll be safe in here until the bond appeal. Whatever it's like, it's got to be better than the jail, don't you think?"

I watched Bobby, racing in a kind of frenzy to the end of the hall, searching the directory. I slowly pushed the elevator button. Too late to hurry, I considered saying, but I didn't want to hurt his feelings. Bobby had worked hard on the memo of facts, on the brief for the appeal. Now they'd probably postpone the hearing.

How much more time would this add to San Antonio? Months, I figured. I'd better go out tomorrow again and look for a job.

A security guard kept staring. Was my hem coming down? Was my slip showing? He finally approached. "Can I help you?"

Bobby explained and asked directions. The guard kept looking me up and down. I knew it, there was something wrong with me. "Both of you stay here," he ordered, "while I speak to security. You're not to go upstairs, you understand?"

Something was going wrong with my heart. It had happened to my father. I imagined all of it, the shortness of breath, the collapse, intensive care next door to Sandy. My mother was safe with David, at least.

Bobby paced. The guard mumbled into his walkie-talkie. Two more guards showed up, led us down the hall, into a small room marked Administration. The chief guard told me to lift my arms. He brushed his hands all over me while the other searched my purse, flipped through my notebook. I wanted to say I'm the wife, but I didn't do it. To say a thing like that would sound too crazy.

When they were satisfied that we weren't hiding any weapons, the head guard rode up the elevator with us to the fourth floor. When the guard announced my name, I watched several doctors disappear, watched two nurses back into the lounge behind their station.

Two jail guards were posted outside Sandy's curtained room. A nurse's desk had been set up in front of the motionless white curtain. Someone had misspelled his name on the log and on the ticker tape scratches from an EEG. I'd started to pull the curtain open when another guard approached.

"You can't go in," he said, his hand on the holster at his hip.

"This is Mrs. Bario," Bobby explained. "I'm one of Mr. Bario's attorneys."

"Fine. But no one's allowed inside that room."

"Wait here," Bobby said, touching my shoulder. "I'll go call the marshal's office."

There were footsteps inside the room, the curtain fluttered. "Sandy?" I said. The curtain moved, a nurse stepped out, pulling the drape closed so quickly that I couldn't really see him, only a form beneath the sheet, the big machines beside his bed. Well then, I guessed he couldn't walk. He wouldn't be coming out to greet us. But he'd be okay. He was probably asleep. They'd pumped his stomach, given him a sedative; they were big on sedatives in hospitals.

"I'd like to peek in," I said to the nurse.

She was a big woman who knew how to look firm. "You'll have to wait," she said. Just then Bobby came back with the chief nurse beside him. "It's all right. Let her in." The chief nurse turned to the guard: "The marshal's on the phone for you."

The mean nurse reluctantly backed off. "One at a time," she cautioned, pulling back the curtain.

Sunlight poured in the window, glinted off bowls and the high steel bed. Sandy's head lay slack against the pillow. I was certain he was dead. "Bobby! Bobby, come!" I said, but he wasn't in the room with me. The respirator chugged, forcing air into Sandy's lungs. I walked slowly toward the bed. He had tubes up his nose, through his penis, a thermal blanket under him to bring his fever down. Somebody had stuck slivers of tape on his lids to hold his eyes open. I touched the sheet, hot and dry, lifted it to touch his legs, bare and trembling. "Sandy," I whispered, and he shuddered. His whole body seemed to jerk away. The blanket slipped off his bare white feet. "No," I said to nobody. His feet were shackled together with heavy chains.

"Bobby!" I called, and he was there, despite the nurse's order. The nurse came in behind him. "You were in such a hurry," she said. "You didn't give us a chance to warn you what he'd be like."

I looked at Bobby, staring down at Sandy's feet, and whispered, "He won't get out of here alive."

The big nurse was angry. "We don't know that. Don't you dare say that. We're still trying to control the seizures."

"Why are his feet like that?" I said.

"You'll have to ask the marshal. I'm not responsible for that."

"Where is his doctor?"

"He has several," she said defensively. "The best in San Antonio. But none of them are here just now."

Bobby held my elbow. "Are you okay? Do you want to sit down?"

I shook my head and looked at Sandy's feet.

"What do you think, Bobby? Any chance he could escape if they didn't chain him down?" Loud enough for the guards to hear, for the nurses in their stations, for the doctors hiding in the lounge. The nurse looked away. The guard kept staring. They're all crazy, I thought—not Sandy, not me.

I went up to the guard. "Take the chains off. I don't care who makes the decision, but they'd better be off before I come back or I'll scream, I swear, so loud the whole town will hear."

The mean nurse had moved behind her desk. "Here's my telephone number," I said, writing it on the top of her log. "I'll be back within the hour to speak to whichever doctor's in charge."

Bobby followed down the hall of intensive care, down the elevator. I led him all the way to Goldstein's office where my car was parked.

"Do you want to come up?" he asked.

"No. I have to go and tell my family."

The expressway hadn't changed. Cars approached, passed without incident. I saw Sandy's spare white ankles on the exit signs, his feet jerking on the chains when another seizure hit. It was a private hospital, a Catholic hospital, Bobby had said. Surely someone must have protested to the guards. Surely the head of the hospital had complained.

I sped off the expressway and onto the interstate. Why hadn't Olivarri called on Saturday night? He could have gotten my number from information. Had the jail or the marshal's office used the extra time to cover themselves and search privately through Sandy's papers? I felt so offended that no one had called. The hospital must have inquired about next of kin. We'd been locked in our three rooms; someone should have told us. I wondered who could have poisoned Sandy—poisoned Sandy, I repeated, as though if I said it often enough it would begin to seem real. Could it have been Claude? I'd have to make a hundred calls: to Sandy's sons in Washington; to Marisa, his sister in Ohio. Olivarri had said strychnine. There would be no prognosis to report, not while the doctors were still hiding from me.

Well, I wasn't keeping quiet any longer. I had tried so hard to be a good girl, to be a young lady. Not any longer.

I parked in my numbered space at the apartment complex. David's push toy had been left outside our door. My parents were sitting at the table. I watched them for a moment without speaking to them. My father was reading want ads in the paper. My mother with her gray hair, her sad blue eyes, was playing solitaire. There were toys spread out on the floor, a lingering odor of dogs from the previous tenants. David came running over to me. How was I supposed to tell them?

"Sandy's in the hospital. He's been poisoned."

40

There is no relief here, no resolution. Even tension can become monotonous. Balled-up tissues on the stained gold rug, the telephone dragged to the center of the floor, its line taut, anticipating action. Brown cushions from the couch, pillows from the beds, have been thrown around and made into a fort. The frantic two-year-old presses his mother's face between his hands, strokes her cheeks. "Don't cry, Mommy. Let me dry your tears." He piles cushions all around her, darts from her knees to the base of the couch, does a double take, and crashes through the pillows. Playing peekaboo to dull red eyes, he never even wins a smile.

The woman waits for the telephone to ring, telling herself she's got to take control to get through this. She's got to stop hanging back, got to stop feeling sorry for herself. Her mother sits at the dinette table, head in hands, more tissues, more sighs. Her father's in the shower. He can't take the idleness any longer. He'll dress, drive her to the hospital, see the patient for himself, though the prospect is disturbing.

She has already placed her calls to family, to friends and friends of friends. The most important call went out to Richard Ben-Veniste, the lawyer who first introduced her to her husband when he'd been a star government witness in New York. Former federal prosecutor who'd received acclaim during Watergate, Richard will help if only she can find him. She has called his parents in New

York, his office in Washington, and left messages in both cities. Why must it be so close to Christmas? Why is half the world on holiday? She's tracked down every doctor working on her husband's case, has left word with critical-care specialists, neurologists, a cardiologist or two. She waits for them to call her back. Newspapers lie open on the cushionless couch. "Poison Suspected in Inmate's Collapse," "Former Narcotics Agent Poisoned in Cell." She's left a message at the medical examiner's office and even at the FBI. Now there's nothing to do but wait.

The calls which come are useless: journalists from news syndicates, from D.C. and New York, craving a human interest story, a splashier case for Christmas than the neediest cases in the New York *Times*. Somebody from a local TV station wants to send a camera crew around, but they're not welcome.

If only the doctors had been kinder, if they had stepped forward to explain the prognosis, grim as it might be. But they won't answer any calls. They fear court orders, lawsuits, publicity.

Finally, the telephone rings. Get hold of yourself, the woman thinks. Please, dear God, let it be Richard.

He says hello. She holds her breath to keep from crying.

"I got your messages," he says softly. "Are you all right?"

She nods as if he's there. It's too difficult to speak. "I guess. Sandy's in a coma, Richard. They're saying he's been poisoned."

With every call there is always that awful moment of silence. Her husband's collapse has taken her where nobody will follow. Richard Ben-Veniste is her only hope. He knows about cover-ups, stonewalling, and secret tapes, but it's too much to ask him. She can't hire him. She has no way to pay him.

"Try not to worry. I'll do what I can. You call Sandy's lawyer this afternoon and tell him I have your authorization to begin making inquiries on your behalf."

After Richard's call the tears came and I could begin to think a little. It had to be Claude, I decided. He was the only one besides the DEA itself to benefit if there were no trial. Much as the DEA might want to scapegoat Sandy, to prove how "honest" the agency was, they couldn't have liked the idea of a trial in which their "normal" practices would come to light. Sandy knew too much.

He had been getting better. If he had gotten out of jail, he would have begun to help with his defense. But no one at the DEA could have been responsible for poisoning Sandy. It seemed too inconceivable. Claude, however, was a different story. If Sandy's case had gone to court, Claude would have had to appear as chief witness for the prosecution. There would be no case if there was no Claude. Yet I couldn't imagine him facing the exposure. No matter how tight the security was, he would have been absolutely vulnerable. The trial would have attracted national publicity. Claude had left a trail of "bodies" in every city he had worked. Somebody would have gotten to him. No matter how much the DEA may have paid him to produce a case against Sandy, I couldn't picture Claude putting his own life on the line at anybody's trial. He'd always worked behind the scenes. He had never testified in court.

But I had no proof against Claude. That woman with her hair disheveled, who batted her toddler away like a fly, she had nothing of substance to produce. The medical examiner wouldn't even say for sure that strychnine had been used. He was still conducting tests.

My father puts on his dark gray suit and drives us to the hospital. He won't let me drive anymore—what if somebody's after me? He's the deliveryman, dropping me off at Santa Rosa. The vending machine in the lobby is selling a newspaper with a half-familiar photograph of someone I once knew—"Murder Try Inside Jail"—but I don't buy one.

My father and I ride the elevator up without any guards approaching. I can't remember Sandy's face, just his lids taped open, his feet in chains. The safe feelings that came after Richard's call are dissipating. Pull yourself together, I tell myself as the doors slide open. This might be your only chance.

They've changed the prison guard in intensive care. The new one won't let my father come inside. But the night nurse assigned to Sandy is kind. "I'll send for the administrator," she suggests. Her name is Mrs. Lee. "I was on duty when they first brought in your husband," she explains. "Please come in."

My father leans against the wall outside the curtain, nodding.

Go ahead. He'll wait; he isn't eager. Mrs. Lee holds my hand, stays close beside me. There's no drawing back from Sandy now. I remember our private session in the small, square room off Chief Olivarri's office and the hopelessness I'd felt. Was that the last time I'd seen Sandy? No, of course not. There was Friday morning in the public rooms, hanging onto the telephone receiver. Sandy had thought the trip to Austin was a fine idea. We shouldn't have gone. I should have never left him. No one would have dared to try such a thing if I'd been there. Perhaps the guards had monitored our visits? Perhaps Chief Olivarri's private little room had been bugged all along? Never mind that, never mind the chief or Goldstein or the prosecutor. The visitor's room, the courthouse, Goldstein's office on the twenty-ninth floor, are all behind us now.

Mrs. Lee's voice is soft as she draws the curtain, drops the bar beside the bed. "Talk to him as if nothing were wrong. He might hear. They sometimes do in coma. Hearing is the final sense to go."

We are alone at last with no partitions. I am careful not to dislodge the intravenous tube up his nose, in his arm, especially careful of the thick plastic tube in his throat where they've performed a tracheostomy. But I must get near enough to touch. His forehead is hot and damp. He's plugged into their machines that count his heartbeats, that make his chest rise and fall mechanically. Beneath the sheets his white legs quiver. At least the chains have been removed.

Remembering Mrs. Lee's advice, I take a deep breath, but the words don't come. I'd speak Italian if I knew enough, so no one else could understand. I'd call him by his family's name—Santino; I'd say *"Mi dispiace."* When my grandmother got old, though she never looked as old as Sandy now, she forgot every word of English. I hoped it was the same with him, that if he heard the guards, the doctors, or nurses, he wouldn't understand. Perhaps he didn't feel the tremors in his legs, the tubes, the fever. He might have lost his memory of feeling. He might not remember carnival in Santa Cruz or any of the names for Claude Picault. He might not remember our meeting in that windowless room with the swivel chairs. He was floating. He was now truly out to sea. For all I knew, he was floating on the Adriatic. I put my face against his ear: *"Mi dispiace,* Sandy."

41

Marisa arrived Tuesday morning from Ohio, tall, skinny, her coat hanging off one arm. She looked so much like Sandy that it took my breath away.

I drove her to the hospital, admired her behavior at the side of his bed. She held his hand, stroked his patchy head, kissed him. She didn't mind the fetid smell of the hole in his throat or his taped eyelids or his blue and swollen fingers. Nurse Lee didn't have to tell her what to do. She held long, one-sided conversations in their Viestano dialect. I stood at the door and bit my lip to keep myself from saying that it was no use.

With Marisa there, I became tougher. We chased down every doctor. When they didn't return our calls, we waited in their waiting rooms for them, waited in Sandy's room for one of them to appear on rounds, closing our ears when the nurses suctioned the mucus from his lungs. On the third day one of the specialists came up to us in the hall, asked our names, led us to a private room behind the nurses station, and showed us Sandy's chest X rays. During the initial seizure he had inhaled peanut butter, causing pneumonia—a dense gray patch on the X-ray film. "We can't give you much hope," the doctor said. "He shows only brain stem activity on the EEGs. He blinks, he coughs, he voids himself."

"What about the poison?" Marisa asked. "You're not just saying that he choked on peanut butter?"

She shook her head. "No, though the tests are inconclusive. The urine sample from emergency shows no strychnine, but he could have voided at the jail before they brought him in. It looks suspiciously like poison. The seizures are classically strychnine, violent, continuous. I don't believe he simply choked on a bit of sandwich, not a grown man. If it's not strychnine, I'd suspect another toxic agent, harder to trace, perhaps."

"Will he go on like this," I asked, "in a coma?"

"I don't think so. You've seen his hands, how blue they are? He's already cyanotic. I don't think he'll last the night."

That same morning we found the neurologist who'd been on call when Sandy was brought in. He wouldn't back down from his original diagnosis. "The medical examiner's more sophisticated tests supposedly showed no sign of strychnine. But I've personally treated eight cases of strychnine poisoning in Mexico. Only tetanus produces seizures this brutal, and we have positively ruled out tetanus."

The other doctors would only talk cautiously by phone. "It's corrupt here," one of them confided. "Who knows if the urine samples tested were even taken from your husband? But what can we do? We live in this town."

Another, strictly off the record, said the case had already become too confusing to sort out. This wasn't a medical case. The federal marshal's office was paying the bills, giving the orders, and the marshal wanted Sandy kept alive. Texas laws on brain death were liberal, but no one here was looking at the laws. The doctors, the jail officials, too, wanted their names kept out of the news, didn't want any part of a courtroom. If he were forced to make an educated guess, he'd call it poison. "But don't quote me," he said, "in a court of law, I'd deny everything I've said."

Marisa camped out on the small brown couch. We didn't sleep. We made long-distance calls to Rome, Naples, Sardinia, Vieste. Every half hour we called intensive care. At 3 A.M. the telephone rang. It was the night nurse from the hospital. "If you want to be here, Mrs. Bario, you'd best come now."

But Sandy didn't die that night, nor on Christmas Eve or Christmas Day. The headlines in the daily papers shrank: "Chemist Rules Out Overdose," "Medical Examiner Finds No Poison," "Narcotics Agent Vegetates."

He was strong, the doctors marveled. His heart would not give out, and each time the pneumonia worsened, a change of antibiotics rescued him. On December 26 the buzzer on the respirator sounded. Sandy was assisting the machine. He'd begun to breathe. Weakly at first, but he was breathing. The EEGs were flat; the CAT scans showed no hope of higher function. He wouldn't live, but he might not die.

On December 30 Marisa went home. We couldn't blame her. There was nothing more to do, and her family needed her. I took her to the airport, came back to the apartment, and called the chief neurologist on Sandy's case.

"How can you let him vegetate like this? Every time he tries to go, you shoot him up with different drugs and leave him hanging."

The doctor was cold and businesslike about it. "You want my advice? Get out of here. I believe I've read that you have a child? Take him home, go back to your life. There's nothing you can do to help your husband here."

"That's it," my father said when I got off the phone. "We're packing up and going home."

I wanted to, so badly. I didn't know how many more visits to Santa Rosa I could take. "Is it all right? I mean, isn't it wrong to leave Sandy here alone?"

"You heard what the doctor said. This could go on for months. What are you going to do? You've got to pay the rent here. It's no good for David. We'll go home, and you'll get Richard Ben-Veniste to help you."

Tell me once more, Daddy, that it's okay to go, that I'm not abandoning Sandy's ship, that I'm not an awful wife for leaving. I'd be going without any answers. Did the DEA really have a case? Did they have any proof from Claude? Did Sandy accidently choke, or was it murder? I should stay, wait, be by his side. But he could vegetate for months—even for years. The longer he went on, the less likely that they'd find any proof of poison in the autopsy.

If we *did* go, there were real things to do, simple chores to occupy me. Clean out the refrigerator, sweep the floors. I'd get the manager of the apartment complex to let the rental company come in to take their furniture away. No reason for us to hang around on the morning of New Year's Eve. Okay, I'm gonna do it, I'm gonna go. Sandy won't know. Sandy isn't knowing anything.

It was a relief to act. I called the doctors, Goldstein, Bobby Ozer. Mr. Blumberg at the hospital promised to call with news of any change. I left my parents' number, their address. I dragged out the shabby Christmas tree, needles shedding, and threw it in the dumpster. I called Bob Hernandez, my last call, asking him to visit Sandy when he could. At two o'clock, over my father's protests, my mother's fear, I drove alone to Santa Rosa to say good-bye.

The respirator chugged in the antiseptic room while I counted three times that Sandy gasped and drew a breath alone. It was horrible to watch him. He didn't twitch any longer—the Dilantin had controlled the seizures. He didn't blink. With his eyes taped open, his plastic tube administering artificial tears, he didn't see.

One last time I went up to the side of the bed, lowered the bar, looked down on him. He was old and white and frail. He had, my mother said, rushed through our lives like a powerful wind in a summer storm. He'd carried me away completely. On his arm on our wedding day, I was sure I had been rescued and lifted out of dailiness, that I was where I wanted to be, part of Sandy's living theater. We would be center stage and overflowing because we had so much. I'd take his name the way he'd taken on so many names, and I'd be changed. No more doubts, no more shilly-shallying. I leaned down into the smell of his infection. I touched his cheek, smooth because somebody shaved him every day. I touched his hair the way Marisa had, with love. It was beginning to grow back. Where the awful holes had been, he had new growth. I kissed each spot. I'm sorry for this end, I whispered, but for the rest of it, I won't be sorry.

I heard a nurse's voice outside the curtain and stood up straight, pulled up the bar. The room was still. The impressive summer storm was over.

42

My father was in the apartment house parking lot, packing his car. Sandy's suits hung from the roof; there were boxes on the sidewalk. By four o'clock both cars were packed. David was settled on a piece of foam wedged in the backseat of my father's car. I watched him spread out his blanket and hug his polar bear. Bob Hernandez came to see us off, tears in his eyes. "I'll take care of Sandy," he reassured me, waving as we left. "Good-bye, good-bye."

As I followed my father onto the interstate, I continued to list the reasons that justified my going: the neurologist's advice, the cost of staying on, my parents, David. Sandy wouldn't miss me because he wasn't really there.

David's fuzzy dime store bear bobbed in and out of view. Browned-out fields replaced the suburbs, flat and neutral under the gray sky. If I didn't know we were still in Texas, I would have sworn the gray sky threatened snow. It was a winter landscape that looked like home.

Forgive me, Sandy, for feeling better, but I was relieved to get out of Texas. In a day we'd cross the line—no more jails, no more doctors hiding. I pretended I could leave San Antonio behind and concentrate on the car in front of me carrying all the family I had left. The day after Sandy's collapse, Goldstein had remarked, "Like you, I'd prefer a brain-damaged Sandy to no Sandy at all," but Goldstein wasn't like me. In three days we would be in Washington, where Richard Ben-Veniste would help me show all of them who Sandy had once been. I didn't want a brain-damaged Sandy. I didn't want to remember him falling apart in the Bexar County Jail. I wanted what I had always wanted from him, the real thing.

San Antonio lay thirty miles back when a misty rain began to fall. I wished I had read some books on coma. How did they know that the patient couldn't feel? I wanted some authority to tell me, but there were no authorities I trusted any longer—not doctors, judges, psychiatrists, or priests.

I smoked a cigarette in the closed-up car, watching my father pass the car ahead of him. I liked these wide, unbroken spaces. The road was flat; we were putting in some distance fast. Three hours from Dallas, and the road was empty. Scrub pines bordered fallow fields; a stunted tree appeared. I hadn't seen a leafless tree in what seemed like years. The branches looked like they had cobwebs hanging from them. The mist hugged the colorless fields, resembling snow. As we drove on, I slowly realized it wasn't mist, but ice, fine as sugar, sticking to the trees. A car in the opposite lane skidded, lost control, and banked on the grass divider before gliding back onto the road. I tested my brakes; the back end slid. I couldn't see my father, several cars up. Then there he was, signaling cautiously as he pulled off the road.

He slipped twice as he came over to my car. "Have you been listening to the radio?"

I shook my head.

"There's a bad ice storm in Dallas, but I haven't seen a decent place to stop. We'll keep going. Keep a good distance from the other cars. If you get in any trouble, blink twice and pull over."

It was almost worth the ice to see my father as himself again. He'd always loved to drive in the snow, terrifying my mother by choosing the steepest hills to climb. The limbs of trees and power lines were encased with ice as we moved on, but it wasn't bad. I'd be like my father, both hands on the wheel. This was something I could do as well as anyone.

Soon the road surface looked like it was waxed. I turned on the radio. They'd closed the Dallas airport. Traveler's warnings had been extended into Arkansas. Flip disk jockeys turned deathly earnest in their appeals: "Don't drink and drive tonight; don't go out if you can stay home." I'd almost forgotten—it was New Year's Eve.

It was dark when we got to the outskirts of Dallas. The exit signs glistened. The ramps and overpasses were dotted with lights that didn't move, silhouettes of trucks that had spun around to face oncoming traffic. My father crawled ahead of me, eased his way around a stalled car on the ramp. Midway up, a car crashed into the safety wall. Ice sparkled on the dented rails.

For the first time in months I stopped thinking about Sandy. My knees locked as my father started across a slick bridge. His tires left a wobbly trail; his car was waltzing. I imagined it sailing off the bridge with David and his polar bear.

I blinked my lights to warn my father, remembering a theory my boss had told me in New York, that getting rich was like finding a mythical river of money, that once you'd found it, you'd never get out of it and would be rich forever. Who cares, I'd thought. But now I understood the theory. Claude, the arrest, Sandy's collapse, and now this storm were all part of some river of bad luck we'd wandered into and would never escape. We had been touched. We were jinxed, and nothing good would ever happen again. Finally, we found a stretch of road where we could stop.

"What is it?" my father asked. "If the driving makes you too nervous, we can stop. But it's just going to get worse. We could be stranded here for days. I think our best bet is to push through it."

After a month of pacing in San Antonio my father's energy had come back. "All right," I said, "let's go."

It was clear in Arkansas. It snowed in Memphis, Knoxville, through the Tennessee mountains. But the snow in Virginia was soft and familiar, like the clean white sheets on the beds my mother made, welcoming us home.

IV

Picault was edgy and with good reason. Bario was caving under from the pressures of the Añez-Vaca case. He wouldn't be able to stall him very long. In time, even with the compromise of the initial sample, Bario would either crack completely or take his story to Kiere. The time had come to blow Bario out of the water.

He had planned it well. He'd scheduled a trip to Montreal on the pretext of meeting Alain Chaillou, a potential dealer, about placing some of the cocaine so they could nab Chaillou in another case. Yes, he'd go to Montreal and blow the whistle to the Royal Canadian Mounted Police, who would call Kevin Gallagher at the DEA's office in Paris.

The DEA would be interested in a case against such a powerful, controversial agent. It might improve their deteriorating image to seem bent on punishing one of their own kind who had "gone wrong." In his weakened condition Bario had confided much about the DEA's state of affairs in Mexico, their problems with the State Department and the Mexican feds. He had unwittingly given Picault a hook to use with the DEA. Picault knew the agency much better than Bario could guess. They had helped him before when he was in trouble in New York after the Castiglione case. They had allowed him to keep the heroin he had brought in as well as the money. They would help him again. He knew Bario had enemies; Bario had been treading on dangerous ground with the CIA and the

DEA's Special Operations group. Bario was used up in Mexico now, and besides, Picault needed the money. He had run up debts with everyone he knew in Mexico's French community; he was flat broke. Sante Bario should be worth a pretty penny.

He had laid it on thick with the RCMP. "This Bario, he's ruining me. He's supposed to be my protector, no? But he's robbing me blind, I tell you. He orders me to bring in drugs. He wants money from me. He's the powerful one, with the United States Government and a Mexican general behind him. It isn't right." He dazzled the Canadian agents with his performance. They had called Kevin Gallagher that very same day.

He had slipped the sample of cocaine into the heel of his shoe before his flight to Paris. He wouldn't tell Gallagher about the sample until he had arrived. He considered it the right touch, the cocaine sample. All he had to do was to appear suspicious when he went through French customs, and they searched him as he'd wanted them to. "No, no, you misunderstand," he'd said to the customs agent. "I work for the American narcotics agency." The French Government would be appalled that the DEA had allowed one of its "agents" to travel into France with illegal drugs without advanced approval. He'd needed that extra bit of insurance in case Gallagher had tried to back out. "Bario was the one. He told me to carry the drugs," he had told Gallagher in front of the French officials. It had been embarrassing to the DEA. They would go the extra mile to get Bario now.

He knew from Campos that there were others in the DEA who wanted Bario out. Campos had his valuable connections. It didn't matter to Picault who paid the bills. As long as he was paid. And this case wasn't going to come cheap. He naturally expected to be paid in cash, but money wasn't all he wanted. He was finished in Mexico, all but burned. He wanted to work in the States. He wanted a new name and genuine papers. American citizenship or at least full residence status. He wanted to be an "agent" for the DEA, guaranteed work and guaranteed protection. He'd give them anyone they'd like for that. He'd give them Sante Bario.

43

Since we'd last met, Richard Ben-Veniste had gained national prominence. Watergate was now behind him. He'd gone into private practice and had as many cases as he could handle. He certainly didn't need me, and I didn't have the money to hire any lawyer, let alone someone in his league. My parents were helping me financially. Sandy's family had made me a generous gift of the money they had sent to be used for the bond. When that was gone, I'd be broke. But Richard took the case without a fee. I don't know what I would have done otherwise. The documents which the DEA eventually produced in court were released because Richard was so shrewd, so canny in his strategy. He outmaneuvered the agency, enabling us to get hold of irrefutable documents which the DEA had hoped to bury permanently.

Our first stop in beginning to sort out the facts of Sandy's arrest was to go to the Justice Department's Office of Professional Responsibility, where we requested an investigation of the "incident" at the Bexar County Jail. We didn't have much to go on. Sandy continued in his coma. There was as yet no proof of poison, no proof that the DEA had acted irresponsibly. We didn't even know the basis of the charges. They had not been dropped by the DEA, though Sandy would never go to trial. He had been accused; we had little hope of vindicating him. After an initial inquiry, the OPR attorneys said they didn't have the authority to retrieve classified documents from the DEA without proof that Sandy's rights had been violated. We had no way to show proof without the documents, couldn't get the documents without the proof.

Our only way to clear Sandy's name was to proceed with an appeal of his suspension and termination from the DEA, initiated in Texas by Goldstein. We were entitled to a hearing before an administrative appeal board, the judicial arm of the Office of Personnel Management, one of the big bureaucracies. According to Richard, this was our only hook to justify a formal inquiry. "It should be interesting," Richard said. "We'll be arguing criminal charges before an administrative judge. But it's our only shot to get DEA into a courtroom, where we can start kicking some ass. Suppose we bring an action for Sandy's posthumous reinstatement on the grounds that he was wrongfully fired? DEA would have to justify the firing—they would be immediately put on the defensive. We might be able to take depositions and get the reports of those DEA agents who ran Claude." Richard began to smile. "They won't lay down and admit they were wrong—it's too sensitive a case for them, but the agency will have to produce Claude to prove its case. We'll have them between a rock and a hard place, but it's going to take time."

That January Richard began implementing his strategy for full disclosure. I stayed at my parents', dreading the idea of looking for a job. I didn't think I could make it through an interview. Somebody was bound to ask about my family situation. How could I explain? It was hard enough explaining to Sandy's family in Italy, who were trying to make sense of San Antonio. In late January two of his brothers arrived in Washington. Peppino, the oldest, was a colonel in the Carabinieri who worked regularly with the DEA in Rome. He came looking for answers from the DEA's director. Pasquale, the youngest, was a doctor in Sardinia, who came to judge Sandy's medical condition. They were planning to fly to San Antonio to see him. They wanted me to go with them. Even if I'd known their language well enough, I never could have explained why I couldn't go. I wouldn't go. I didn't ever want to see Texas again. But there they were in my mother's house, eyes I recognized, the hint of a face I knew. "I will," I said, "if Marisa comes, too."

We took a taxi from the San Antonio airport, on the expressway, past road signs I remembered, familiar clumps of trees. I blacked out on the drive.

Mr. Blumberg and the attending physicians reviewed the X rays and the EEGs. Blumberg announced with pride that Sandy was being weaned from the respirator, gradually day-by-day. Still, the pneumonia lingered. The hospital accepted Pasquale's credentials and allowed him to take his own black bag inside for the examination. Marisa helped flip Sandy over. The pain collected in Peppino's eyes as we waited in a room outside.

We stayed that night in a motel half a block from the jail, but we didn't go back to the hospital. Pasquale agreed there was no reason. "Will he go on like that?" I finally got up the nerve to ask. Pasquale shook his head. "I'd give him a month, two at the most. The pneumonia will kill him."

After our flight back to D.C., Peppino met with Peter Bensinger, the DEA's administrator. They had a thirty-minute session, formal and polite, but the DEA admitted nothing. Their official line was that Sandy was an agent who had gone bad. The two brothers returned to Italy, Marisa to Ohio. The waiting continued.

I made daily calls to Santa Rosa, fourth-floor intensive care. The nurse's voice might as well have been recorded. There was never any change. One night in February Blumberg called. "At last, good news to report. Your husband's sitting up," he boasted. "We have him strapped to a Sears reclining chair. The nurse feeds him mashed potatoes through the tube up his nose."

March came. The DEA was fighting hard against disclosure, arguing that they couldn't and wouldn't produce Claude. They denied knowing his whereabouts. Four years later we would learn he'd continued working for them until he'd done to them what he'd done to Sandy.

The DEA's hardline position was no surprise to Richard. What he couldn't believe was the agency's lack of finesse. He had demanded that the DEA produce all evidence in its possession that Claude had misled or lied to the agency in other matters, records of DEA's contacts with Picault after Sandy's arrest, and any rewards promised Picault for making a case against Bario. Administrative Law Judge John J. McCarthy ordered the DEA to produce the information requested by Richard, as well as any evidence supporting the bribery claim. Yet the DEA took the astonishing stance that it would only produce that evidence used to get the indictment, those documents implying Sandy's guilt, while holding back any which would exculpate him. They argued their responsibility to protect Claude.

In March a nurse from intensive care called to offer her report. Sandy breathed, blinked, could void himself. Every half hour they flipped him like a flapjack to prevent bedsores.

By April the calls from Texas became confusing. He was better, and he wasn't. Blumberg was cautious, had his orders as I had mine. We were playing out a delicate charade. I pretended delight to hear that Sandy was propped up with pillows in his vinyl chair, and Blumberg pretended hope for a miraculous and Catholic cure. The truth was, Sandy wouldn't give up his ghost. He held us all in the palm of his blue, swollen hand. If his lungs missed a beat, the doctors plugged him in again. If his temperature climbed, they slid his cooling blanket under him, injecting him with a different class of drugs. Lying in bed in the suburbs of Virginia, I swore I could hear his labored breathing.

I began believing Sandy might exist in his coma for years. The hospital called, eager to move him to a nursing home near me. They were giving him only custodial care. A week later Goldstein called to ask who would represent us when the autopsy was done. I couldn't figure out what was happening, but I was accustomed to others knowing more than they'd tell me. I didn't want to believe that Sandy would really go. I'd gotten used to waiting. I wanted our hearing with the Merit Systems Protection Board. I wanted Sandy to be cleared before he died. Then I might have gone to San Antonio again. Having rescued him, I would have claimed him. Those were not my finest hours. On April 19 Blumberg called to say it was almost over. This time I believed him. He dropped his game. He offered to collect me at the airport, but the appeal hadn't yet been heard. I wasn't ready. I couldn't go. What about my son? I didn't want to leave him. I couldn't take him there. Richard might need me. The case might be heard. There might be time if we just waited. No, insisted Blumberg, there wasn't time.

I called Marisa. She said she understood why I couldn't go, but a brother was different from a husband. She left for San Antonio the next day, relieved to get a flight. It was Rodeo Week in San Antonio. The hotels, the airlines, were booked solid. She promised to call as soon as she got in. Late that night David woke up crying. Nothing so strange about that, I thought. Nightmares were a fact of life for two-year-olds. I got him back to sleep at 2 A.M., and still Marisa hadn't called.

At two forty-five the telephone rang. I was sure her flight had been delayed, that it had taken hours to check into her hotel, that the thick-headed guards wouldn't let her into Sandy's room.

"Hello?" I whispered.

"Joanne," she said, "it's over."

Hospital business occupied us completely. Should they release the body to the medical examiner or keep it in their morgue till morning? What was Sandy's social security number? I had my own questions that I wanted to ask: What time had she arrived? What was he like? Had he suffered?

"I can't really talk," she said. "I have to go down to sign the releases. I've placed a call to Italy which will soon come through. I'll call back later."

I sat on the edge of the bed in the house I'd rented with my son. The buses down our block had finished their nightly runs. The room, the house, the street were quiet. I felt like an empty jar turned over. I'd soon call my parents and awaken them. I'd called Franco and my best friend in New York. Not yet, though. I went downstairs, put the kettle on, sat in the living room in the dark. Maybe the hearing would be scheduled before the funeral. They would do the autopsy first. How long did an autopsy take? I'd call Richard in the morning to see if Sandy's case was on a docket somewhere. Maybe he could tell the judge we had to have our hearing soon.

Finally, Marisa called again. "I just came down from the empty room," she said. "They'd already stripped his bed, but I was glad I went back up. The room is so much lighter now. You were right not to come."

"Tell me everything. I have to know."

"Blumberg was very nice. He offered me a room at his house if I wanted to sleep. I didn't even check into a motel. It's impossible here with this rodeo. Bands have been playing in the street all night long. They had moved Sandy up to the eleventh floor. They didn't say so, but I think that's where they take them to die. I got here just in time. Even with the window closed, even on the eleventh floor, you could hear the music. They played country music in the street while he was dying."

"And his face?" I asked. "Did you see anything in his face?"

Her voice was like gravel. "They had to suction him every fifteen minutes. It didn't help. I finally asked the nurse to stop, there wasn't any point. It was horrible. Every time he strained to breathe, his whole body shuddered."

"What about his face? Do you think he knew?"

"I know you're not religious. I know you'll think I'm crazy, but I believe he waited for me." She paused, as if she knew what I wanted to ask. "I don't know what to say about his face," she said, "but his hair had all grown back. They had taken the tape off his eyelids. On their own, his eyes stayed closed."

I was afraid David would wake up again. Bad dreams plagued him every night as though he knew I hadn't told him the whole story. I'd said over and over again to him that his father was sick and wouldn't live. But it did no good. "When will my daddy come back from dying?" he kept asking.

At 4 A.M. my mother came. I watched headlights moving up the empty road, knowing it was she. We spoke in whispers in the living room. Neither of us cried. There were birds outside, singing in the dark. We couldn't decide whether to make coffee or tea and in the end had nothing. There was the quiet, the awful singing of the birds, and the emptiness around us.

The emptiness was yawning space. I kept waiting for something to happen. I watched the clock and waited for the buses to rock the house again. I felt tremendous energy and had nothing to do.

"You'll have to have a service," my mother said.

"I know. I've thought about it." I'd begun to plan it after Goldstein's call about the autopsy, though I didn't admit it to myself. I didn't want to believe I could be that unfaithful, planning a funeral when no one had died. I'd kept my image of Sandy in that antiseptic room, breathing uneasily, biding his time. The nurses had passed along rumors. One had told Marisa that he coughed on command. A guard said he swore Sandy's eyes had followed him around the room. To plan a funeral was too hard-hearted, worse than giving away his clothes or tossing out his boxes of news clippings. As Blumberg always said so cheerfully, we couldn't give up hope.

Throat bandaged, bony knees like saucers, Sandy could come home. A blue hand opening the front door, his eyes breaking through their tape, artificial tears streaming down his face, he would survey the scene in the strange house I'd chosen. Where are the photographs that always hung on the kitchen walls? When did his favorite clay statue lose its nose? There are ink stains on the quilt and cracker crumbs between the sheets in our bedroom.

I imagine the church decked out in flowers, the organist playing some sad tune, the guests lined up in pews. The minister would be the first to see us. I can picture his sad expression. Dressed somberly in navy blue, I rush down the aisle to warn him and our guests. Sandy hangs back, a gauze necktie where his breathing tube should be. You'll have to change the hymns, I say. Rethink your sermon, select some happy readings, put a smile on your face. We're making our grand entrance as bride and groom.

44

Richard hired a toxicologist in New York to assist the medical examiner in San Antonio with the autopsy. To no one's surprise, nothing irregular was found. Any toxic substance would have long ago metabolized. The medical examiner ruled probable accidental death. The blood and urine samples preserved from the initial seizures were checked again. They showed only traces of Elavil, the antidepressant prescribed by Rosenthal. Perhaps someone at the jail had altered the dose of Elavil; who knew if the original blood and urine samples had been switched? There were a hundred questions but no answers.

After the autopsy the body was cremated; Sandy's ashes were flown to Washington in a small bronze box wrapped in brown paper and tied with string. Marisa, our children, and I were to fly the urn of ashes to Rome and from Rome to Vieste for burial.

Sandy's brothers and sisters met us in Rome with a small Mercedes hearse waiting in the parking lot. I hadn't expected the hearse but wasn't as shocked as the driver was by the tiny box of ashes. He laid the box on a satin pillow, carried it to the back of the car where it disappeared among the flowers. How weird, he must have thought, and positively foreign.

We were a three-car procession pulling out of Fumicino, Peppino's car, Anna's, and in the rear, the tiny black Mercedes hearse. Peppino was driving. Marisa sat beside me in the back. "Were we wrong?" Peppino asked, "not going to Texas when Santino was alive?" No, Marisa said, chipping at her lip with a fingernail. Santino lost himself in Texas and didn't want to be seen in that place. None of us could help. The children sat between us, batting their bears against the seats, giggling as that name hung in the smoky air. Santino, Santino. Before the other names he'd used, Sandy had been Santino. I could see him in the pines at Anna's house in his cutoffs, bare-chested on the highest limbs, hear the children on the dusty ground: "Zio Santino, Zio Santino, higher still!"

Peppino dried his eyes, looked back at the road again. "How could this have happened to Santino?"

The far-off hills were indigo. The car was quiet. I watched my face in the mirror on the door, mascara tracks under my eyes, pale lips in double image. I wanted to abort this eight-hour drive to Vieste. I wanted to sleep. Without sleep I couldn't be responsible for what I did or said.

"Marisa, could we stop for coffee?"

The question changed languages as it changed hands. Marisa, please, some coffee. Stop these children jumping; make that silly hearse disappear.

Anna unfolded herself from the other car, her shiny dark hair falling in her eyes. *"Come stai, Giovanna?"* Holding my arm, she led me into the coffee shop. *"Vuoi un caffè?"* I let her take me over, though it wasn't really coffee that I wanted. I wanted to tell her I was sorry, that I'd tried, that I loved Santino, but I didn't know the words to use.

After coffee Anna took us to the restroom. She had a suitcase with her and was talking in short, quick, sentences to Marisa. "They're clothes for us," Marisa explained, "black skirts and sweaters. Vieste's an old-fashioned town. It would please my father if we'd wear them."

Punch-drunk on sleeplessness in my new black duds, I climbed back in the car again. David slept three hours on my lap, through Foggia, up into the mountains. Santino used to ride his Vespa in these hills, used to ride the train from Rome through this same landscape. It was Santino who had captivated me, Santino who grabbed hold of a room, absorbing everybody's doubts. He'd always wanted to live by the sea, and suddenly the sea appeared, Vieste's sea where his ashes would be laid.

The road wound around the cliffs. I grew dizzy from the height, from the glitter and swell of the water. In another few miles, Vieste would appear.

"Marisa?" I whispered. Was she sleeping? We'd switched seats at the café. She was behind me now. "Marisa?"

"Hmm?" she said.

"Marisa, I'm afraid I'm going to be sick."

"What?"

"We'd better stop. I'm going to throw up."

Mumbo jumbo from Marisa to Peppino. I held my breath, afraid I'd heave or wet my pants. This wasn't any way to put Santino to rest. I had no good news to give his family. Where was the classy widow all in black? I shifted on the seat, and David woke up crying, pressing on me, trying his best to leap off my lap.

"There's no place to stop," Marisa said. "We're almost in Vieste. Can't you wait?"

One boy cried, so the other started. "No. We have to stop."

Peppino found a stretch of road, signaled to the others. I watched Anna's car and the hearse behind it come down the mountain. A bus appeared on the crest of the hill, pausing before beginning its long dive. We'd be an amuscment for the bored riders—look, a hearse! When will the ceremony start? We'd be dots and dashes against the backdrop of the sea. They'd watch us emerge, black squiggles in the dirt. Anna jumped out, came up to me again. She pointed to me as she touched Marisa on the arm. *"Che fa?"* she asked. When Marisa whispered in her ear, she smiled.

"Vieni qua, Giovanna," Anna said, leading me onto the rocky precipice. Peppino had chosen well. Rocks jutted from the cliff like balconies where olive trees had sprouted dwarfed and cunning in the sun. I followed Anna to the farthest rocks, raised my skirt, watched the bus careening faster. The chauffeur sauntered from his hearse, his disdain showing. The foreign widow has to take a leak; the widow's gonna toss her lunch.

Go on, Anna encouraged me. It's okay, we're here. I peeked

from behind the ledge of rocks. I'm better now, thank you. Could I be alone a minute?

They left and I got up off my rumpled knees. Anna had left a box of Kleenex beside a silver flask of cognac. Soiled tissues rippled on the ground. I opened the flask and took a sip.

I couldn't let myself be such a disappointment to Vieste, especially to Sandy's father or his maiden aunt. I couldn't let them think that little box of ashes was all I'd brought them from America. I had promised some denouement, answers from Claude and the DEA. Someone collected the flask and box of tissues at the car. Peppino stood beside the door to let me in, eyes red from the effort of not crying. He took my arm, leaning into the car to whisper, *"Piano, piano,"*—softly, gently, easy does it.

We finally reached sea level and the town. I remembered the route now, through the old section of the city, past the new hotels, the kiosk in the square. But we turned off the main road almost immediately, onto a dusty driveway that curved into the mountainside and ended in a clearing. There was a parking lot, a huge stone arch, rose-colored in the setting sun. It was the cemetery.

"What are we doing here, Marisa?"

"We're going to leave the urn. There'll be some prayers in the chapel, a few friends, that's all."

But I wasn't ready. I saw them waiting for us, all in black—Sandy's aunt, his sister Rita, and in the rear with a man on either side to steady him, Papà. We pulled to a stop; the group of mourners came slowly forward.

"But the children, Marisa. This is going to frighten the children."

"Pasquale called ahead to warn them, no keening or scenes in front of the children."

Car doors slammed. Anna wrapped Zia Francesca in her arms. Peppino and Pasquale took their places with Papà. David and I hung back in the car, staring out the windows. Even with the windows closed, we heard the whimper of their softened voices, the sighing that accompanied their tears. Marisa opened her door behind me. "Wait, Marisa—" But her door slammed shut. Someone took the child from her arms. Sandy's father slowly approached the car, his shuffling feet kicking up sand. He wasn't well, Papà. He had Marisa in his arms. David started crying, "Mommy, let's go home." "It's all right," I crooned, closing my eyes, "it will be all right."

Sandy's father smelled of liniment. Viviana, Pasquale's wife, took David from my arms. "Mommy, Mommy—" Sandy's father linked his arm in mine. The gravel gnashed beneath our feet. The driver opened the back of the hearse. There was a rush of gladioli, their wedged-in stems breaking off like bits of ice. In the center of the small black car blanketed with flowers was the small, square box tied up with string, the parcel that was once Santino.

Sandy's father didn't wince. He took the package in both hands. The sound of pebbles gave way to the silence of grass. I followed him through the carved stone arch, past monuments and mausoleums, wild poppies growing everywhere.

The chapel was cold and dark, lit only by the setting sun burning orange through the windows. I kept turning from the altar to the back of the room to check on David. He was a small, dark silhouette hiding his head in Pasquale's shoulder.

The priest began to pray as Sandy's father set the box on a table near the altar, lit the candles on either end. I wanted to cut the string, still dangling. I wanted to scratch out the waxed immigration seal with my bitten nails, to find a small screwdriver, open the box, and scatter Sandy's ashes on the water where he'd wanted them. But Peppino, who could read my mind, leaned forward in his pew and whispered, "Leave him be, Joanne, *lascialo stare.*"

45

"I won't give up. We'll find out something," I promised Sandy's father, and painstakingly we did. But the DEA fought us all the way, facing contempt of court and adverse rulings in three separate court actions rather than produce their files.

The documents which were released to Judge McCarthy had been sanitized and carefully selected. The agency refused to comply with the judge's order to turn over all exculpatory materials in its files, the very documents we needed to prove Sandy's innocence.

Still, Richard Ben-Veniste was hopeful. "Don't worry. This is just round one," he said. "We now have their full damage report, everything negative that DEA could scrape together. To say the least, it's 'underwhelming.'"

Though Claude had innumerable opportunities to tape his conversations with Sandy under the auspices of the DEA's inspection service, not a single tape released by the DEA corroborated the indictment's charges. Most importantly, the pivotal conversation at the Chicago airport—when Claude gave Sandy the four thousand dollars which was later mistakenly returned to me—had never been recorded. According to Richard, this was ironclad circumstantial corroboration of Sandy's explanation that Claude gave him the money with that feeble story of keeping it for him so Claude's girlfriends wouldn't find it.

"Sandy didn't know that the tape of that conversation would end up blank," Richard explained. "And there's no way an experienced informer like Claude would get his equipment so tangled up that the microphone wire would 'accidentally' be pulled out of the jack. Put that together with the fact that Sandy had kept the money in his office safe—hardly what a corrupt agent would do with a bribe, and the whole goddamned case boils down to Claude's word against Sandy's. There isn't a shred of corroboration for Claude's story except that he put the money in Sandy's hands. Now DEA admits they never even made Claude take a lie detector test."

DEA's arrogance, together with its meager "proof" against Sandy, incensed Richard. "There isn't any question that this whole case stinks. I can't believe DEA would arrest its own agent on the little that it had. I'm not letting this end here."

The DEA denied knowing Claude's whereabouts and refused to produce him or Campos as witnesses, even in closed chambers with the judge. They coolly told Judge McCarthy he had no authority to subpoena witnesses or force production of DEA files.

By June 1980, Judge McCarthy had been pushed beyond his limits. Citing the DEA's refusal to comply with the Merit System Protection Board's discovery order, he ruled that the DEA's partial production of documents failed to meet due process requirements. He listed several conditions justifying full sanctions: our disadvantage in being denied Sandy's testimony since his death, our inability to uncover the basis of the government's case without the DEA's cooperation, the agency's refusal to produce any witnesses, and their refusal to release documents after we had, in good faith, released our documents to them. On June 10 Sandy was posthumously reinstated as a federal narcotics agent. The charges against him were formally cleared.

But the judge's ruling couldn't give us answers to our questions. Eventually, David would want to know what had happened to his father—had he taken a bribe or not? There were two other sons involved as well, already old enough to wonder. How much had the government paid Claude Picault to make a case against one of its most decorated agents? Where had they hidden Claude? How had he lived while Sandy was in San Antonio waiting to die?

Two years after the autopsy, after our burial trip to Vieste, the telephone rang in my Washington house; a voice in French asked for the Café Français. I panicked, convinced that it was Claude. "You have the wrong number," I mumbled. *"Pardon?"* "The wrong number." I hung up. There were other such calls, each one precipitating a sleepless night. It was crazy. What reason could Claude possibly have to get in touch with me? He'd already taken from me what he'd wanted. Did I imagine an apology from him? A change of heart? But he had no heart. Everything he'd ever done, he'd done for money. In some ways his life was very simple. Even if he had called, what could I have said to touch him? I couldn't hurt him. I didn't even know his name any longer. But I hated those wrong numbers. I considered having my number changed. One day I finally looked up the Café Français in the telephone directory; its number was one digit off from mine. It wasn't Claude. It would never be.

I was as naïve as Sandy, believing that if I had Claude on the phone, he'd confess—believing Claude would give me something to tell David when he called me into his room each night: "See, Mom, that rip in the wallpaper, the way the closet door won't close? I see eyes there, a face trying to climb in." I used to see them, too, those half-collapsing eyes of Sandy.

I'd never know for certain if he was innocent or guilty. Maybe in his own mind he had crossed a permanent boundary when he let the sample pass. It was all over as soon as he'd made that first mistake, and from that moment on his entire world began crashing down on him—because he was too straight, too much the police chief's son to admit his failure at the start when he could have been saved. Perhaps his mother had been right in that letter she'd sent him long ago. What was best about Sandy, what made him so compelling, had cost him his life. His charm, his eagerness, his need to win at the wrong game, in the wrong place—in Mexico with Claude. He was too ambitious, too impatient, his mother had said. He was too much. I would have liked to tell her I was grateful for him.

Or perhaps I'd gotten it all wrong. I didn't understand a thing, and the true story of Sandy's death involved characters far more sinister than the likes of Claude Picault, turned on a plot whose complexities I'd never penetrate. There had been rumors. Reporters had approached me. Government agents offered through third parties to meet me secretly. Sandy was a man who had known too much, and I was a woman who hadn't known him at all. "He was murdered," one of the reporters glibly suggested, "by the government. Isn't that your theory?" I sipped my coffee, lit another cigarette, and admitted what shocked the reporter most of all: "I don't have a theory." It wasn't that I didn't want to know the truth, but more that I didn't want the truth to be too awful. I didn't want to live with theories of conspiracy and paranoia. I didn't want to be forced to recognize the fear in Sandy's eyes for what it really may have been—naked terror. I didn't want to believe he had kept so many secrets from me. Speculative stories came and went: Sandy worked for the CIA in Mexico, Sandy was part of a DEA secret operation as he had been in Operation Croupier in the Bahamas. He had found out things that had turned him against the agency. They had done away with him. The rumors filtered through my dreams. If the stories were true, Sandy had kept them from me in order to protect me. Maybe that dumb girl I'd self-consciously projected when Sandy was in jail wasn't just an image after all, wasn't just a way to hide when I was frightened; maybe I had really been that dizzy dame. In the world where Sandy lived, that was all that I could be. I shook off the fuzzy dreams I didn't want to remember, the half-felt truths I didn't want to understand. I preferred the scraps of "facts" we were thrown by DEA in court.

While David and I tried to cope with our bad dreams, Richard figured out how to get us into a federal courtroom. He would use the DEA's own evidence, the four thousand dollars in marked fifty-dollar bills that they were trying to reclaim. They had written to Goldstein about their money, and Goldstein quickly passed the message on to Richard. In late 1982, the DEA wrote to us directly. "This is really burning them up," Richard said amusedly. "First, they have to acknowledge that they screwed up in sending you their crucial evidence, now they're having apoplexy because I won't give it back to them. But Sandy didn't get the cash from DEA—he got it from Claude. There's nothing wrong with that—unless the money was a bribe. If it was a bribe, DEA is finally going to have to prove it. In court. Federal District Court."

In early 1983, just as Richard hoped, the DEA filed in U.S. District Court in Washington, D.C. The money was duly placed in the registry of the court for safekeeping until the outcome of the case. "I think we just heard the bell for round two," Richard said with a smile. He began writing motions, requesting everything he could think of, the same information DEA had previously withheld, all documents pertaining to Claude and Campos, any documents the DEA had in its possession in the matter of Sante Bario.

The young Justice Department attorney who was handling this particular twist in the Bario case took court orders seriously. Though the agency was sensitive to any aspect of the Bario investigation, she believed she had a good case and didn't want to jeopardize it by refusing to comply with the judge's routine orders to provide discovery. She began producing the documents requested. Though she hadn't released many before the higher-ups at the DEA closed the floodgates, what we learned was explosive.

Ben-Veniste was dumbfounded at first, then angry. "I can't believe this is part of the same Justice Department I worked for with pride. The stuff we've gotten is enough to make me sick."

It was indeed sickening. The DEA had paid Claude Picault fifty thousand dollars for a three-week investigation that ultimately led to Sandy's death. The last installment of seven thousand dollars was paid less than a month after Sandy went into a coma. Memos from DEA Inspection revealed that Claude had been relocated to Miami, where he received U.S. immigration papers, a new name, and orders for other DEA operations. Claude Picault, alias Kercadio, Hernandez, Pichambert, would soon become a U.S. citizen. While Sandy chugged along on his respirator, Claude went to work for the DEA in San Juan, Puerto Rico. He set up the usual confusing situations. When in doubt, he'd always obfuscate. Names here, suggestions there, the promise of a bigger case just around the corner, when his biggest cases were never for the record.

According to the documents released by the DEA, Claude began working behind Inspection's back. They had asked him how much was left from the five kilos he had smuggled in from Bolivia in April 1978 in the Bario investigation. Only five hundred grams in Mexico, Claude swore, though he couldn't tell them exactly where the coke was hidden. A friend had held it. He wouldn't agree to fly to Mexico with a DEA agent to pick it up—he could easily be killed as soon as he crossed the border. Bario had been a favorite of General Mendioleya; the DEA couldn't expect the MFJP to protect Claude Picault. It must have hurt him to think of his narcotics stash just out of his reach.

Claude called on a "friend" to help him. Alain Chaillou, mentioned by Claude to Sandy as a possible buyer in the Añez-Vaca case, was a purchaser of South American television programs for export to Mexico. He and Claude had met in Montreal. He asked Alain to do a favor for the U.S. Government. "I am a DEA agent," Claude said. "I have certain cocaine in Mexico which the DEA needs for a big case. Carry it to Bogotá for me—you can make an extra stop on your routine trip. DEA and I would be very grateful and could make it worth your while."

Tinged with the glamour of secret-agent work, it had seemed aboveboard to Chaillou when Claude explained that someone would deliver the coke to him at a hotel in Mexico City and retrieve the merchandise at another specified hotel in Bogotá. Claude would call Chaillou in Colombia to make sure the goods had safely arrived. "Don't worry about anything," Claude had reassured him. "You probably won't even be checked. Colombia isn't an import country, the cocaine originates from there. Customs will be busy checking departing passengers. But if anything should go wrong, don't panic. The DEA will help. The whole idea in this kind of situation is to convince the Colombian Government that a Colombian citizen I know is a genuine dealer."

Chaillou must have scratched his head a little. "You see, *hermano*," Claude continued, "here's how it will go—I'll fly to Bogotá and use the cocaine to implicate this Colombian national, to persuade the Colombian officials to let this same suspect export another fifteen kilos to San Juan, under the DEA's and my protection, so I can arrest the guy in U.S. territory."

It was the same kind of game that Claude had played on Sandy. Claude would end up with his Mexican stash—about two kilos— plus a reward for producing a Colombian trafficker in San Juan, where he would be tried under U.S. laws. All he had to do was fabricate his tales and confuse them all a little.

Claude instructed Chaillou to hide the coke in the lining of his suitcase. "If anything goes wrong," he said, "give the authorities this Colombian's name as the trafficker who hired you to make the trip and the true owner of the drugs. But don't tell the Colombians that you're working for DEA. These diplomatic things are delicate, you know. Sit tight. DEA will get you out of trouble."

One month into Sandy's coma, in February 1979, Alain Chaillou was arrested at the El Dorado Airport in Bogotá, Colombia. Chaillou requested an interview with the DEA agent who routinely accompanied the Colombians on a drug arrest. The DEA agent asked to see Chaillou's passport, his address book, and other documents. In the address book he saw the names of two DEA officials, one of whom was the head of Internal Security in Washington, D.C. "You see," Chaillou tried subtly to explain. "I'm on a mission for the DEA in San Juan, Puerto Rico, supervised by your agent, Claude Picault." It couldn't be possible that DEA-San Juan denied any knowledge of this case.

"Incredible," Ben-Veniste said after I'd read the first report. "Less than a month after Sandy goes into a coma, Claude is running another scam on DEA, involving the very same cocaine that Claude told DEA he'd sold with Sandy's approval. The bribe money was supposed to be Sandy's cut of what we now know was a nonexistent sale. The worst part is that DEA knew in February 1979 that Picault's accusation against Sandy was a lie. They just sat on their information, hoping it would never come out."

Sandy had heard of Alain Chaillou through Claude. Chaillou had also heard of Sandy. While the DEA was preparing its criminal case against agent Bario, Chaillou had received a call from Claude.

"I need a routine favor," Claude said. "It's nothing, really. I want you to appear at a trial I'm preparing to corroborate certain statements I've made to DEA about Sante Bario. I want you to testify that you carried cocaine from Mexico to Canada and that you delivered it to Vierzon on the instructions of Sante Bario."

Chaillou had been flattered to be asked to appear as a witness for the U.S. Government, but how could he testify against Bario when he had never even met him?

The DEA interviewed Chaillou on February 22, 1979 at the El

Modelo prison after his arrest in Bogotá, Colombia. Chaillou's interrogator, DEA Special Agent Rafael Aguirre, couldn't believe what he was hearing. He asked Chaillou to repeat Claude's perjury request. Internal Security in Washington must have been shaken when its agents read Aguirre's report. DEA Inspection couldn't have ignored the fact that its star witness, its only real witness, in the Bario case had tried to suborn perjury. Christ, imagine if such a fact had gotten out. A report on the interview was slipped into Internal Security's file on February 28. It must have been embarrassing to the DEA, especially when Bario hadn't yet died. The agency could have released the information and helped clear his name then. But of course it couldn't. How would Bario have looked in Mexico during the Añez-Vaca investigation if he'd admitted that Claude Picault carried in more than his reported sample? How would Inspection look now? The DEA and Bario responded much the same to the prospect of public embarrassment like that, to the idea that such disclosure would wreck their respective cases, cases which affected their reputations.

Claude had conned Internal Security as he had conned Sandy. Unless it were possible that Claude was working as a DEA agent when he approached Chaillou—but the idea of that was preposterous. In March 1979, citing serious violations of the controlled substances law, Claude Picault was blacklisted by DEA Internal Security, his informant file permanently closed. The agency could have chosen to prosecute Claude in San Juan, Puerto Rico, but the trial would have been an embarrassment to the DEA. Better to cover their tracks, to close Claude's file quietly and let him go.

Richard Ben-Veniste wasn't surprised when the DEA refused to comply with any further discovery orders in federal court. "What can we expect when they sat on Claude's subornation of perjury and his other free-lance dope deals since before Sandy's death?" he asked. "At least this part of the cover-up is over."

Ben-Veniste had predicted to U.S. District Judge Joyce Hens Green that the DEA would never comply with an order to produce the relevant evidence in its files. But we'd gotten more than Richard had hoped for. Judge Green, like Judge McCarthy before her, condemned the DEA to forfeit its case for failure to comply with her production order. We got to keep DEA's marked bribe money.

Richard said he might have a few bills framed to hang on his office wall.

The civil service sanctions, the marked money, the shocking report about Claude and Chaillou are not enough. I want a far more satisfactory ending. I tell myself I need more facts to tell David when he asks me what happened to his father. My son is almost eight years old now; when will he be old enough to learn the truth? I'm almost thirty-eight and not yet old enough myself. I am now the age that Sandy was when we first met, when I looked admiringly at him for having lived so passionately, so close to the edge. Perhaps I've become too much like him and can no longer be satisfied by facts. I refuse to accept the obvious lesson from his death—that it's dangerous to have too many dreams, to want too much high drama. Instead, I long for what I lost in losing him: those charged moments, the intensity he brought to everything he touched. No facts about his death can demonstrate those qualities to David. If I want them, I'll have to take them for myself.

The rumors persist. Some reporters won't give up. Two of them believe they are close to piecing together the whole story. Part of me wants to help them in their search. I agree to meetings, dig out documents, go through my cartons of papers again, but I'm not sure my heart is in it. They have collected so many pieces in the Bario puzzle that they need a computer to sort them out. They are convinced Sandy was involved in a highly secretive mission in Mexico whose main objective had little to do with drugs. There are stories that the DEA almost successfully managed the assassination of General Omar Torrijos in Panama. How many other coups and murders have been engineered by secret DEA forces abroad working behind the front of narcotics interdiction? They ask me, as if I knew. They have deeply felt political motives, these reporters. They think in terms of scoops. I look at them across a sea of feeling I have for a man they analyze but never knew. I feel disloyal, guilty because I'm not sufficiently excited as they get close to pinning down their story. If I really wanted facts, my enthusiasm would match theirs. They're on the verge of giving me definite answers, absolute proof, yet I get lost in their details, my mind wanders. I light a cigarette, and my fingers shake. What bothers me about them? Surely I'm not afraid of what they'll finally write about

Sandy. They see him sympathetically. They make him into a kind of hero, the perfect gift to give his sons. Yet I'm caught by the small ways they modify him in fashioning their view of his life. Is that what I've done, too—subtly made him over to make him more like me?

Sitting with these reporters in a Washington café, I feel sad suddenly, knowing both our portraits fail. Neither their facts nor my memories can "capture" Sandy. There is no neat way to sum him up. I am left with only sharp, vivid sparks of Sante Bario in the way my son charges into a room, in his eyes at times, in the way his shoulder blades jut out. Some day, when David is old enough to ask, I'll tell him what I know and that I don't regret the brief, strange life I once lived with his father. Given the chance again, I'd dive headlong and go with Sandy.

IMPERIAL PUBLIC LIBRARY
P.O. BOX 307
IMPERIAL, TEXAS 79743